Representing the Holocaust

By the same author

Emile Durkheim: Sociologist and Philosopher
A Preface to Sartre
Madame Bovary *on Trial*
Rethinking Intellectual History: Texts, Contexts, Language
History & Criticism
History, Politics, and the Novel
Soundings in Critical Theory

Editor
The Bounds of Race: Perspectives on Hegemony and Resistance

Coeditor
Modern European Intellectual History: Reappraisals and New Perspectives

HISTORY, THEORY, TRAUMA

REPRESENTING THE HOLOCAUST

∾ ∾ ∾

Dominick LaCapra

Cornell University Press   *Ithaca and London*

First published 1994 by Cornell University Press.

Printed in the United States of America

♾ The paper in this book meets the minimum requirements of the American National Standard for Information Sciences— Permanence of Paper for Printed Library Materials, ANSI Z39.48–1984.

Library of Congress Cataloging-in-Publication Data

LaCapra, Dominick, 1939–
    Representing the Holocaust : history, theory, trauma / Dominick LaCapra.
        p.   cm.
    Includes bibliographical references and index.
    ISBN 0-8014-2997-8
    1. Holocaust, Jewish (1939–1945)—Historiography.   I. Title.
D804.3.L33   1994
940.53′18′072—dc20
93-33885

With deepest affection, for Rae, Faye, and Harry

As we already know, the interdependence of the complicated problems of the mind forces us to break off every enquiry before it is completed—till the outcome of some other enquiry can come to its assistance.

—Sigmund Freud, "Mourning and Melancholia"

The Holocaust threatens a secular as well as a religious gospel, faith in reason and progress as well as Christianity. It points, in that sense and that sense only, to a religious upheaval. It challenges the credibility of redemptive thinking. . . .

Our *sefer hashoah* [the response to the missing Book of Destruction commissioned from seventy elders by a king "who made himself sick reading and reading, and decreed that there be no more accounts of the destruction"] will have to accomplish the impossible: allow the limits of representation to be healing limits yet not allow them to conceal an event we are obligated to recall and interpret, both to ourselves and those growing up unconscious of its shadow.

—Geoffrey H. Hartman, "The Book of Destruction"

CONTENTS

PREFACE

In the recent past, history and theory have often been construed as mutually exclusive (or at least as necessarily divergent) approaches to problems—for example, in terms of the binary opposition that correlates history with diachrony and theory with synchrony. Critical of the unmediated application of such a stark opposition in defining research as well as of its implications for understanding history, I insist instead on an active, sustained, and critical interaction between theoretical reflection and historical investigation, and I try to bring this insistence to bear on the problem of representing the Holocaust. Only through such an interaction can history and theory pose mutually provocative questions.

The Holocaust has been both repressed and "canonized" in the recent past, and it often functions as a more or less covert point of rupture between the modern and the postmodern. Careful inquiry into it may reveal often concealed aspects of the genealogy of various postmodernisms and poststructuralisms, and it may also help to provide a different way of seeing and raising questions about certain pronounced tendencies in contemporary thought, such as the near fixation on the sublime or the almost obsessive preoccupation with loss, aporia, dispossession, and deferred meaning. Moreover, such an inquiry prompts one to ask whether psychoanalysis, which has recently met with a variety of responses ranging from subtle rethinking to extreme condemnation, should itself be understood not primarily as a psychology of the individual or as the basis for a generalized therapeutic ethos but as an inherently historicized mode of thought intimately bound up with social, political, and ethical concerns.

Making a specific use of psychoanalysis, I investigate the transferential relation between the historian or theorist and the object of analysis. Victims of severely traumatizing events may never fully escape possession by, or recover from, a shattering past, and a response to trauma may well involve "acting-out" (or emotionally repeating a still-present past) in those directly affected by it and at least muted trauma in attentive analysts and commentators. While thoroughly acknowledging these important considerations, I maintain that what Freud termed "working-through" has received insufficient attention in post-Freudian analysis, and I stress the importance of working through problems in a critical manner. I also suggest that a vital question for present interpreters of such figures as Heidegger is how to situate dubious, symptomatic, at times insensitive or insufficiently empathic aspects of their work while distinguishing and elaborating further valuable, critical dimensions in an active engagement with the past. How, in other words, may one eschew rewriting or apologetically glossing history yet "brush [it] against the grain" (in Walter Benjamin's phrase) to recover different possibilities for the present and future? And how may this be accomplished in a secular historiography or criticism that distinguishes—without totally dissociating— itself from religion or theology and employs the "weak messianic power" of values not projectively to refigure or redeem the past but to prompt inquiry into it that critically confronts explicit normative issues?

In the course of the following chapters, I also address the role of canons in various disciplines, the import of noncanonical readings of canonized texts, and the relation between canons and problems (such as those posed by the Holocaust) that cannot be reduced to questions of canonicity. I endeavor to place in a different perspective such specific, controversial issues as the historians' debate over ways of representing the Shoah, the attempt to historicize extreme events, responses to the discovery of Paul de Man's World War II journalism, the implications of Heidegger's Nazi turn for the reading of his texts, and the role of Holocaust testimonies in historical interpretation. Throughout there is an emphasis on basic issues in historical inquiry and self-understanding that should be of interest not only to historians but also to philosophers, literary critics, and social scientists for whom the problem of history has recently become a renewed concern.

Versions or parts of certain chapters appeared in the following places: parts of the Introduction in the *American Historical Review* 97 (1992); a version of Chapter 1 in the *Intellectual History Newsletter* 13 (1991) and substantially its present form in Lloyd Kramer, Donald Reid, and William Barney, eds., *Learning History in America: Schools, Cultures, and Politics* (Minneapolis: University of Minnesota Press, 1994); a version of Chapter 2 in Saul Friedlander, ed., *Probing the Limits of Representation: Nazism and the "Final Solution"* (Cambridge: Harvard University Press, 1992); a version of Chapter 3 in *New German Critique* 53 (1991); and Chapter 4 in *History and Memory* 4 (1992). Chapters 5, 6, and 7 are published here for the first time.

In closing, I want to acknowledge Carol Betsch, of Cornell University Press, and Victoria Haire, for their excellent editorial assistance. I also thank Kathleen Merrow for her assistance in preparing the Index.

DOMINICK LACAPRA

Ithaca, New York

Representing the Holocaust

INTRODUCTION

The general concern of the following chapters is the relation between history and theory, while the leitmotif (and often the specific focus) is the difficult question of how to address issues bearing on the Holocaust or Shoah. Virtually everything in the book pertains to the problem of historical understanding. It may be useful to observe at the outset that by theory I mean sustained critical and self-critical reflection addressed to practices, texts, or sets of facts. Ideally, such reflection increases self-understanding and provides a measure of critical distance on problems without implying a denial of one's implication in them. It also tests (or contests) existing formulations and may indicate the need for more desirable modes of articulation (even when the theorist is able to provide only components or indications rather than fully developed paradigms of the latter).

The first chapter tries to reformulate the problem of reading canons, and it extends the notion of significant texts beyond the purview of high or elite culture. The Holocaust or Shoah is of course a problem that itself requires a mode of inquiry not confined to classically canonical texts although this problem certainly encompasses the issue of the role of certain of these texts with respect to it. It is in a sense a problem that has itself been both avoided or repressed and in certain ways "canonized" in the recent past—a problem that should be a concern of both history and critical theory but whose understanding often poses seemingly insuperable obstacles or holds out dubious temptations to the historian and theorist. The bulk of this book is devoted to recent "representations" or uses of the Holocaust in history and theory as well as to debates concerning the pertinent writings of major theorists such as Paul de Man and Martin Heidegger. Only in the chapter on Heidegger, however, do I address directly and in a sustained fashion certain issues raised in the first chapter on canons, to wit, the extent to which canonized texts are symptomatic, critical, and potentially transformative with respect to their relevant contexts of production and reception or use.[1] Since so much of the book is addressed to specific matters pertinent to the Holocaust or Shoah, I would here—without simply losing sight of these matters—like to devote some attention to the preliminary, more general question of the relation between theory and history—a question often implicitly at issue in the following chapters. (Readers who are not interested in this type of question might consider going directly to the first chapter.)

On a general level, the attempt to relate history and theory has at least three manifest implications. First, this relation should not be seen in merely additive terms or as a purely associative link. The idea of "history and theory"—a title that in fact graces an important journal—may authorize a mere assemblage of reflections on history from a rather conventional perspective and on theory from relatively ahistorical or narrowly analytic points of view. Although I cannot promise that I always deliver on this assertion or that the relationship I seek is nonproblematic, I would nonetheless maintain that the relation between history and theory should be dialogic and mutually provocative—a relation in which the terms are interinvolved and in part transformed by their implication and interaction.

Second, the conjunction of history and theory implies a critique of history without theory or in which the theoretical component remains unarticulated if not resisted and repressed. An atheoretical or even antitheoretical approach has often characterized conventional historiography, and it has engendered the idea of history as a craft. The historian's craft, in Marc Bloch's phrase, has indeed produced much admirable work, and I would in no sense want to jettison the norms of meticulous research and careful testing of propositions that have become ingrained as common sense in the historical profession. In fact, I think that even the most theoretically sophisticated approach should

---

[1] I treat comparable problems in the work of Paul de Man in *Soundings in Critical Theory* (Ithaca: Cornell University Press, 1989), pp. 101–32.

have more than a nodding acquaintance with common sense, which can check and bring down to earth its more speculative or involuted gestures. But the procedures of established disciplines such as professional historiography should also be rendered more explicit and thus more open to questioning, revision, and supplementation. Otherwise the misleading understanding of history as an alternative to theory may well induce one to hypostatize history, essentialize context, and confide in an unmediated or crude idea of the manner in which "historical" information is supposed to explain various features of texts.

The unfortunate tendency in some recent work has been to become familiar with theoretical perspectives only to be better able to criticize and fend them off. This rather unconstructive, defensive strategy leads at best to containment by partial incorporation and to rather unreflective tensions in the work of the historian. In the recent past, this tendency has characterized the work not only of professional historians but of literary critics who, at times under the mantle of "new historicism," have utilized theoretical sophistication in a movement "against theory."[2] This bizarre form of antitheoretical theory may lead to the intentionally unearthshaking conclusion that theory makes no difference in practice, that it amounts to spinning one's wheels in the void—a danger that should be resisted and not a possibility that should be invoked (or even indulged) in a way that jeopardizes the significance of theoretical reflection in general.

Third, conjoining history with theory does not lead to theory without history or, more precisely, theory in which the historical dimension is extremely attenuated, abstract, unspecified, or fetishized. For just as there is in reality no history without theory, there is no theory without history. But the relations between the two may be implicit or even repressed with the result that the problems and potentials of a more explicit and critical relationship may be obviated or misconstrued. Although there is always the risk that theory will develop

---

[2]See, for example, Steven Knapp and Walter Benn Michaels, "Against Theory," in W. J. T. Mitchell, ed., *Against Theory: Literary Studies and the New Pragmatism* (Chicago: University of Chicago Press, 1985), pp. 11–30. For a restricted and at times antitheoretical use of theory by historians, see, for example, Donald R. Kelley, "Horizons of Intellectual History: Retrospect, Circumspect, Prospect," *Journal of the History of Ideas* 48 (1987), 143–69; Anthony Pagden, "Rethinking the Linguistic Turn: Current Anxieties in Intellectual History," *Journal of the History of Ideas* 49 (1988), 519–29; and especially Bryan D. Palmer, *Descent into Discourse: The Reification of Language and the Writing of Social History* (Philadelphia: Temple University Press, 1990).

beyond—or fall short of—its object and become self-referential, the relationship between theory and history should not be seen solely in terms of a self-propelled theoretical movement that engenders its own resistances or that construes history in extremely theoreticist terms as referential aberration, aporetic impasse, and radical discontinuity or fragmentation. The latter view accords with the recent fixation on an (an)aesthetic of the sublime, and in my judgment it runs the risk of fetishizing or compulsively repeating what is indeed one important and unavoidable possibility in thought. The larger problem is, however, to explore the interaction between various dimensions of language use and its relation to practice, including the relationship between "constative" historical reconstruction and "performative" dialogic exchange with the past as well as between "sublime" excess and normative limits that are necessary as controls in social and political life. Indeed, as I try to show in certain of the chapters below, a fixation on the aporetic or the sublime may in certain contexts unintentionally have apologetic functions.

In line with the effort to conceive of history with theory, one should try to relate in as sustained a manner as possible the reading of texts and artifacts to specific historical and sociopolitical problems. In fact, the notion of specificity is vitally at issue in the three implications I have drawn from the conjunction of history and theory, and it is an insistent motif of the chapters in this book. One should also try to indicate precisely how historiographical studies and debates might profit from closer, more critical attention to rhetorical and textual matters and to the kinds of theory that provide perspective on these matters. Here, as elsewhere, one needs a translation between disciplines and areas of culture. But any effective translation must be sensitive to the different traditions and protocols of interpretation in areas that come (or are brought) into contact. A translation that is premised on the understanding of only one tradition (say, conventional historiography on the one hand or deconstruction on the other) is necessarily an insufficiently complex, at times one-dimensional appropriation that fails even to register as relevant in the terms of those within the other interpretive tradition. One should not, however, valorize complexity for its own sake or glorify "high" culture as the sole sanctuary of resistance in an administered society. Defensible complexity is related to dialogism in the basic sense of the interaction of mutually implicated yet often contestatory traditions or tendencies that have provocative relations to one another. These traditions or tendencies indicate why texts in which they are at issue cannot be reduced to mere symptomatic documents insofar as texts perform critical and transformative work or play on their contexts of production and reception. In this sense, these texts demand a response from the reader that cannot be confined to contextualization or mastery through the accumulation of information.

In addition, contexts themselves may well involve mutually contestatory tendencies that significantly complicate the problem of relating them to texts. But there is no need to postulate a dichotomy or simple choice between an interest in texts and in contexts, although the work of different historians and critical theorists may legitimately show different stresses and strains in addressing them. Nor need one posit an opposition between dialogization in textual and in intersubjective senses, that is, between forces operative in texts and in readers or social agents. There may be tension between textuality and intersubjectivity, and the role of intention is always problematic in its relation to what a text may do or perform. But highly dialogized texts may be argued to require a dialogic and self-critical response from the reader that is intimately related to the subject-positions he or she occupies and is attempting to forge. The basic point here is that one should not hypostatize the text, the context, or the reader but attempt to understand the relations among them in tensely interactive terms. Even more basically, one should construe one's own position as inserted within that interaction in relation to which text, context, reader, and subject are themselves more or less useful abstractions.

In *Rethinking Intellectual History*,[3] I attempted to engage various old historicisms whose hegemonic role in professional historiography is not entirely a thing of the past. The book employed a limited or circumscribed strategy that is, I think, particularly defensible in a discipline such as historiography. It attempted to give a significantly different twist to a traditional approach to problems that was and is familiar within intellectual history, for it looked to established canons but insisted on critically noncanonical readings of canonical or, more precisely, canonized texts.

In later work[4] as well as in the first chapter of the present book, I render more explicit and to some extent revise the strategy employed in *Rethinking Intellectual History*. It is important to distinguish between

[3]Ithaca: Cornell University Press, 1983.
[4]See especially *Soundings in Critical Theory*.

canonization—a basically conservative practice in the reception or appropriation of artifacts—and the potentials of those artifacts to be brought out through critical readings that, in Walter Benjamin's words, brush history against the grain. It is only through a rigidified and misplaced ritual process that one apprehends canonization as totally and irredeemably contaminating texts or artifacts. By contrast, it is, I think, necessary to understand canonization critically as a historical process through which texts are made (however problematically) to serve hegemonic interests both in ways they invite and in ways they resist more or less compellingly. The process of canonization requires that the critical or even potentially transformative—noncanonical or anticanonical—dimensions of texts and other artifacts be repressed or radically downplayed.

It is indeed vital to attend to the way more symptomatic artifacts are able to reinforce ideological needs and desires or even to hold out a more or less distorted image of utopia. But it is equally vital to elaborate an approach in which one can address this problem critically, and certain texts may be particularly valuable in cultivating this approach. There is no simple formula that will enable one to decide which texts these are, but the process of education—and of educating oneself as educator—requires that this be a topic that is recurrently debated. Here dialogic relations both within and between texts and selves have a continually renewed role to play in elaborating different vantages on textual and cultural processes.

It might still be plausible to suggest that, at least in the recent past, certain texts of "high" culture have had a particularly powerful critical charge in part because they have not entered fully into the commodity system and are instead objects of relatively small capital investment. (To account for that critical charge, Adorno's ideas about "autonomous" art and the role of negative textual space in an administered society would have to be revised in important or even drastic ways, notably in the direction of a better understanding of the divided tendencies or differences within any text or artifact and the interactions among various artifacts in different "levels" or areas of culture.) Mass culture, by contrast, is heavily capitalized and commodified, and popular culture in industrial societies has been largely absorbed into the commodity system. The fact that we often use the terms "popular" and "mass" culture interchangeably is one index of the extent to which popular culture has been integrated into the commodity system. This usage is distortive and anachronistic with respect to other forms of popular culture, which existed and functioned under significantly different conditions and might at times have critical, transformative, or legitimately affirmative tendencies. But even with respect to more recent commodified popular and mass culture, we should avoid blanket categorizations or condemnations that always skirt essentialization, elitism, and self-defeating cultural pessimism. Instead we should attempt to work out sustained and careful analyses of the way artifacts always to some extent affect social and cultural stereotypes and ideological processes, even when they insistently attempt to reproduce and reinforce banality.[5] We should also be not only open to the possibility but actively alert to the manner in which artifacts of mass culture may indeed have popular and even critical dimensions either through creative modes of consumption or through more thoroughgoing and even collective procedures in which commodified artifacts are reproduced or refunctioned.[6]

In addition, it is difficult to deny that the counterpart to the relative resistance of aspects of "high" culture to commodification is frequently their hermetic quality, including their tendency to recycle older and more popular forms, such as the carnivalesque, in largely inaccessible ways. At times this difficult or hermetic quality may be justifiable.[7] But it is also possible—particularly when certain strategies have become routinized—that texts employing them, even when

[5]For a discussion of some of these issues, see Alice Yaeger Kaplan, *Reproductions of Banality: Fascism, Literature, and French Intellectual Life* (Minneapolis: University of Minnesota Press, 1986). I would like to note what should be obvious. A critical process need not be purely negative. It may reinforce established principles or policies precisely insofar as they are able to stand up to criticism and prove worthy of affirmation. But then their reproduction is not simply ideological.

[6]See, for example, Andrew Ross, *No Respect: Intellectuals and Popular Culture* (New York: Routledge, 1989).

[7]One of the more interesting and valid reasons for the appeal of a difficult or hermetic style as a strategy of resistance is given by the Tunisian writer Abdelwahab Meddeb: "We will defend ourselves with arabesque, subversion, labyrinthine constructions, the incessant decentering of the sentence and of language so that the other will lose the way just as in the narrow streets of the *casbah*"; quoted in Jean Dejeux, *Situation de la littérature maghrébine de langue française* (Algiers: Office des publications universitaires, 1982), pp. 103–4. Compare Adorno: "What everybody takes to be intelligible is in fact not intelligible at all. Conversely, what our manipulated contemporaries dismiss as unintelligible secretly makes very good sense to them indeed. This recalls Freud's dictum that the uncanny is uncanny only because it is secretly all too familiar, which is why it is repressed. [. . .] The accessibility of past art spells its doom. To validate this, one only has to look at the fact that there are many dark and doubtlessly misunderstood works among those enshrined for ever in the pantheon of classics"; *Aesthetic Theory*, trans. C. Lenhardt (1970; London: Routledge and Kegan Paul, 1984), p. 262.

they attempt to subvert the high/low opposition and explicitly attack both the stratification of levels of culture and their own "high" or "elite" status, may be elitist, for example, in their function as symbolic capital and social reinforcement for a restricted in-group or cenacle. (Needless to say, the object of analysis may be popular culture, but the position of its students, the functions of their activities or modes of networking, their methods of analysis, and their performative styles may be "high-cultural" in nature and very confined in terms of actual or even potential audiences.) Indeed, we in the academy may be rewarded for saying the most radical things insofar as they remain intellectually inaccessible to most people and have little effect on existing power structures. How such a state of affairs may be conjoined with the type of democratic values and politics often advocated by relatively hermetic critics poses a significant problem.

This problem is not confined to any one theoretical tendency, and its sources are connected with advanced forms of the division of labor and professionalization both in the academy and in the larger society. Here the challenge is not to dismiss these forms or to believe that one can return to some putative earlier and simpler state; it is to do something appreciably different, more comprehensive, and engaging with them. An awareness of this challenge should at least indicate that the necessary difficulty required by rigorous and self-critical thought should not itself be fetishized or correlated with some prejudicial ranking of types of thought such as that which presents accessibility as necessarily a feature of a degraded, pejoratively vulgar, or popularizing mode of thought. Indeed, one aspect of traditional historiography that is worth preserving in a transformed manner is the idea that all forms of writing—and certainly all forms of academic writing in the humanities—should ideally make contact with diverse social groups. This ideal requires a style of address and a type of social reconstruction that should be affirmed, however difficult they may be to elaborate in a sustained and cogent fashion. Another directive one may take up and reformulate from traditional historiography is that we should insistently relate the reading of texts and other artifacts to the interpretation of significant problems in history and social life. In the chapters of this book, I try to provide related perspectives on how this reformulation should be undertaken and the import it may have for the elaboration of theory that is not self-contained but open to a sustained interchange with historical research.

A theoretical tendency with which I am particularly concerned is psychoanalysis.[8] I am intent on showing why psychoanalysis is misunderstood as merely a psychology of the individual, and its basic concepts are overly reduced when they are confined to a clinical context, however important the latter may be. In addition, certain key psychoanalytic concepts (such as transference, denial, resistance, repression, acting-out, and working-through) are crucial in the attempt to elucidate the relation between cultures that come into contact as well as between the present (including the analyst) and the past. One manifest goal of this book is to forge a stronger link between psychoanalysis and history in which the relation between individual and society is not prejudged on the basis of current ideologies to be purely analogical. The processes referred to by the basic concepts of psychoanalysis undercut the opposition between individual and society insofar as they involve social individuals whose relative individuation or collective status should be a problem for inquiry and argument. I would, moreover, observe that a psychoanalytically informed notion such as repetitive temporality (or history as displacement), as it is used in these pages, should not be read as a dogmatic return to a philosophy of history. On the contrary, it counteracts historicist teleology and redemptive or messianic narratives, and it has a hypothetical, revisionary status that is always in need of further specification and open to debate.

With regard to deconstruction, which is also at issue in these pages, I would like to make a point that I have repeatedly made elsewhere but that deserves restatement and elaboration here. The critique of pure binary oppositions or sheer dichotomies (themselves essential for a scapegoat "mechanism") eventuates in problematic distinctions—not in utter confusion, free play, or homogenization of all differences. Indeed, when the security and self-certainty of pure oppositions are placed in doubt, distinctions become more rather than less important, and their ethical and political bearing is of crucial significance. In addition, more hangs on certain distinctions than on others. In some cases one may want to reinforce distinctions, in others, to question them further. I am touching on difficult matters of judgment in which ethical and political issues are very much at stake.

For example, there is a sense in which less rides on the distinction between history and other disciplines than on that between perpetra-

---

[8]Here it is useful to refer to my "Psychoanalysis and History," in *Soundings in Critical Theory*, pp. 30–66.

tors and victims in the Holocaust. Even to compare these distinctions may be symptomatic of a crisis in judgment. But it may still be worth noting that at present there are good reasons to problematize even further the distinction between history and other disciplines insofar as one argues that certain practices, such as critical reading that resists simple reductionism, warrant a larger place in history whereas other practices, such as careful historical research into contexts of discourse, should be more prominent in fields such as literary criticism and philosophy. In this sense, one might want to emphasize the point that the role of the historian is not a full identity but at most a subject-position that should be complemented, supplemented, and even contested by other subject-positions (such as critical reader and intellectual).

By contrast, one may point to the dubious nature of certain attempts to problematize further the distinction between perpetrators (or collaborators) and victims of the Holocaust. This is not to say that ordinary people under given conditions or in certain contexts may not become perpetrators; they clearly may. Nor is it to argue that perpetrators were destined to play that role because of their intrinsic personality type or peculiarities of their national history. But it is to say that once people become perpetrators, an important distinction exists between them and those whom they victimize. Of course there are complex and ambiguous cases, for example, victims who cooperated with perpetrators. But here important questions include the representativeness of such cases, the conditions in which victims were induced to participate in victimization, the degree to which they did so, and the very motivations of the analyst in focusing on such cases. In any event, there is a significant difference between those put in an impossible situation—however questionably they may have responded to it—and those who put them there. In addition, there were victims (and in large numbers) who were not perpetrators or collaborators in any significant sense.

It might be argued that all Nazis were to some extent accomplices in victimization, and many Germans during the Nazi regime were collaborators or largely nonresisting bystanders. Moreover, collaborators in general cannot be identified with victims; their complicity varies in degree but counteracts any such identification. Additional distinctions and qualifications are of course necessary, for example, with reference to the role of Allied leaders as nonresisting bystanders and the dubious postwar uses of the Shoah as "symbolic capital." Nor can those born later be placed in a guilt-ridden lineage or made to bear the stain of a secularized original sin, although they may well have a special responsibility in confronting a specific past. Furthermore, the issue of what distinctions should be stressed or elaborated in a present context, especially if one is concerned with working through the past, is always debatable. My basic point, however, is that the deconstruction of binary oppositions need not result in a generalized conceptual blur or in the continual suspension of all judgment and practice. It should be accompanied by a careful inquiry into the status and role of resulting distinctions as well as by research into their actual historical functions, knowledge of which is crucial for even the most tentative moral and political judgments. The latter should never serve as testimonials to one's own ideological purity, transcendent status, moral self-righteousness, or sense of certitude, but they are important insofar as they are bound up with practice in the present and future that may help to avert or resist possibilities to which one is indeed liable.

It is, moreover, not a defense of a generalized "nonjudgmental" attitude to observe that, in cases where one has not oneself been tested by comparable circumstances, one may be in no position to judge particular individuals. The judgments one seeks through an exchange with the past are related instead to more general questions of interpretation and argument that become specified not as one plays imaginary God or just judge vis-à-vis others in the past but as one confronts difficult challenges in the present and future. As Geoffrey Hartman has aptly noted with reference to the case of Paul de Man: "The aim of judgment in historical or literary-critical discourse, a forensic rather than juridical sort of inquiry, is not that of determining guilt or innocence. It is to change history into memory: to make a case for what should be remembered. This responsibility converts every judgment into a judgment on the person who makes it."[9]

---

[9]"Judging Paul de Man," in *Minor Prophecies: The Literary Essay in the Culture Wars* (Cambridge: Harvard University Press, 1991), p. 148. On the problem of history and memory, see the excellent book of Yosef Hayim Yerushalmi, *Zakhor: Jewish History and Jewish Memory* (New York: Schocken, 1987). Yerushalmi argues that until the sixteenth century Jewish thought was concerned not with history but with collective memory in a living ritualistic and liturgical tradition. He also postulates a very sharp division between memory and history in the present that creates a tragic subject-position for the Jewish historian, notably the Jew with a nostalgia for the traditional past but a commitment to the criteria of secular historiography. (For a related variation on the theme of the "godless" Jew, see Yerushalmi's *Freud's Moses: Judaism Terminable and Interminable* [New Haven: Yale University Press, 1991].) Yerushalmi in a sense provides a specifica-

I would also like to note that the term "subject-position," which I use in the following pages, should not be equated with a notion of full identity. A subject-position is at best a partial, problematic identity, and it is intricately bound up with the other subject-positions any social individual occupies. Certain subject-positions may become especially prominent or even overwhelming, for example, those of victim or perpetrator. But a subject-position becomes a total identity only in cases of extreme "acting-out" wherein one is possessed by the past and tends to repeat it compulsively as if it were fully present. Here identity is imaginary and may be related to pathological disorders. The tendency for a given subject-position to overwhelm the self and become a total identity becomes pronounced in trauma, and a victim's recovery may itself depend on the attempt to reconstruct the self as more than a victim. More generally, the process of coming critically to terms with the past requires perspective on subject-positions and the ability to resist the total consumption of the self by a given identity that threatens to prevent any form of renewal. This process is not purely individual or psychological but linked, in however undogmatic and mediated a manner, with ethical, social, and political concerns. Hence it is eminently open to discussion and argument in the effort to arrive at cogent judgments. Furthermore, the critique of full identity along with the affirmation of a notion of subject-positions does not entail the simple rejection of either the role of responsible agency or the goal of a viable articulation of subject-positions in social individuals enjoying a significant measure of control in action. Instead it raises the question of conditions in which these values be-

tion of Max Weber's notion of disenchantment that applies to certain Jewish historians and those of other backgrounds who find themselves in a comparable position. His account is lucid and moving, and I would agree that a tension exists between memory (notably memory with a ritualistic, liturgical character) and critical, secular historiography. But Yerushalmi tends to take this tension to the point of dichotomy; he does not investigate how it might be addressed and worked through without the promise of redemption, full transcendence, or elimination of its tragic dimensions. One reason for his insistence on dichotomy or unsurpassable binarism is his tendency to remain within an unanalyzed and relatively conventional understanding of historiography as a basically historicist (if not neopositivistic) reconstruction of the past. He does not explore the relation between objective reconstruction and dialogic exchange in ways that would generate a mutually provocative interaction between "history" and memory. Such an interaction might lead to a revised notion of legitimate memory as that which is argued to stand the test of critical historiography and evaluative judgment—both a memory of the undesirable, indeed traumatic, past that is recalled so that its repetition may be combatted and a memory of that which is worth passing on and reworking as a basis of individual and collective life.

come operative and points to the desirability of furthering their gence.

In other words, the notion of subject-position is a beginning, end point, in analysis and argument. I later insist that, especially in cases of severe trauma, one may never fully transcend the past and that one should be both respectfully attentive to the voices of victims and wary of certain extreme, negative reactions to acting out problems. But the function of critical thought is not to rationalize the tendency simply to enact one's positionality or to benefit from the unearned authority one's background may at times furnish. It is to provide perspective on subject-positions and to assist in coming to terms with them, not only by thematizing them and tracing their "voices" but also by helping to transform their articulation and interaction in desirable ways. In this sense, it is to abet responsible practice and even a revised sense of objectivity in discourse insofar as one works out a more lucid and effective relationship to constraining forces.

Finally, I would like to make explicit something that is implicit in the course of this book. Especially in Chapter 1, I return to a notion of historical understanding in terms of a problematic combination of reconstruction of, and dialogic exchange with, the past or the object of study. I dwell on the necessity and the limits of contextualization as a dimension in both reconstruction and dialogic exchange. I would also note the limits as well as the necessity of the attempt at "dialogue." Any literal dialogue is always affected and at times undermined or rendered deceptive by differences in power and authority between interlocutors. And dialogism in the sense of an interaction of mutually implicated and perhaps contestatory forces (including subject-positions) itself involves differences in strength between these forces. Any discursive attempt to brush history—or contemporary culture—against the grain by attending to subdominant or oppressed voices itself requires structural change to make those voices register effectively or (with respect to contemporary problems) attain a stronger and more effective institutional position.

There is, moreover, a sense in which the limits of both literal dialogue and the process of dialogism are most evident in the face of the traumatic and the sublime. Indeed, the sublime is a kind of transvaluation of the traumatic that becomes most dubious when it is figured as sacrificially redemptive or salvational, and it is at issue both in the most exigent, question-worthy, at times questionable forms of art and in extreme experience or "limit" cases such as the Holocaust.[10] I intimate that a negative sublime was itself an element of national socialist ideology, in which unheard-of, traumatizing transgression exerted a deeply ambivalent fascination for the fanatically committed Nazi. Not only was the Nazi sublime (as evidenced, for example, in Heinrich Himmler's 1943 Posen speech) linked to a numbingly extremist, transgressive (an)aesthetics, equivocally combined with an aesthetic ideology of identity or "beautiful" wholeness; it was also related to a distorted secular religiosity involving scapegoating and victimization.

Dialogue, indeed language in general, may break down in the attempt to come to terms with limit cases. But another insistent motif in this book is that one should not become fixated on this possibility (indeed eventuality) or restrict "theory" to what itself may threaten to become its compulsive or melancholic "acting-out."[11] Nor should one

[10]On trauma, see the important work of Cathy Caruth, "Unclaimed Experience: Trauma and the Possibility of History," *Yale French Studies* 79 (1991); Introduction, *American Imago* 48, no. 1 and no. 4 (1991). What is unclear in Caruth's approach is whether trauma not only is postulated as the condition of possibility of history but tends to be generalized and conflated with history. This uncertainty may itself perhaps be seen as a symptom of posttraumatic stress in which the recognition of a crucial problem (both the prevalent role of trauma in history and trauma as a possibility that may unexpectedly happen at any time in history) is rendered in a hyperbolic fashion that seems to equate history and trauma. I would further note that the notion of time as repetition with change allows for a recognition of the need to act out problems "symptomatically" in a posttraumatic context and for the significance of trauma in history which may be particularly marked in the recent past. It also allows for the way in which trauma limits history and historical understanding, notably in its disruption of contextualization and dialogic exchange. But one need not conflate trauma and history. Indeed, one may entertain the possibility of modes of historicity in which trauma and the need to act out (or compulsively repeat) may never be fully transcended but in which they may to some viable extent be worked through and different relations or modes of articulation enabled.

[11]In the tradition of Western Christianity as well as in secular forms that have a complex relation to it, notably romanticism, there is a marked tendency to valorize positively not only sublimity but melancholy and even self-victimization. The abjection and suffering of the melancholic may itself reach sublime heights (or depths), notably when one sees all forms of renewal or reinvestment in life as unacceptable compromises and betrayals of an unattainable ideal or an irreplaceable lost love. Intense intellectuality and ascetic saintliness, whether religious or secular, have often been linked to melancholy. (See, for example, the analysis in Julia Kristeva, *Black Sun: Depression and Melancholia* [1987; New York: Columbia University Press, 1989].) As Freud noted, melancholy may be combined or alternate with states of manic agitation and exaltation. (See especially "Mourning and Melancholia," *The Standard Edition of the Complete Psychological Works of Sigmund Freud* 14, trans. James Strachey [London: Hogarth, 1957], pp. 237–60.) The "narcissistic" identification with the other, which Freud saw as regressive in its ultimate denial of alterity, may even be affirmed not only as inevitable in identity-for-

see it as simply eliminating the need for a dialogic relation to the other that is vital for any process of understanding and working through problems, however limited and partial such a process may be. Rather the very relation between the sublime and the dialogic poses a ques-

---

mation but as an undecidable meeting of self-effacement and self-discovery through *imitatio*.

One may be unable—or even find it undesirable—to overcome the allure of sublimity or the valorization of melancholy, particularly when they attest to an extreme situation and are combined with arresting insights that are otherwise denied or obscured. Indeed, melancholy may be a warranted response to crisis and a traumatic past, and the sublime is a possible correlate of estrangement, uncanniness, and dislocation. But one may nonetheless insist on the desirability of limits in any process of imitatio— limits that are necessary to bring critical judgment to bear on the issue of what does or does not deserve to be followed (or relived) with respect to a seemingly redemptive leader or even a secular *maître à penser*. And one may question the role of melancholy and the sublime insofar as it becomes prepossessing, leads in dubious directions (such as the excessive valorization of radical transcendence or self-victimization), and is fixated upon as the ne plus ultra of thought and action.

In "Mourning and Melancholia" Freud himself says much less about mourning and working-through than about melancholy (or melancholia), and the intellectual complexities and aporias of the latter have also tended to captivate the attention of later theorists, often inducing an insufficient analysis of their relation to other possibilities. Without either dismissing the importance of melancholy or pretending to be able to provide answers that satisfy even myself, I nonetheless think it is necessary to raise and explore further the questions of mourning and working-through in their complex relations to phenomena such as melancholy and the sublime. In any case, what is especially questionable is the political and social analogue of a religious view of apocalyptic conversion: the view that only by acting excess out to the end (or succumbing to the abyss) can one reach the end of excess (or attain the heights). This view easily leads either to arbitrary declarations of a political propensity or to a *politique du pire* in which all effective agency, judgment, limits, and counterforces in the present are denied and their deficiencies aggravated rather than confronted critically and struggled against.

The sublime may also be correlated with an invidious distinction between the (narcissistic) self and the other wherein the affirmation of the autonomy and freedom of the self depends on a radical constructivism (or secular creationism) requiring a nihilating relation to the other (nature, history, the past, the maternal, and so forth). Such a view of extreme transcendence is often bound up with the idea that humans (typically through a "dreadfully free" but "effective" act of sovereign will) create all meaning and value; it may also involve gendered fantasies about self-genesis and creation ex nihilo. Moreover, it may be based on the assumption that any utopian politics of vision as well as "whatever dignity and freedom human beings could lay claim to could come only by way of what Freud called a 'reaction-formation' to an apperception of history's meaninglessness"; Hayden White, "The Politics of Interpretation: Discipline and De-Sublimation," in *The Content of the Form: Narrative Discourse and Historical Representation* (Baltimore: Johns Hopkins University Press, 1987), p. 72. Such a visionary politics, however, may be indistinguishable from blindness insofar as it complements an apperception of the past as abysmally meaningless with one of the future as an utterly blank (sublime?) utopia that may be addressed at most in hyperformalistic terms (for example, through hyperbolically pure affirmations of human creativity or collective praxis).

tion in which the limit to understanding—or the point at which understanding or even language in general breaks down—cannot be established once and for all because it is recurrently a matter for thought that is not simply divorced from practice.[12]

It should of course go without saying that what follows is in no sense an attempt at anything approximating a comprehensive account of the Holocaust or uses and abuses of it. Vis-à-vis those engaged in these important projects, I at most examine some important approaches to problems and attempt to bring out issues that may prove thought-provoking. While in no sense reducing these projects to the status of mere examples, I also attempt to touch on ways in which research into the Shoah may pointedly raise certain questions about the relation between history and theory. The reader should, however, be forewarned that Chapter 1 on canons has only a general relation to the issue of representing the Holocaust. It tries to bring such an issue into a viable relationship with the practice of reading texts by indicating how reading may keep alive the critical potential of certain texts and counteract the ways in which canonization mitigates or represses the role of texts in stimulating legitimately thought-provoking questions in the reader. Indeed, texts may undergo minor traumas or trigger them in the reader, and preeminently open to debate is the validity of the manner in which texts come to terms with their own disorienting potential and its import for the major traumas

[12]There is a sense in which Paul Celan wrote a poetry of almost unmitigated trauma that (especially with the canonization of "Todesfuge") became extremely hermetic. But it is noteworthy that, while feeling that he addressed no one, he still affirmed the value of dialogue: "The poem intends another, needs this other, needs an opposite. It goes toward it, bespeaks it. [. . .] The poem becomes a conversation—often desperate conversation"; "The Meridian" (1960) in *Paul Celan: Collected Prose*, trans. Rosmarie Waldrop (Manchester: Carcanet Press, 1986), pp. 48, 50. Celan also saw obscurity as "bestowed on poetry by strangeness and distance (perhaps of [poetry's] own making) and for the sake of an encounter" (p. 46). It is significant that this uncanny "encounter" was not conceived in abstract structural or linguistic terms but involved a notion of specific context or "date": "Perhaps we can say that every poem is marked by its own '20th of January'?" (p. 47). (Celan refers earlier to Georg Büchner's figure of Lenz "who 'on the 20th of January was walking through the mountain.' " It is also noteworthy that 20 January 1942 was the date of the Wannsee conference where Nazi officials, under the chairmanship of Reinhard Heydrich, coordinated and finalized plans for the extermination of the Jews.) But it is open to question whether the "other," sought in an "encounter," was human, for Celan linked the problematic "strangeness," on whose behalf poetry was written, to the "altogether other" in a way that seemed to have displaced religious connotations: "The poem has always hoped [. . .] to speak on behalf of the *strange*—no, I can no longer use this word—*on behalf of the other*, who knows, perhaps of an *altogether other*" (p. 48).

of social life. The broader problem I address is how to link reading and research so that the former does not become an involuted, formalistic undertaking and the latter a pretext for obliterating the significance and educational value of reading certain texts. In this sense, my argument in Chapter 1 bears on one of my long-standing concerns: how cogently to relate text-oriented fields such as intellectual history or literary criticism to research-oriented fields such as general history or the social sciences.

ONE

∽

Canons, Texts, and Contexts

Advocacy of a canon of "great books" in education and in the study of culture in general has recently become the object of renewed affirmation as well as attack. Unfortunately, the most heated affirmation has been part of a neoconservative revival that has placed the blame for contemporary problems on education and educators, especially in the humanities, and has seen the return to "great books" as the true path to salvation. The plaints of Allan Bloom, William Bennett, and Lynne Cheney chime with a long-standing tendency in American culture to divert attention from the socioeconomic and political sources of problems by scapegoating intellectuals; they also reaffirm a displaced religious sense of the sacred text as the beacon of common culture for an educated elite.

The neoconservative defense of an authoritative and culture-building canon has exacerbated the desire to decenter or even demolish canons. This desire has been pronounced among various groups, including neo-Marxists, feminists, students of popular culture, and proponents of ethnic and Third World studies.[1] To the extent that the ex-

---

[1] See, for example, Terry Eagleton, *Literary Theory: An Introduction* (Minneapolis: University of Minnesota Press, 1983); Peter Stallybrass and Allon White, *The Politics and Poetics of Transgression* (Ithaca: Cornell University Press, 1986); Jane Tompkins, *Sensational Designs: The Cultural Work of American Fiction* (New York: Oxford University Press, 1985); Henry Louis Gates, Jr., *Figures in Black: Words, Signs, and the "Racial" Self* (New York: Oxford University Press, 1987); and Houston Baker, *Blues, Ideology, and Afro-American Literature: A Vernacular Theory* (Chicago: University of Chicago Press, 1984).

clusionary bias of canons is aggravated rather than mitigated by the neoconservative initiative, the critique of canons acquires increased plausibility and appeal. Moreover, the broad issue of cultural and sociopolitical practice can in no sense be reduced to a debate over canonicity. At the very least, there is the prior question of access to literacy and, even more basically, the issue of equality of opportunity in general. Indeed, debates about the canon, especially when they are conducted without an awareness of their limitations and assumptions, may serve as a displacement of, or even a diversion from, a broader analysis of social and political structures.[2] The question, however, is whether the limited significance of the issue of canonization and the valid objections to certain social, political, and cultural functions of canons—or of overcharged debates about canonicity— entail the simple abandonment of careful study of texts and artifacts that have traditionally been included in canons. I would answer that question in the negative but insist that recent discussions raise the question of precisely how one should undertake both a critique of canonicity and a qualified defense of the careful reading of certain canonical texts.

I begin with a few general considerations that serve as a framework for my other comments. One should distinguish between the texts or artifacts that have been included in canons and the process of canonization that entails acts of inclusion and (explicit or implicit) exclusion. The latter has, I think, been the primary object of both attacks on and defenses of the canon. Through canonization texts are presumed to serve certain hegemonic functions with reference to dominant values

---

On canonization in general, see Robert von Hallberg, ed., *Canons* (Chicago: University of Chicago Press, 1983). See also Joseph Gibaldi, ed., *Introduction to Scholarship in Modern Languages and Literatures* (New York: Modern Language Association of America, 1992), especially Robert Scholes, "Canonicity and Textuality," pp. 138–58, and David Bathrick, "Cultural Studies," pp. 320–40.

[2]For an elaboration of this argument, see John Guillory, "Canonical and Non-Canonical: A Critique of the Current Debate," *ELH* 54 (1987), pp. 483–527. In *Professing Literature: An Institutional History* (Chicago: University of Chicago Press, 1987), Gerald Graff questions the extent to which processes such as canonization have in fact been effective in successfully inculcating dominant values, at least in the United States. He writes: "Literary studies have been no beacon of political enlightenment, but they have not been an instrument of dominant ideology and social control either—or, if so, they have been a singularly inefficient one" (p. 14). Scholars with political concerns are prone to overestimate the actual impact of their own areas of study even if only to criticize the results. But one obviously has here a problem that requires extensive empirical research on the level of dissemination and reception.

and structures, and the extent to which they do depends upon the way in which they are interpreted and the uses to which they are put. The process of canonization raises the question of the reception of texts with regard both to the constitution of disciplines or professions and to processes, such as socialization, operative in the larger society and polity. The open question is the degree to which texts that are canonized may be argued to invite or resist canonical functions.

A critique of a canon may proceed in two fashions. First, it may insist on the noncanonical reading of canonized texts in order to bring out the ways in which those texts resist or contest the canonical functions they are presumed to serve. For what may be quite forceful in canonization is the tendency to bracket the critical and even transformative potential of texts. Ideally, noncanonical reading examines the manner in which canonized texts must be interpretively bowdlerized to make them adjust to canonical functions. It also brings out their critical sides and investigates their relations to whatever ideologically reinforcing functions a text may be argued to have.

A second and equally important mode of criticizing canons is to insist on the importance of sets of texts and artifacts that have been not simply bowdlerized but marginalized or altogether excluded with the effect that certain counterhegemonic traditions are effaced from the historical record. Until recently, texts of women and minorities have undergone this process of suppression and repression. The effort to include formerly excluded or marginalized texts is altogether crucial, as is the historical and critical study of how and why processes of exclusion take place. I maintain, however, that the two modes of criticizing canons which I have mentioned should be seen as mutually reinforcing rather than as mutually exclusive options. Choices have to be made between these procedures not on a theoretical level but on pragmatic and problematic grounds when one confronts the issue of assigning material in a course or treating it in a study. But the unavoidable difficulties these choices pose should not be made to obscure the point that both procedures raise comparable problems and hold out similar promises.

One problem is that critiques of the canon may share a propensity with defenses of a canon — the tendency to fetishize the canon and fixate attention on it. The result is a monolitic idea of the historical role of canons as well as an inclination to consign to the shadows issues that cannot be centered on the question of canonicity. To the extent that a canon is dominant or at least prominent in a field of study, concern about its composition and functions is warranted. Still, one should not lose sight of the point that the goal—indeed, the promise—of a critique of canons should be the displacement of the very problem of canonicity and the realization that the important factor in the selection and interpretation of texts is their relationship to a set of crucial issues. The emphasis should be on certain issues and what texts may be argued to disclose or conceal with reference to them. Among the most intensely pressing issues we confront today are those relating to gender, race, class, and species—issues that involve the legitimate rights of women, oppressed minorities and classes, and animals other than the human being. These and comparable issues, such as the relation of work and play in society and culture or, in another register, between texts and contexts in interpretation, should be the focus of our concern and the guides in our debates, and the issue of the selection and interpretation of texts and other artifacts should be decentered in the sense that it becomes one limited but not unimportant subject of discussion and controversy in the light of significant problems. One would still have to select certain texts or artifacts for special attention, but one would be constrained to make arguments and provide reasons for one's choices. Although co-optation is always a clear and present danger in a commodity system, the resultant choices would not *simply* amount to a canon in the conventional sense insofar as they are self-critical and do not serve—or may even actively resist—canonical functions and reappropriations. Indeed, until we start asking certain questions about significant issues, we do not know how the texts of the past will respond. Moreover, we ought to be open to the possibility (in certain cases the likelihood) that in the reading of a text our very conception of significant issues will be challenged or changed—shown to be too restricted or simplistic. This outcome of reading is itself a hallmark of texts from which we may have most to learn and to which we should be inclined to return.

When one discusses a phenomenon such as the Shoah, one broaches issues of a distinctive order of magnitude. The general problems in reading texts and analyzing processes of canonization become particularly demanding, and one confronts almost intractable difficulties in formulation and presentation. The Nazis did indeed "canonize" certain texts, such as those of Nietzsche, and subject them to specific ideological interpretations. And important intellectuals, such as Heidegger, read their own work in a selective and ideologically tendentious fashion in order to adapt it to their conception of the needs and promise of the regime. The Nazi appropriation of the intellectual and artistic heritage of Germany and the West was often crude and blatantly reductive, but it was also of great political importance and closely bound up with genocidal policies. Furthermore, to the extent that the Holocaust itself comes in some sense to be "canonized," one may expect that (as in the case of texts) certain issues tend to be avoided, marginalized, repressed, or denied. Indeed, a mutually re-inforcing relation exists between canonization and the role of forces such as the repression of significant dimensions of the canonized object—dimensions that may place in question the process of canon-ization itself. In the case of traumatic events, canonization involves the mitigation or covering over of wounds and creating the impres-sion that nothing really disruptive has occurred. Thus one forecloses the possibility of mourning, renders impossible a critical engagement with the past, and impedes the recognition of problems (including the return of the repressed). How to come to terms with this coincidence of "canonization" and its seeming opposites—and with the Nazi re-gime in all its dimensions—has posed an extremely difficult problem in the postwar period, especially (but not only) for Germans and Jews.

In view of these observations and contentions, one should recog-nize the need to criticize the very concept of "great book," which is encrusted with neoconservative and Arnoldian connotations. This concept should be displaced in the direction of text and artifact in gen-eral. (Often I shall use "text" in its expanded sense as a metonym for artifact or signifying practice in general.) This process of substituting "text" for "great book" is already well under way, especially in liter-ary criticism and certain forms of intellectual history. Texts in the lit-eral sense are not the only and not the most important objects of study or of life. I contend, however, that without careful, critical at-tention to at least certain literal texts, one's own intellectual and po-litical culture (at least in the context of modern Western societies) may prove to be rather thin, if not superficial, and one may well be in no position to reconstruct past—or to analyze contemporary—social, po-litical, and cultural practices with any degree of subtlety and acumen. In fact, one may find oneself implicitly relying on the perspective of an overly restricted subset of more or less canonical figures (or "mod-ern masters") whose limitations are not offset by the arguments and perspectives that could conceivably be elaborated on the basis of the work of other, unread figures. This is not, however, to say that the sole guide to critique is the written text or, for that matter, the artifact of traditional elite culture in general. On the contrary, the very opposition between elite and popular culture should be both investigated historically and questioned politically. And one should be open to the critical potential of noncanonical artifacts or traditions (including oral traditions) that may deserve broader dissemination if not centrality. Indeed, attention should be directed to an important but problematic distinction that may help in salvaging the valid component in the notion of especially significant texts (in the expanded or general sense).

I propose that all texts are worth thinking *about*, but some texts are especially valuable to think *with*, and in certain cases they have proven this value in renewed ways over time. The texts that are worth thinking with enable a more pointed discussion of texts or aspects of texts—including aspects of texts worth thinking with—that are less deserving of emulation. They may also assist in the recognition of those critical aspects or utopian possibilities that may at times be found in even the most debased or commercialized cultural artifacts. Despite its problematic nature and the difficulty in applying it to specific artifacts, this distinction between that which is worth thinking with and that which is worth thinking about is required as a general guide in coming to terms with texts in ways that actively invite continual self-questioning. It would, however, be a mistake to take this distinction as a binary opposition, and its variable application to specific texts is always open to reconsideration. But critical thought is in a worse position without this distinction than with it. The danger in certain reading technologies, including deconstruction and the new historicism, is that this distinction may be obliterated insofar as all texts and artifacts are read in the same terms either as self-deconstructive or as culturally and politically symptomatic.[3]

How does one identify the texts that are particularly worth thinking

[3]On these problems, see my *Soundings in Critical Theory* (Ithaca: Cornell University Press, 1989) as well as Chapter 4 of the present book. In the controversy over the early World War II journalistic articles of Paul de Man, some commentators sympathetic to deconstruction have tended to read markedly symptomatic, propagandizing texts as if they were self-questioning—indeed to read de Man as if his very early texts were as intricate and self-contestatory as his later ones are. To some extent, this tendency was unfortunately authorized by Derrida in "Like the Sound of the Deep within a Shell: Paul de Man's War" (*Critical Inquiry* 14 [1988], 590–652; reprinted in Werner Hamacher, Neil Hertz, and Thomas Keenan, eds., *Responses: On Paul de Man's Wartime Journalism* [Lincoln: University of Nebraska Press, 1989], pp. 127–64).

with—texts that help to develop critical abilities in cultural studies? No text entirely transcends an uncritical implication in contemporary ideologies and prejudices. No text in this sense is without its blind spots. But certain texts are submerged in blindness and regenerate or even reinforce ideologies in relatively unmodulated fashion. Propaganda on the political level and advertising on the commercial level tend to be ideologically reinforcing or to employ potentially critical modes, such as irony and parody, only within safe and self-serving limits.

In significant but not total contrast, some texts help one to foreground ideological problems and to work through them critically. And they may assist one in elaborating a critically self-reflective approach to a field of study as well as procedures for investigating contexts in an other than narrowly historicist manner. For these texts may be argued to frame their ideologies and prejudices in a specific fashion and to help put the reader in a better position to confront them critically. No text or cultural artifact can in and of itself critically rework or transform society. But some are particularly effective in engaging critical processes that interfere with the regeneration or reinforcement of ideologies and established contexts in general; they provide bases for the critique of their own blindnesses by helping to initiate a process of reflection that may educate us as readers and have practical implications. These are the texts and artifacts that have a special claim to be included in self-contestatory "canons" that are themselves always open to questioning and renewal, particularly as we discover blindnesses and limitations in what we earlier thought were exemplary texts or dimensions of texts. A challenge in the reading of any text or artifact is to ascertain the specific configuration of symptomatic (or ideologically reinforcing), critical, and potentially transformative forces it puts into play—a challenge that involves us as readers in both reconstruction of and dialogic exchange with the past. This objective should never be divorced from close, formal inquiry into the manner in which a text does what it does, for this mode of inquiry is crucial in delineating precisely how a text relates to its contexts or reworks its contents. Formal inquiry is not simply formalistic to the extent that it does not confide in a simple separation of form from context or content. Such inquiry is necessary not only for the critic but also for the historian who recognizes what should be obvious: texts or artifacts are events that cannot be reduced to contextual forces or employed as mere documentary sources insofar as they make a historical difference by refiguring their contexts or reworking their material. To make this point is not to subscribe to a quasi-transcendental notion of textuality or "literariness" that relegates contexts to an ancillary status and affirms a purely performative or abysmally self-canceling conception of language. It is rather to insist on a careful, historically specific, and self-questioning inquiry into the manner in which texts interact with their contexts of writing and reception.

There is clearly a need in historiography to address the question of the contexts of reading and interpretation over time. Indeed, there is no simple choice among contextualization, textual interpretation, and self-critical dialogue with the texts of the past. To oppose the reconstruction of contexts to textual analysis or dialogic exchange is to create an artificial and debilitating dichotomy. But historical understanding should not for that reason be conflated with contextualism in its narrowly historicist and documentary sense.

Although no text transcends an implication in contexts, one cannot read all texts indiscriminately as straightforward signs of the times. "Context" easily becomes a procrustean bed on which we cut all artifacts to the measure of our familiarizing, preestablished modes of understanding and satisfy our hunger for hefty "factoids" and thick descriptions. What is thereby eliminated is the manner in which certain texts make claims on us and may even disrupt the explanatory or interpretive molds in which we try to contain them. For the contextualizing historicist, history—understood in a very conventional manner—is the answer. For the historian, history should be a problem, that is to say, something that calls for critical reflection and for continual reinvestigation as to its very nature.

It is, moreover, important to note that one cannot essentialize the nature of the work performed on ideologies and contexts by texts that are worth thinking with. Or, to put the point another way, one cannot essentialize or fetishize the notion of critique itself. In this sense, it would at best be of limited value to try to arrive at a uniform, purely formal, or universally determining set of criteria with which to identify texts worth thinking with, for what might serve critical thought in certain circumstances might not in others. For example, at a given point in history, it might be both aesthetically and politically challenging for a member of an oppressed group to make use of a traditional literary form, such as the *Bildungsroman* or the autobiography—a form that might serve a critical function for a member of a privileged class only if it were subjected to certain telling variations. And, within a given reference group, a technique (such as free indirect style or montage) that was experimental and thought-provoking at one time may become banal and accommodating at another. In this sense, a concern for context is directly related to the appreciation of the critical or at least provocative potential of given texts or procedures at a given time and over time. Moreover, on the level of reception, one must try to understand as fully as possible why it is that even the most heinous and disastrous ideologies or the most stereotypical texts have been able to exercise a hold over people, including some of the seemingly most critical intellectuals. When critique becomes autonomous and emerges as one's own form of naïveté, the very appeal of ideologies may escape one's grasp. One may thus become blind not only to the limits of one's own thought but also to the way in which certain aspects of an existing set of contexts may in fact be worth preserving, reinforcing, or reworking. (This point applies, for example, to civil liberties in our own context.) Other aspects of a status quo may by contrast be ready for radical criticism and major reconstruction. In addition, one's perspective on which contextual aspects fall into one or another category may change over time, thereby indicating that understanding has a delayed or belated—what Freud termed a *nachträglich*—dimension. This unsettling dimension, whereby one is able to see things or ask questions that were not available to oneself or others in the past, is bound up both with traumatic effects and with the very ability to learn from an exchange with the past. *Nachträglichkeit* (belatedness) would be utterly misconstrued if it became a pretext for simplistic teleological narratives in which earlier phenomena are portrayed as causing or leading unilaterally to later ones. But the attempt to reduce its role to the vanishing point (for example, by an indiscriminate dismissal of "anachronisms") may itself be criticized as an extreme manifestation of a certain kind of historicism that attempts to evade present contexts in favor of total empathy with, or autonomized reconstruction and pure interpretation of, an excessively restricted and idealized idea of past contexts.

With respect to existing disciplines, the departure from canons has had some dubious consequences that underscore the need to be attentive to the nature and implications of one's critique. Canons have been more evident in literary criticism, philosophy, and art history than they have been in history or social science. In addition, the former fields have had canons both on the level of so-called primary texts and on the level of theoretical texts or commentaries taking "primary" texts as objects of analysis or emulation. The critique of canons has for obvious reasons also been more vociferous and forceful in these fields than in history or social science. The near-fixation on canons in the traditional humanistic disciplines tended to obscure an entire range of important problems, including the very problem of the emergence, institutionalization, and often dubious functions of a canon.

Still, there is one function of a canon that is difficult to gainsay. A canon does provide a shared set of reference points for discussion, even when one insists that these reference points should be not only approached critically but also selected in part because of their very ability to stimulate critical thought that may be applied elsewhere. The role of such a set of reference points would seem to be directly related to the importance of theory and of traditions of theorizing in a field not modeled on the natural sciences. In other words, it is difficult to see how one could relegate texts to an instrumental status and elaborate an autonomous body of theory in fields in which meaning, interpretation, and critical self-reflection are at issue. In these fields, specific texts would seem to be inextricably bound up with problems and have a special status as media of dialogic exchange. In them the question, have you read so-and-so? always has a marked relevance.

There is an obvious but nontrivial sense in which any common program of studies with requirements institutes a canon that may well exclude or underemphasize certain topics. And the effects of such a program, on however local or evanescent a level, can be very constraining. But disciplines or fields taken as a whole do reveal some noteworthy divergences, at least with reference to a canon in the weightier sense of a pantheon of authors and a long-standing list of consecrated texts believed to be privileged objects of reading for generations. Certain fields have for some time not had a canon in this delimited sense, and in them the movement toward a more critically defined set of textual reference points would not involve dismantling such a traditional edifice. In fact, it might well involve arguing for the necessity of nontraditional, self-contestatory "canons."

One sign of a science is that it no longer reads its canonical authors. To put it another way, it does not have a textual canon or even competing canons. It has relatively autonomous theories, textbooks, and problems; a disciplinary matrix; and occasional papers in which the valuable findings—in contrast to the texts—of earlier figures are assumed to be integrated. To the extent that science has exemplary texts, they lead a very short life and would seem to have a largely instrumental value. Hence a contemporary physicist qua physicist need not read Newton or Einstein. I would be inclined to object that reading Newton and Einstein, as part of a broader definition of a historically informed, self-reflective physicist, should be prevalent and valued within the profession, but the dominant criteria for good physics do not require it.

The social sciences have in large part attempted to follow the natural sciences in this dimension of self-understanding. In this minimal sense, they seem to have become more "scientific." Yet the consequences are questionable. It is problematic in the extreme to believe that whatever is valuable in Marx, Weber, Freud, and Durkheim has been integrated into the state of the art in a manner that releases social scientists from the need to read carefully the texts of these figures and to offer courses on them. Other crucial figures such as C. L. R. James and W. E. B. DuBois are often excluded and therefore ignored as parts of the history of the discipline. The belief that the social sciences may emulate the natural sciences in this "noncanonical" respect helps to void them of a critical, self-reflective dimension and fosters a narrowly scientistic self-conception. It also tends to make them adaptive to the status quo in an extremely confining manner.

One may argue that an attempt to come to terms with the past of a discipline is part and parcel of a broader cultural, philosophical, and self-critical understanding of that discipline; it requires some sense of a "canon" of relevant texts as a shared but critically appropriated and essentially contested set of reference points. Yet one may question the extent to which professional historiography itself has had a theoretically informed relation to its own past, in which certain texts provide a basis for argument and self-reflection. The "research imperative" often appears to be dominant—an imperative in accordance with which past texts are documents having an instrumental value as sources of information that is used to test a hypothesis or to flesh out a narrative. When it exists at all as part of an undergraduate or graduate program, the "theory" seminar may stress works that are of restricted methodological interest in furthering research rather than those that stimulate more basic critical and self-critical reflection, and it may be even more narrowly geared to immediate, practical payoffs in the assignment of very recent historiography that may be directly emulated (or "trashed") by aspiring professionals. Of course, a seminar cannot do everything; difficult choices have to be made, and a great deal depends on how assignments are discussed. But the conflation of methodology with theory and the neat separation between recent historians and those who wrote more than a generation ago may induce both diminished self-understanding and the relegation of past historians to the history of historiography, thereby inhibiting a tense interaction between contemporary work and a dialogue with the past. In addition, one often slights the possibility that attention to the nature and role of the historian's own discourse entails not an "aestheticization" of history or a simpleminded reduction of history to fiction but rather a cognitively responsible effort to achieve critical understanding of theoretical problems with implications for historical practice—problems such as subject-position, voice, and the negotiation of the transferential relation between the historian and the past.[4]

In philosophy, the analytic turn, while not eliminating entirely the rereading of past philosophers, tended to reduce their work to quarries for insights into present problems. In this sense, Plato not only would be treated very selectively but might just as well have published—after the requisite editorial work—in *Mind* or the *Philosophical Review*. The study of the past could not in this sense aid in providing perspective on the present or even in generating a reorientation of significant questions. Thus, when Richard Rorty argued for a conception of philosophy as a conversation with the past, his initiative came as something of a shock, even though it was still very much indebted to a now-familiar analytic idiom and often kept conversation within rather gentlemanly parameters and bourgeois-liberal assumptions that tended to downplay more intense modes of controversy and conflict.

[4]See, for example, Perez Zagorin, "Historiography and Postmodernism: Reconsiderations" (*History and Theory* 29 [1990], 263–74), in which rhetorical analysis of historical texts tends by and large to be reduced to—and dismissed as—an "aestheticization" of history, and any attempt to foreground the problem of the historian's use of language is seen as diverting attention from the central concerns of historiography. For a contrasting view, see Philippe Carrard, *Poetics of the New History: French Historical Discourse from Braudel to Chartier* (Baltimore: Johns Hopkins University Press, 1992). See also my review of this book in the *Journal of Modern History* 66, no. 3 (1994). On the problem of transference, see my "Psychoanalysis and History," in *Soundings in Critical Theory*, pp. 30–66. See also Saul Friedlander, "Trauma, Transference, and 'Working Through' in Writing the History of the *Shoah*," in *History and Memory* 4 (1992), 39–59, and Peter Loewenberg, *Decoding the Past* (New York: Knopf, 1983). In transference as I adapt the term from psychoanalysis, the historian or analyst tends to repeat with more or less significant variations the problems active in the object of study. The point is not to deny transference or simply to act it out but to attempt to work through it in a critical manner.

Recently, history and philosophy have become somewhat more open to debates about their orientation. Philosophers have become more attentive to the possibility that the manner in which one comes to terms with the past is crucial to one's activity in the present and future.[5] In historiography, debates about theory and method are no longer confined to a small group of intellectual historians. A significant number of historians believe they must be up on current controversies about theory and method, if only at times to resist the allures of newer orientations and reaffirm an established convention or the tried-and-true proclivities of a mentor. And historians in general are increasingly apprehensive not only about the threat of invading troops but also about the deceptive maneuvers of invading tropes. The fact that the *American Historical Review*—until recently not notable as a forum for self-reflection—could devote almost an entire issue (94 [June 1989]) to methodological and theoretical debates is a surprising and welcome turn of events.[6]

With respect to a critical and self-critical historiography, I maintain that there is, and ought to be, a tension between two related approaches to which I have already alluded. Although both are in certain ways necessary, they cannot be simply integrated or subsumed in a classical synthesis. Rather, the two exist in a tense and open dialectical relationship that may be negotiated with greater or lesser success. Indeed, they may—and perhaps should—take different inflections in the work of different scholars (or even in different dimensions of the work of the same scholar). Each approach involves a claim about how to construe texts and implies how implausible it is to maintain that texts simply read themselves. These two approaches are contextualization in terms of the conditions of production and reception in the past, and dialogic exchange with texts in terms of an

[5]Especially significant in this respect is the "Ideas in Context" series edited by Richard Rorty, J. B. Schneewind, Quentin Skinner, and Wolf Lepenies for Cambridge University Press. For the more interpretive approach to social science, which has probably been strongest in professional anthropology, see, for example, Paul Rabinow and William M. Sullivan, eds., *Interpretive Social Science: A Reader* (Berkeley: University of California Press, 1979), and James Clifford and George E. Marcus, eds., *Writing Culture: The Poetics and Politics of Ethnography* (Berkeley: University of California Press, 1986).

[6]Discussion of theoretical and methodological problems has continued to be combined with monographic research in subsequent issues of the journal under the excellent editorship of David L. Ransel. With particular reference to certain arguments in the present chapter, see Russell Jacoby, "A New Intellectual History?" *American Historical Review* 97 (1992), 405–24, and Dominick LaCapra, "Intellectual History and Its Ways, 425–39.

interaction between past and present with possible implications for the future.

The contextualizing approach stresses the detailed embeddedness of texts in their own time and over time. It frequently relies on the provision of extensive background information that cannot be derived from the text itself, and it typically insists on a very broad sampling of texts from the same or related genres. In the form given to it by such recent figures as Quentin Skinner, J. G. A. Pocock, and David Hollinger, it aims to reconstitute an idiom or discursive framework that formed the broad yet particularized context for the text or corpus of texts under consideration. This approach has resulted in notable achievements, and the reconstruction of a shared field of discourse is both important in itself and necessary in the appreciation of how certain texts rework or transform common assumptions. But at times there is a tendency in the profession to identify contextualization with historical understanding itself. For many historians, to historicize is to contextualize. Careful and well-informed contextualization is, as I have intimated, an altogether necessary dimension of historical understanding, but it should not be equated with historical understanding *tout court*. The limitations of contextualism emerge most sharply when it becomes historicist in the sense criticized by Walter Benjamin in his "Theses on the Philosophy of History."[7]

The second approach is prevalent among literary critics and philosophers. It stresses our dialogic exchange with the past, and it may emphasize if not focus exclusively on the performative and creative way in which we rewrite the past in terms of present interests, needs, and

[7]*Illuminations*, ed. with an introduction by Hannah Arendt (1955; New York: Schocken, 1969), pp. 253–64. Benjamin writes in Thesis 7 (p. 256): "To historians who wish to relive an era, Fustel de Coulanges recommends that they blot out everything they know about the later course of history. There is no better way of characterizing the method with which historical materialism has broken." It is often easier to know what Benjamin is criticizing in the Theses than what he is advocating. But I take his critique of full empathy in the attempt to reconstruct the past purely in its own terms and for its own sake to imply that it is only through a diacritical comparison with later times that one can even attempt to reconstruct and understand what something meant at its own time. I also take it to imply that contextualization is most thought-provoking when it brings out obscured features or submerged possibilities of the past that still (if only by contrast) raise questions for us. And contextualization must be supplemented by critical dialogic exchange if we are to elicit and probe the past's unexamined assumptions and belated effects, thereby enabling us to put them in self-critical contact with our own assumptions (whose very disclosure may be facilitated by our attempt to articulate past assumptions).

values. On this view, we awaken the dead in order to interrogate them about problems of interest to us, and the answers we derive justifiably tell us more about ourselves than about a context we could not fully recreate in the best of circumstances even if we wanted to. Here priority is given to the novel and stimulating interpretation that tests our methods and theories and enables the texts of the past to be read as addressing us, whether in an intemporal sense or in a more disorienting and uncanny manner in which conventional notions of time may be unsettled. What is often lost sight of, however, is the caveat that the ability of a powerful reading method to reprocess in its own terms any object of inquiry should not be seen as a solution to problems but as itself a deeply problematic and disturbing phenomenon.

In philosophy, this second approach has at times led to "rational reconstructions" in which the work of past philosophers is rethought to make it relevant to present concerns, at times by working out more coherently lines of inquiry that were either cut short or poorly elaborated in the texts under scrutiny. In literary criticism, new criticism and more recent approaches such as deconstruction differ in how they interpret texts, but they converge in showing little interest in past contexts for their own sake. For example, Rousseau's status in the Enlightenment and his relation to the French Revolution—problems that have traditionally preoccupied historians—may not even be mentioned or in any case are not given a privileged status. In Jacques Derrida's *Of Grammatology*, for instance, the history of primary concern is the long and tangled heritage of metaphysics, and Rousseau is an exemplary figure in a problematic in which we are still very much implicated.[8]

A somewhat different formulation of the various stresses of recent interpretive approaches would distinguish those who read for the plot and those who plot for the read.[9] Those who read for the plot are concerned with eliciting patterns that actually or potentially characterize a set of texts, and their emphasis could be seen as a mode of contextualization in the form of intertextuality—one that may be adjusted in a variety of ways to contextualization in terms of social, political, and cultural matters. Those who plot for the read may refer to

[8]Trans. Gayatri Chakravorty Spivak (1967; Baltimore: Johns Hopkins University Press, 1974).
[9]*Reading for the Plot* is of course the title of Peter Brooks's important book (New York: Knopf, 1984). The book is dedicated to Paul de Man, one of the exemplars of plotting for the read.

contextual forces, including intertextual ones, but their objective is to provide as fine-grained a reading of specific artifacts as possible, and this emphasis may well induce a creative exchange that at times seems to depart from what might plausibly be argued to be happening in a text. Instead, the exchange prompts imaginative or intricately theoretical initiatives on the part of the reader. Structuralists often seem to read for the plot, whereas deconstructors plot for the read—typically the read that brings out the paradoxes or aporias of plotting itself and indicates how we are read by what we attempt to read.

I have oversimplified somewhat, and a closer investigation of the figures and movements I have mentioned might lead to a fuller appreciation of how they may be of use in elaborating the perspective I am about to enunciate. I contend that contextualization and dialogic exchange, reading for the plot and plotting for the read, supplement each other in several important and, at crucial moments, tense and even conflict-ridden ways in our attempts to read and interpret texts. For one thing, they are different inflections of the transferential relation that binds us to the past and through which the problems we investigate are repeated in displaced and sometimes disguised form in our very discussions of them. Extreme contextualization of the past in its own terms and for its own sake may lead to the denial of transference through total objectification of the other and the constitution of the self either as a cipher for empathetic self-effacement or as a transcendental spectator of a scene fixed in amber. By contrast, unmitigated "presentist" immersion in contemporary discourses, reading strategies, and performative free play may at the limit induce narcissistic obliteration of the other as other and the tendency to act out one's own obsessions or narrow preoccupations. An analogue of working through problems in interpretation would at the very least require a critical and self-critical way of putting into language the tense and shifting relation between contextualization and dialogic exchange. In other words, we must attempt to listen attentively to the voices of the other as we respond in voices that necessarily bear the imprint of our own formative and at times conflict-ridden contexts. But to construct the point this way is not to make apostrophe a pretext for mythologization or to reify the text as the autonomous bearer of its own readings. It is rather to insist on our implication in a complex interactive process whereby readings and interpretations must be defended by arguments that direct attention to features of the object and engage contrasting understandings of it.

In addition, the very manner in which texts of the past responded to their own multiple contexts makes radical or historicist contextualization a relatively adequate mode of interpretation only with respect to the most banal and reproductive artifacts. Even in these artifacts, reproduction is not simple replication of contexts but does something to them (typically in terms of reproducing and further legitimating an ideology or stereotype) that must be examined carefully. If a text could be totally contextualized, it would paradoxically be ahistorical, for it would exist in a stasis in which it made no difference whatsoever. It would be immobilized in its own era. If contextualization were fully explanatory, texts would be derivative items in which nothing new or different happened. But especially with texts that are good to think with, the work or play on contexts is far ranging, and it necessarily engages us in dialogic exchange. By giving of themselves, certain texts are especially effective in inducing us to give of ourselves. Thus, certain texts may be exemplary in demonstrating that historical interpretation requires not only contextualization but also the insistent investigation of the variable and never-to-be-fixated limits of contextualization.

Another way to put the point concerning transference, dialogic exchange, and working-through is to say that if we probe far enough, no significant problem is purely anachronistic. Anachronism takes two inversely related forms: projection of the present onto the past and projection of the past onto the present. Objectivity requires that we check projection, but the process of projection cannot be entirely eliminated. It is related to commitment and to intense interest and investment in what we do. In a basic sense, it is entailed by the fact that we are always implicated in the things we analyze and try to understand. The ideal of objectivity should not be made to neutralize the problem of the historian's voice in narration or analysis. Checking projection requires that we listen to the other, not that we efface or transfix the self. It may also require that we examine carefully the complex manner in which the other is in the self and the self in the other. Here an example may be helpful. David Hollinger writes the following in defense of contextualization as the more "authentic" way to understand William James historically:

> Advocates of this or that currently popular epistemology or metaphysical doctrine will claim James as their own, or set him up as a representative defender of some opposing doctrine. The anachronistic readings of James that sometimes result are not difficult to live with, but a more

accurate comprehension of what James himself was doing can make a more authentic James available for use in these contemporary debates. This authentic, historical James is also the one we must have if we wish to get right the intellectual history of the United States.

A truism about James is that he worried over the relation of science to religion. Yet this concern has been distant from the minds of most of the philosophers and scholars of the last fifty years who have drawn inspiration from, and sought to interpret, James's work. . . . [A]n accurate reading of James requires that we not screen out as an irrelevant curiosity the anxiety about the fate of religion in an age of science that James frankly shared with most of the people who heard him lecture and bought his books during his lifetime. By taking this anxiety seriously, we can more easily discern in James's texts what I argue here was James's center of intellectual gravity: A radically secular, naturalistic vision of the process by which knowledge is produced, and a hope that religiously satisfying knowledge might still be forthcoming if only enough people would bring to inquiry—and place at risk in it—their religious commitments.[10]

Hollinger is convincing when he points out the limitations of even anodyne "presentist" rational reconstructions that filter out concerns deemed to be irrelevant and reconfigure the past to serve an excessively truncated idea of contemporary interests. And he may well be correct in asserting that "anxiety about the fate of religion in an age of science" was not a concern in the James scholarship to which he refers. But one can criticize these tendencies without identifying contextualization as authentic and confining historical understanding only to the reconstruction of past contexts. One may instead conclude from Hollinger's remarks that philosophers who eliminated religion from the picture were misled and that the historian need not covertly corroborate or at best invert their form of anachronism by identifying authentic historical understanding with an interpretation that itself situates religion and the concern about the relation between science and religion squarely in the past. Moreover, one may ask whether a "radically secular, naturalistic vision" may conceal displaced religious elements in the thought of its proponents and itself induce an underestimation of the role of religion in contemporary social life. Hollinger wrote at a time when the revival of religion, at times in its most fundamentalist forms, was already becoming obvious as a feature of con-

[10]*In the American Province: Studies in the History and Historiography of Ideas* (1985; Baltimore: Johns Hopkins University Press, 1989), pp. 3–4.

temporary American culture and politics. And he says enough about the historical role of religion in America to indicate that the very belief that religion is a thing of the past is a shortsighted historical judgment. In fact, the relevance of Emerson to the pragmatic tradition may be in placing in the foreground the union of pragmatism and evangelism in American culture—a topic that is both studied and reenacted in Cornel West's 1989 book, *The American Evasion of Philosophy: A Genealogy of Pragmatism*.[11] I would even be tempted to say that if you scratch a pragmatist, you may well find an evangelist (or at least an edifying "discourser").

There is, however, another observation to be made in this regard. The fixation on anachronisms tends to obliterate the ways in which the past is repeated in the present with more or less significant variations. This process is crucial to our transferential relation to the past, and only by investigating it closely can we hazard a judgment about just how different a past context or period indeed was. With respect to religion, the obvious question is whether the so-called secularization thesis should be reformulated not in the simplistic form of an identity between religion and secular ideologies or in the tendentious form that leads one to reject as nefarious heresies ideologies one opposes. Rather, secularization should itself be understood as a typically conflictual process of repetition with change—at times disruptive or traumatic change. In opposing a simplistic version of the secularization thesis, Hans Blumenberg may well have offered a better and more psychoanalytically acute interpretation of secularization in terms of reoccupation: an older, typically religious or theological cultural territory or set of concerns is reoccupied or reinvested ("recathected" in Freud's sense) by contemporary modes of thought and practice, which may in the process be deformed or disfigured in unconscious ways.[12] In this sense, the very notion of anachronism,

---

[11]Madison: University of Wisconsin Press, 1989.

[12]See *The Legitimacy of the Modern Age*, trans. Robert M. Wallace (1966; Cambridge: MIT Press, 1985). The notion of reoccupation offers an obvious way of reading the first of Walter Benjamin's "Theses on the Philosophy of History": "The story is told of an automaton constructed in such a way that it could play a winning game of chess, answering each move of an opponent with a countermove. A puppet in Turkish attire and with a hookah in its mouth sat before a chessboard placed on a large table. A system of mirrors created the illusion that this table was transparent from all sides. Actually, a little hunchback who was an expert chess player sat inside and guided the puppet's hand by means of strings. One can imagine a philosophical counterpart to this device. The puppet called 'historical materialism' is to win all the time. It can easily be a match

while having certain obvious but significant uses, may be superficial insofar as it diverts attention from the intricate process in which older forms are regenerated or reaffirmed with more or less significant differences over time. One might even venture to say that old problems never die, or even fade away. They tend to return as the repressed. Coming to terms with them requires a process of working-through that is cognizant of their role and the possibilities or difficulties it creates for interpretation and for life.

The line of thought I have tried to sketch leads to a conception of differential economies of loss and gain that should become objects of debate and options to be actively engaged in various departments and disciplines. Even if one recognizes the claims of both contextual particularization and dialogic exchange, one may strike different balances or imbalances under different circumstances. To the extent one emphasizes the insertion of a text or problem in past contexts, one may well be interested in elaborately detailed features of the inferentially reconstructed past. And one may insist that only through contextualization will one be able to provide the perspective on problems or artifacts that is altogether necessary (although not sufficient) in critically understanding them. At times scholarly erudition may take precedence over criticism and dialogic exchange. And the focus on context—especially on the grand panoramic picture of the immediate time and place—may lead to excessively reductive readings of texts or at least to a directed and very selective use of them.[13] By contrast, an

---

for anyone if it enlists the services of theology, which today, as we know, is wizened and has to keep out of sight"; *Illuminations*, p. 253.

[13]Excessively reductive reading has, I think, been prevalent in the historical profession. An especially impressive example is Richard Wolin's important book *The Politics of Being: The Political Thought of Martin Heidegger* (New York: Columbia University Press, 1990). Wolin succinctly and cogently puts forth contextual considerations that must be taken into account in a reading of Heidegger, and he convincingly argues that recent disclosures concerning the significance of Heidegger's affiliation with the Nazis should foster a hermeneutics of suspicion in reading Heidegger's texts. But he also pursues the more dubious goal of employing Heidegger's Nazi affiliation to thoroughly discredit all of his thought from *Being and Time* (1927) to his latest writings, thereby denying the role of all tensions and counterforces in his work, including those that might be argued to question the bases of his affiliation with the Nazis. Wolin in effect reverses the tendency to read markedly symptomatic, ideologically saturated texts as if they were self-critical by emphatically reading even texts with certain critical currents as if they were predominantly if not totally symptomatic. His procedure may be partially justified to the extent that there has been until recently a tendency to underplay if not ignore the problem of the relation between Heidegger's Nazi commitment and his thought. But it suffers from the limitation of a strategy of reversal that is not supplemented by an in-

interest in criticism will typically be linked to a desire for pointed, provocative, even micrological readings that renew or at least upset prior ways of understanding a text or problem. One may emphasize the need to generalize within cases, that is, to draw out the implications of local knowledge for larger themes and grander theories. Yet one may also be drawn into the text and its complexities in ways that limit or downplay the role of extensive research into more immediate contexts—perhaps the role of historical understanding in general. Even in the best of cases, the concern for dialogic exchange will probably induce one to stress basic, long-term contexts as they are reworked in texts or to raise the very issue of contextualization in a manner that underscores our implication in the problems we treat.[14]

I have already intimated that the partial contrast between a dialogic exchange with texts and an insertion of them in past contexts should not be promoted to the status of a sheer dichotomy.[15] In fact, it may be mitigated and displaced in a manner I have signaled at certain points—a manner that is becoming a concern among historians and theorists.[16] Aside from stressing the need to work through the tensions among contextualization, textual interpretation, and dialogic ex-

---

quiry into the overdetermined nature of interacting and at times mutually self-questioning tendencies that are especially pronounced in certain texts—tendencies that make texts significant objects of dialogic exchange and open them to differing or even divergent interpretations and uses. On these issues, see Chapter 5.

[14]The concern with dialogic exchange has in different ways characterized the work of Mikhail Bakhtin, Martin Heidegger, Hans-Georg Gadamer, and Jacques Derrida. I have tried in my own work to explore selectively and critically the relevance of their approaches for historiography and to relate them to the problem of contextualization.

[15]I offer the following incomplete list of texts in which the tension between dialogic exchange and contextualization is addressed or negotiated in a thought-provoking manner: Roger Chartier, "Intellectual History or Sociocultural History? The French Trajectories," in Dominick LaCapra and Steven L. Kaplan, eds., *Modern European Intellectual History: Reappraisals and New Perspectives* (Ithaca: Cornell University Press, 1982), pp. 13–46; Saul Friedlander, *Reflections of Nazism: An Essay on Kitsch and Death*, trans. Thomas Weyr (New York: Harper and Row, 1984); François Furet, *Interpreting the French Revolution*, trans. Elborg Forster (Cambridge: Cambridge University Press, 1981); Martin Jay, *Fin-de-Siècle Socialism and Other Essays* (New York: Routledge, 1988); Joan Scott, *Gender and the Politics of History* (New York: Columbia University Press, 1988); Eric L. Santner, *Stranded Objects: Mourning, Memory, and Film in Postwar Germany* (Ithaca: Cornell University Press, 1990); and Richard Terdiman, *Discourse/Counter-Discourse: The Theory and Practice of Symbolic Resistance in Nineteenth-Century France* (Ithaca: Cornell University Press, 1985). Deserving special mention are Karl Marx's *Eighteenth Brumaire* and (despite its very reductive reading of Enlightenment figures) Alexis de Tocqueville's *Old Regime and the Revolution*.

[16]See, for example, Carrard, *Poetics of the New History*, especially pp. 121–33.

change, I would note the importance of providing a close, critical reading of contexts themselves that might enable a self-critical exchange with them. In this respect, documents, while not losing their evidentiary function, would be objects of interrogation and analysis, and inquiry into their specific situation and workings would complement and complicate the necessary use of them as sources of information about the past. Instead of restricting one's use of documentary sources to quarries for facts, one might even find it desirable to thematize the problem of the nature of documents (notably, such documents as inquisition registers and police reports) in relation both to their historical role in networks of power and authority and to the more or less warranted inferential reconstructions one bases on them. Instead of simply assuming that one's goal is to find order in chaos, to structure and fully explain one's material, or to discover meaning in the past, one would, rather, try to set up an exchange between sources and inferential reconstructions such that the elaboration of a context—including the crucial issue of the appropriate use of language in rendering it—would be constituted as a genuine problem in historical inquiry. This effort, for example, in the study of the Holocaust, might enable one to combat more effectively revisionist abuses that only accentuate the deficiencies of both positivistic method and theories about the "fictive" nature of all interpretive structures and inferential reconstructions.

It would also be desirable to include in one's account selections from unpublished sources and archival material that are sufficient to allow the reader to evaluate one's analysis or narrative. At least equally desirable would be an attempt to give a context to one's approach in terms of one's own subject-position and relation to the contemporary conflict of interpretations and reading strategies. Especially with respect to controversial topics, nothing is more misleading for a reader than the impression that an account simply relates the facts or explains a problem without having a formative and ideologically weighted relation to other accounts. This effort to read documents as texts, to pose as a problem the question of the relation between various sources (including memory) and the inferential reconstruction of contexts, and to offer the interlocutor or reader some perspective on oneself in terms of a present context of debate would not transcend all tensions; on the contrary, it would place them in the foreground. It might, however, further the chances of working out a more comprehensive account of problems that would at least counteract the one-sidedness of both historicist contextualism and presentist reprocessing of the past in and through contemporary forms of reading. It would also indicate how various options may engage one another most provocatively and constructively when they incorporate an active awareness of the claims of other interpretive modes and the differential stresses and strains attendant upon any choice in interpretation. Indeed, such a field of forces may give rise to hybrid modes of thought, of delicate hue and complex configuration, that attest to the way critical thinking is positioned on thresholds, open to its own historicity, and prone to unforeseen transitions.

TWO

❧

Reflections on the Historians' Debate

The *Historikerstreit*, or German historians' debate, erupted in the summer of 1986. It was occasioned by the article published in the *Frankfurter Allgemeine Zeitung* by the historian Ernst Nolte.[1] Its promotion to the status of a heated public controversy if not a cause célèbre was provoked by two articles in *Die Zeit* by Jürgen Habermas.[2] As Habermas recognized, the Historikerstreit evoked many basic issues ranging from the nature of historical understanding to the self-conception of the Federal Republic of Germany. Whatever their personal motives or agendas, the views of revisionist historians were, for Habermas, symptomatic of a neonationalist resurgence that was most prominent on the part of conservative forces that wanted to rewrite the Nazi past in order to provide a "positive" or affirmative German identity in the present. This larger context of the controversy among historians

---

[1]"Vergangenheit, die nicht vergehen will," *Frankfurter Allgemeine Zeitung*, 6 June 1986. References to this article as "Vergangenheit" are included in the text. Contributions to the Historikerstreit have been collected in Ernst Reinhard Piper, ed., *"Historikerstreit": Die Dokumentation der Kontroverse um die Einzigartigkeit der nationalsozialistischen Judenvernichtung* (Munich: Piper Verlag, 1987). See also the invaluable special issue of the *New German Critique* 44 (Spring/Summer 1988).

[2]"Eine Art Schadensabwicklung. Die apologetischen Tendenzen in der deutschen Zeitgeschichtsschreibung," *Die Zeit*, 11 July 1986; translated by Jeremy Leaman in *New German Critique* 44 (1988), 25–39, as "A Kind of Settlement of Damages (Apologetic Tendencies)." "Vom öffentlichen Gebrauch der Historie," *Die Zeit*, 7 November 1986; translated by Jeremy Leaman in *New German Critique* 44 (1988), 40–50, as "Concerning the Public Use of History." References are to the English translations, and page numbers are included in the text.

provided the crucial code or subtext for arguments that might otherwise seem to be purely methodological and run-of-the-mill.

The Historikerstreit should not be conflated with the issue of "historicization" (*Historisierung*) in general. But a close examination of the historians' debate does help to accentuate the question of precisely how historicization takes place and the functions it fulfills in specific contexts. The neoconservative idea that history as a secular surrogate for religion provides satisfying meaning (*Sinnstiftung*) for those who have been uprooted by modernizing processes diverts attention not only from negative aspects of the past but from modern problems that are not totally dissociated from earlier difficulties and dilemmas. As Nietzsche saw long ago, history as a surrogate for religion is clearly ideological in its dubiously providential role as provider of unearned, compensatory meaning.

In his 1988 book, Charles Maier formulated a prevalent conception of the more specifically historiographical issues in the Historikerstreit —a conception with which Maier basically agrees:

> The central issue has been whether Nazi crimes were unique, a legacy of evil in a class by themselves, irreparably burdening any concept of German nationhood, or whether they are comparable to other national atrocities, especially Stalinist terror. Uniqueness, it has been pointed out, should not be so important an issue; the killing remains horrendous whether or not other regimes committed mass murder. Comparability cannot really exculpate. In fact, however, uniqueness is rightly perceived as a crucial issue. If Auschwitz is admittedly dreadful, but dreadful as only one specimen of genocide—as the so-called revisionists have implied—then Germany can still aspire to reclaim a national acceptance that no one denies to perpetrators of other massacres, such as Soviet Russia. But if the Final Solution remains noncomparable—as the opposing historians have insisted—the past may never be "worked through," the future never normalized, and German nationhood may remain forever tainted, like some well forever poisoned.[3]

[3]*The Unmasterable Past* (Cambridge: Harvard University Press, 1988), p. 1. See also Richard J. Evans's well-informed and lucid account, *In Hitler's Shadow: West German Historians and the Attempt to Escape the Nazi Past* (New York: Pantheon, 1989). Evans's book is perhaps best read as a complement to Maier's, for it fills in background that Maier's more pointed and conceptualized analysis often takes for granted, and it devotes relatively little attention to facets of the Historikerstreit, such as Habermas's role, that Maier elaborates. Evans, however, often seems to proceed on the assumption that an argument may be effectively countered by adducing and evaluating the evidence germane to its discrete claims. This approach, while certainly necessary, is not sufficient to

Maier's insightful and balanced account provides an excellent place to begin any contemporary discussion of the Historikerstreit. It is noteworthy that Maier invokes the binary opposition between the unique and the comparable (or the general)—one of the oldest such oppositions in historical thought. Yet this opposition takes on a specific, albeit debatable, significance in the context of the Historikerstreit. Maier's initial paragraph has a manifestly contradictory structure: uniqueness is not the issue; uniqueness is the issue. I think this contradiction is not debilitating, but the aporia it conceals must be subjected to further analysis. For it may indicate that the point is both to deconstruct the binary opposition and to see precisely how it functions historically and ideologically. Seeing how the opposition functions is necessary in the analysis of how "uniqueness" and "comparability" are coded in a historically and ideologically specific situation. Deconstructing the opposition is necessary in the attempt to elaborate a different way of posing the problem and even of defining the "central" issue.

I maintain that one crucial—perhaps the central—historical issue is whether (and how) the Holocaust[4] is attended to or whether attention is diverted from it in a manner that decreases chances that it will be "worked through" to the extent it can possibly be worked through. The attempt to provide a historical account of the Holocaust offers a limit case of a problem that confronts historians in general. This problem

---

addresss less rational aspects of certain "arguments" I focus on in my analysis.

[4]The term "Holocaust" is of course problematic. But here one is in an area where no easy, uninvolved, or purely objective choices are available. There are, I think, at least three reasons for using the term "Holocaust" even if one is aware of its problematic nature and resists giving it a privileged status: (1) Given the unavailability of innocent terms, "Holocaust" may be one of the better choices in an impossible, tension-ridden linguistic field. The possibility exists that resorting to terms such as "annihilation" or "final solution" will inadvertently repeat Nazi terminology. "Holocaust" is both less bureaucratic and less banal than certain alternatives. (2) The term for various reasons has had a role in the discourse of the victims themselves, and there are ritual and ethical grounds for honoring their choice. (3) The rather prevalent use of the term, including its use by nonvictims, has to some extent routinized it and helped to counteract its sacrificial connotations without entirely reducing it to cliché, although one must beware of its role in what Alvin H. Rosenfeld has called "a pornography of the Holocaust" promoted especially by popularization and commercialization in the mass media. See "Another Revisionism: Popular Culture and the Changing Image of the Holocaust," in Geoffrey Hartman, ed., *Bitburg in Moral and Political Perspective* (Bloomington: University of Indiana Press, 1986) pp. 90–102. See also Saul Friedlander, *Reflections of Nazism: An Essay on Kitsch and Death*, trans. Thomas Weyr (New York: Harper and Row, 1984).

is perhaps best formulated in psychoanalytic terms: how should one negotiate transferential relations to the object of study whereby processes active in it are repeated with more or less significant variations in the account of the historian?[5] The Holocaust presents the historian with transference in the most traumatic form conceivable—but in a form that will vary with the difference in subject-position of the analyst. Whether the historian or analyst is a survivor, a relative of survivors, a former Nazi, a former collaborator, a relative of former Nazis or collaborators, a younger Jew or German distanced from more immediate contact with survival, participation, or collaboration, or a relative "outsider" to these problems will make a difference even in the meaning of statements that may be formally identical. Certain statements or even entire orientations may seem appropriate for someone in a given subject-position but not in others. (It would, for example, be ridiculous if I tried to assume the voice of Elie Wiesel or of Saul Friedlander. There is a sense in which I have no right to these voices. There is also a sense in which, experiencing a lack of a viable voice, I am constrained to resort to quotation and commentary more often than I otherwise might be.) Thus, while any historian must be "invested" in a distinctive way in the events of the Holocaust, not all investments (or cathexes) are the same, and not all statements, rhetorics, or orientations are equally available to different historians.

How language is used is thus critical for the way in which a transferential relation is negotiated. It is also decisive in determining the manner in which subject-positions are defined and redefined. Certain voices seem unavailable for certain historians and more possible for others. But no historian should be content with a conventional voice that levels or routinizes problems that make particular demands and pose special challenges. I do not think that conventional techniques, which in certain respects are necessary, are ever sufficient, and to

[5]A fruitful beginning in addressing this problem is made by Theodor W. Adorno in "What Does Coming to Terms with [*Aufarbeitung*] the Past Mean?" trans. Timothy Bahti and Geoffrey Hartman, in Hartman, ed., *Bitburg in Moral and Political Perspective*, pp. 114–29. As Adorno observes (p. 125): "Enlightenment about what happened in the past must work, above all, against a forgetfulness that too easily goes along with and justifies what is forgotten." It should be noted that I use a concept of transference based not on a simple analogy with the analytic situation but on the much stronger claim that the latter is a condensed version of a general transferential process characterizing relationships—a process of which the Oedipal situation is one variant. On these issues, see my "Psychoanalysis and History," in *Soundings in Critical Theory* (Ithaca: Cornell University Press, 1989), pp. 30–66.

some extent the study of the Holocaust may help us to reconsider the requirements of historiography in general. Conventional techniques are particularly inadequate with respect to events that are indeed limiting. In our addressing of these events, language may break down, and the most appropriate form of representation may be minimalist. Still, I contend that it is more possible to indicate what has not worked than to legislate what approach must be taken in trying to write or speak about the Holocaust. In addition, silence here is not identical with simple muteness, and the way language breaks down is itself a significant and even telling process. In any event, the language-user—including the historian—is under special constraints and obligations, which he or she avoids through a reliance on standard operating procedures. Positivism in general may be seen as an abuse of scientific method through an autonomization of the constative or empirical-analytic dimension of discourse in a way that denies the problem of transference. (Indeed, one way to define positivism is as a denial of transference.) Nowhere more than in discussions of the Holocaust do positivism and standard techniques of narrowly empirical-analytic inquiry seem wanting. How the historian should use language with reference to the subject-positions that he or she occupies and is attempting to forge is a pressing issue with no prefabricated or pat solutions; the issue cannot be obviated through a reversion to type. To make this point is not to deny an important role for objectivity. Objectivity does, however, become a more difficult and problematic undertaking redefined in terms of the attempt to counteract modes of projection, self-indulgence, and narrow partisanship in an exchange with the past. (Here one has the possibility of a "postdeconstructive" notion of objectivity that resists absolutization or foundational status but has its valid uses in conjunction with the socially sensitive, psychoanalytically informed concept of subject-positions.)

In view of what I have been arguing, there is a sense in which the "Nazi crimes" are both unique and comparable. They are unique not only in that they affect people in a distinctive way insofar as they have a specific "lived" relation to them and occupy different subject-positions. They are unique in that they are so extreme that they seem unclassifiable and threaten or tempt one with silence. But they will be compared to other events insofar as comparison is essential for any attempt to understand. The problem is how this process of comparison takes place and the functions it serves. To see the Holocaust in terms of transference is to some extent to make it comparable, but the value of the concept of transference is to enable one to stress the differences in traumatizing potential of events and to situate the Holocaust as a limit case that tests and may even unsettle categories and comparisons. When employed in a certain fashion, comparisons may serve manifestly leveling functions.

I propose that the greatest danger at the present time, at least in the context of the historians' debate, is that certain comparisons may function as mechanisms of denial that do not enable one to "work through" problems. Indeed, they may misleadingly conflate normality with a leveling normalization. The seemingly balanced account of an unbalanced situation—particularly the appeal to comparisons that evenhandedly show the distribution of horror in history—may well be coded in a specific manner as mechanisms of denial that seek normalization and a "positive" identity through an avoidance or disavowal of the critical and self-critical requirements of both historical understanding and anything approximating "normality." The emphasis on uniqueness has the virtue of opposing normalization and may be contextually effective as a limited strategy of reversal. But it may also be conducive to "acting out" problems rather than working them through. With respect to any extremely traumatic situation, and clearly with respect to the Holocaust, some "acting out" may be unavoidable and even necessary. In fact, critiques of "acting out"—critiques that may at times have a partial validity (notably when they address the problem of the self-legitimating or self-righteous use of the Holocaust as "symbolic capital")—may themselves function to reinforce tendencies toward denial. Still, a historical and critical account should attempt to provide a measure of distance on events in order to deal with them with a degree of objectivity and self-critical perspective.[6]

One critical role of comparisons in history is to bring out not only similarities but also significant differences. Comparisons that accen-

---

[6]"Working-through" is a translation of Freud's term "durcharbeiten." "Denial" or "disavowal" (*Verleugnung*) is of course meant here not in its ordinary sense but in its psychoanalytic sense, which may involve intricate and subtle modes of evasion, often through relatively complex (if at times paranoid and circular) modes of argumentation. (These more sophisticated modes of revisionism do not simply deny the existence of gas chambers.) In "acting-out," the past is compulsively repeated as if it were fully present, resistances are not confronted, and memory as well as judgment is undercut. The therapeutic goal is to further the movement from denial and "acting-out" to "working-through"—a recurrently renewed and easily impaired movement that may never be totally or definitively accomplished.

tuate only similarity are ipso facto dubious. Despite certain of his disagreements with Habermas, Eberhard Jäckel has offered a succinct and justifiably oft-quoted statement of the manner in which the Holocaust was "unique" in this sense: "The Nazi extermination of the Jews was unique because never before had a state, under the responsible authority of its leader, decided and announced that a specific group of human beings, including the old, the women, the children, and the infants, would be killed to the very last one, and implemented this decision with all the means at its disposal."[7] Jäckel here underscores the significance of official, political anti-Semitism involving a systematic, state-sponsored policy of extermination directed against an entire people for the express scapegoating purpose of eliminating a putative source of pollution.

In the course of my discussion, I try to give more substance to the schema I have suggested. I begin with a brief discussion of two of the foremost revisionist historians: Ernst Nolte and Andreas Hillgruber. (I do not address complications introduced by the consideration of other revisionists such as Michael Stürmer.)

The larger philosophical premise of Nolte's analysis is his peculiar concept of transcendence by which he means the radical emancipation of the individual from tradition. The "transcendent" individual becomes atomized and deracinated and requires history as the replacement of lost tradition, particularly lost religious tradition. The daunting task facing the historian in Germany is to furnish a binding answer to anomy through a conception of tradition that may be taken up and affirmed by the individual in quest of roots and a feeling of being at home in the world. The comparative method is one key means of making one's nation more available as an object of sustaining commitment and a bulwark against communist threats to the West.

Through rhetorical questions, Nolte takes comparison in the dubiously metaphysical (perhaps magical) direction of making Nazi crimes derivative or mimetic of a more basic original, and he even suggests that they were preemptive with respect to the archetypical Bolshevik menace. He thereby resuscitates the hackneyed apologetic claim that at least the Nazis opposed the Bolsheviks and thereby defended the interests of Western civilization. In Nolte's words: "Did the National Socialists, did Hitler carry out an 'Asiatic' action perhaps

[7]"Die elende Praxis der Untersteller," *Die Zeit*, 12 September 1986.

only because they regarded themselves and their kind as potential or real victims of an 'Asiatic' action? Was not the Gulag Archipelago more original [*ursprünglicher*] than Auschwitz? Was not the 'class murder' of the Bolsheviks the logical and factual precondition of the 'racial murder' of the National Socialists? Was it not a scientific mistake to focus on the latter and neglect the former, although a causal nexus is probable?" ("Vergangenheit")

Thus, for Nolte, the Gulag may have "caused" Auschwitz: the Nazis did it because the Russians did it first, and the Nazis were afraid that the Russians would do it to them. The identification of the Holocaust as an "Asiatic" action performs the astonishing feat of projecting guilt away from the Germans in an act of racial slander that is particularly offensive in view of its context. The distancing effect of quotation marks with respect to Nolte's own voice is at best moot. The concluding invocation to science is a sheer propaganda ploy in the attempt to lend credibility to an outlandishly speculative and implausible causal imputation; it too is reminiscent of Nazi tactics. With consummate insensitivity, Nolte also intimates that the "Final Solution" was itself not substantively different from other pogroms of mass annihilation "but for the sole exception of the technical procedure of gassing." In an earlier essay, Nolte even went to the extreme of suggesting that Hitler might have been justified in interning Jews as prisoners of war because of Chaim Weizmann's "official declaration in the first days of September 1939, according to which Jews in the whole world would fight on the side of England."[8]

Nolte is nonetheless to the point in warning against indiscriminate conceptions of German "guilt" that unconsciously replicate the kind of thinking by which the Nazis convinced themselves of the "guilt" of the Jews. Nor would one want to deny the prevalence of atrocity in the twentieth century. But Nolte insists on this prevalence not so much to emphasize its importance as to mitigate if not evade that of specifically Nazi behavior. In light of his premise (or fixation) whereby communism is the ultimate cause of all modern evil, Nolte's argument takes on a circular, paranoid structure which makes it impermeable to counterevidence. His argument also has the earmark of uncontrolled transference in its uncritical repetition of features of his object of study.

[8]"Between Myth and Revisionism? The Third Reich in the Perspective of the 1980s," in H. W. Koch, ed., *Aspects of the Third Reich* (London: Macmillan, 1985), p. 27.

Habermas himself recognized that one could not simply amalgamate the views of Nolte and Andreas Hillgruber. In the two essays he published together in book form in 1986, however, Hillgruber did to some extent relativize the Holocaust, especially through comparisons, for example, with Stalin's "extermination and resettlement practices [*Ausrottungs-und Umsiedlungspraktiken*]."[9] The ill-chosen subtitle of Hillgruber's book is itself telltale in its ambiguous association of "the shattering of the German Reich" and "the end of European Jewry." Both the euphemism of "the end" (in contrast to the decidedly emphatic "shattering") and the impersonality of "Jewry" (creating a false parallelism with the Reich) attest to a process of normalization and routinization.

Hillgruber traces the roots of anti-Semitism in Germany, and he notes (p. 96) the priority of the destruction of the Jews in Nazi policy even in the later portion of the war. At one point (p. 98) he even refers to the historical uniqueness of events (*historische Einmaligkeit des Vorgangs*). But he insists that while others went along and might even be culpable in their indifference, the "Final Solution" was Hitler's distinctive venture. Indeed, within the compass of a relatively short essay, Hillgruber devotes a disproportionate amount of space to the question of Hitler's role in the "Final Solution." Hillgruber, moreover, argues that the Allies were prompted by power politics and misled by a crude image of Prussian militarism—not moved by Nazi crimes—in their presumably long-standing ambition to dismember Germany and destroy its heartland, Prussia. In this sense, Germany was victimized. The events on the eastern front during the final phase of the war were themselves aspects of a normal struggle for dominance and of a heroic yet desperate attempt to save as much of German culture and as many German lives as possible from the atrocity-mongering Russian Army. For Hillgruber, the historian must empathize with Germans in the East, notably including German soldiers fighting against overwhelming odds on the eastern front— soldiers who were victims in their own right as fighters for a cause that had been sacrificed to power politics. Hillgruber's plea for empathy is remarkably one-sided, especially in view of the fact that the continuance of the war on the eastern front prolonged the operation of the death camps. It is facilitated by the generalizing and

[9]*Zweierlei Untergang. Die Zerschlagung des Deutschen Reiches und das Ende des europäischen Judentums* (Berlin: Siedler, 1986), p. 67.

essentializing nature of his account of the plight of German soldiers and, at least in this book, by the limitations of his inquiry into the degree of the military's complicity in Nazi policy and the extent of their own atrocities against both Russian soldiers and civilians on the eastern front.

Hillgruber's reasoning about the path the historian's empathy must follow is symptomatic of an unself-questioning identification with hegemonic forces in Nazi Germany: "The concept of liberation implies . . . an identification with the victors, and naturally the concept is fully justified for victims of the Nazi regime liberated from concentration camps and prisons. But with respect to the fate of the German nation as a whole, it is out of place [*unangebracht*]" (p. 23). One can perform the ideologically mystifying and tendentious feat of subtracting an apparently negligible part ("the victims of the Nazi regime") and still end up with the whole ("the German nation as a whole") only from a hegemonic, state-conservative point of view that seems blind to its exclusionary implications in this context. Making a distorted use of a distinction drawn by Max Weber, Hillgruber also contrasts what he sees as the commendably realistic ethic of individual responsibility upheld by German party, state, and military leaders in the East with the unrealistic ethic of inner conviction that motivated those who plotted against Hitler's life.

I have treated Hillgruber's account selectively by singling out some of its features without addressing the important rhetorical issue of the way in which they are embedded in the erudite and at times intricate analysis of a historian with a strong and solid professional reputation. It is nonetheless important to recognize that Hillgruber's account is at times questionable even though, when compared to Nolte's, it is apparently more "historical," less "philosophical," more securely "authorized" by previous publications, and hence more professionally "reputable." (Most historians would probably agree with Habermas in thinking that Nolte's status is not enhanced by the fact that he was Heidegger's student.) Indeed, at least for certain audiences, Hillgruber's approach may be more effective than Nolte's in legitimating a more guarded and sophisticated relativization. In fact, it is very tempting to be taken in by Hillgruber and to begin playing his game. For one to understand Hillgruber's role in the historians' debate, it is, however, insufficient to isolate and evaluate the truth-value of his claims one by one; it is necessary to analyze how these claims function in his account. Otherwise one runs the risk of displacing normalization onto one's understanding of Hillgruber's text and perhaps un-intentionally participating in a larger process of relativization.

Nolte's conception of transcendence is in certain respects the photographic negative of the notion of emancipation and Enlightenment of which Jürgen Habermas has made himself the champion.[10] At times Habermas's own self-image and his understanding of the tradition of critical rationality he wishes to defend induce him to caricature more substantial questioners of that tradition (such as Jacques Derrida, whom Habermas often interprets misleadingly as a mere mystical, anarchistic opponent of reason); they also lead him to make allowance in his own approach only for rather reduced variants of notions that disorient rationality without simply denying it (such as Freud's notion of the unconscious). But Habermas's intervention in the Historikerstreit enabled him to bring important problems to public attention and even to elaborate in more telling fashion certain of his basic arguments.

In one of his interventions, Habermas puts forth a striking formulation of the relationship between collective responsibility and the public role of memory:

> There is the obligation we in Germany have—even if no one else is prepared to take it upon themselves any longer—to keep alive the memory of the suffering of those murdered at the hands of Germans, and we must keep this memory alive quite openly and not just in our own minds. These dead have above all a claim to the weak anamnestic power of a solidarity which those born later can now only practice through the medium of memory which is always being renewed, which may often be desperate, but which is at any rate active and circulating. If we disregard this Benjaminian legacy, Jewish fellow citizens and certainly the sons, the daughters and the grandchildren of the murdered victims would no longer be able to breathe in our country. ("Concerning the Public Use of History," p. 44)

Habermas also argues for a critical rather than a blind appropriation of traditions; this critical appropriation would validate only traditions that "stand up to the suspicious gaze made wise by the moral catastrophe"

[10]Bitburg forms part of the larger context in which the Historikerstreit must be seen. In the article he wrote on Bitburg, Habermas prefigured some of the points he would make in the salvo that opened the Historikerstreit. See "Die Entsorgung der Vergangenheit: Ein kulturpolitisches Pamphlet," *Die Zeit*, 24 May 1985; translated by Thomas Levin as "Defusing the Past: A Politico-Cultural Tract," in Hartman, ed., *Bitburg in Moral and Political Perspective*, pp. 43–51.

(p. 44). Instead of a particularistic nationalism, Habermas calls for a "postconventional identity" based on universal norms and a constitutional patriotism. In themselves these ideals may seem rather ineffective and overly indebted to the abstract aspirations of the Enlightenment and German idealism. But the passages I have quoted indicate that the larger project may be to join these ideals to the selective appropriation of traditions, including those of the Enlightenment, that in their own way also carry historical sedimentation and concrete commitments. In still another intervention in the debate—an address delivered in Denmark—Habermas extended his inquiry into the complex transformations of embeddedness in a traditional lifeworld. While insisting on a complementary rather than analogical relation between individual and collective identity, he stresses the postconventional implications of Kierkegaard's notion of a conversionlike existential choice that consciously and responsibly transforms one's life history. This choice puts the individual in the ethical position of an editor deciding what should be considered essential and worth passing on in his or her past. The counterpart in the life of a people would be the decision, conscious of the ambivalence in every tradition, that publicly and critically determines which traditions or aspects of traditions one wants to continue and which one does not.[11] The reference to Kierkegaard might itself be read to indicate that, with respect to the tense conjunction of universalizing constitutional principles and more specific—to some extent nonreflective—bonds, there is a need for continual rethinking and renegotiation rather than speculative synthesis, or *Aufhebung*.

One obvious problem is the use made of any notion of unquestioned or nonreflective attachments as well as the manner in which this use interacts with a critical approach to problems. Indeed, any justifiable sense of responsibility for the past would not rest on passive acceptance of a burden; it would require both a nonreflective involvement in a shared history and a critical and self-critical attempt to come to terms with that history. In this sense, there is still much of value in Habermas's earlier critique of the kind of uncritical, customary identity that seeks an affirmative conception of the past and self-

[11]"Geschichtsbewusstsein und posttraditionale Identität. Die Westorientierung der Bundesrepublik," in *Eine Art Schadensabwicklung. Kleine politische Schriften 6* (Frankfurt am Main: Suhrkamp, 1987). All of Habermas's writings on the Historikerstreit may also be found in *The New Conservatism: Cultural Criticism and the Historians' Debate*, ed. and trans. Shierry Weber Nicholsen, intro. Richard Wolin (Cambridge: MIT Press, 1989).

confirming normalization or national identity even at the price of denial and distortion. The power of the following questions is enhanced when they are contrasted with the earlier-quoted questions rhetorically raised by Ernst Nolte:

> Can one assume the legal succession of the German Reich, can one continue the traditions of German culture without also assuming historical liability for the form of existence in which Auschwitz was possible? Is it possible to remain liable for the context in which such crimes had their origins and with which one's existence is interwoven, in any way other than through the solidarity of the memory of that which cannot be made good, in any way other than through a reflective and keenly scrutinizing attitude towards one's own identity-creating traditions? Is it not possible to say in general terms: the less communality such a life-context allowed internally and the more it maintained itself by usurping and destroying the lives of others, the greater then is the burden of reconciliation, task of mourning, and the self-critical scrutiny of subsequent generations? Moreover, doesn't this very sentence forbid us to use levelling comparisons to minimize the non-transferability of the shared responsibility imposed on us? This is the question concerning the singularity of Nazi crimes. ("Concerning the Public Use of History," p. 47)

Habermas sees no simple dichotomy between memory and history, and his concept of conventional identity is more probing than is a stereotypical idea of "mythical memory" that is at times tendentiously opposed to "authentic" history. (Indeed, as we shall see, those who put forth this idea of mythical memory only to reject it are themselves at times close to a conventional identity at least in their conception of "authentic" historiography.) It would, moreover, be a mistake to identify Habermas's specific and limited notions of historical liability and solidarity of memory with an indiscriminate conception of German guilt that is visited on each and every German as irrational fate or pathogenic stain, even though those born later may at times unjustifiably feel guilty about the past.

Yet Habermas himself lends too much credence to the standard opposition between the citizen and the expert, and he is thus unable to elaborate a conception of the validly mixed or hybridized role of the historian both as a professional scholar and as a critical intellectual engaged in dialogic exchange with a past that he or she attempts to reconstitute as "scientifically" as possible. Habermas is led to make an argument that underwrites a very conventional identity for the historian and seems particularly inappropriate for a field that is not formalized but instead remains in many significant ways very close to public discourse in its own protocols of explanation and interpretation:

> We are addressing the dispute about the right answer from the perspective of the first person. One should not confuse this arena, in which it is not possible to be a disinterested party, with discussions between scientists who, in the course of their work, must adopt the perspective of the third person. The political culture of the Federal Republic is without doubt affected by the comparative work of historians and other academics within the humanities; but it was only through the sluice gates of publishers and the mass media that the results of academic work, with its return to the perspective of the participants, reached the public channels for the appropriation of traditions. Only in this context can accounts be squared by using comparisons. The pompous outrage over an alleged mixing of politics and science shunts the issue onto a completely wrong track. ("Concerning the Public Use of History," p. 47)

Habermas is of course well advised in noting his lack of special expertise in the historiography of the Nazi period and in taking exception to the reaction of certain members of the historical profession to his articles. But he concedes too much to those historians who took offense at his intervention rather than seeing it as a stimulus to public discourse and a prod for them to assume certain responsibilities not excluded by professional expertise but, on the contrary, demanded by it. One may even raise the question of whether Habermas's own general conception of the division of modern society into rather neat spheres or areas obviates critical thought about the more difficult problem of the nature of valid combinations or hybridizations of roles in different fields such as history, philosophy, literary criticism, and social theory—at times even journalism.

There are other questionable aspects of Habermas's argument, including a tendency to conflate or at least implicitly to correlate a normative conception of Western democratic values with the existing Western political alliance. Moreover, in view of his defense of modernity as an uncompleted project of enlightenment, Habermas has strategic as well as more deep-seated philosophical reasons for not placing too much emphasis on the ambivalence of Western traditions and the possibly dubious role of a critique of revisionism in lessening awareness of the implication of other Western countries in massively destructive or even genocidal processes. Given the history of the United States, this danger is clear and present for an American, and identification with Habermas's position may be facilitated by the narcissistic and self-justificatory gains it brings. It would nonetheless be a mistake simply to process all of Habermas's arguments in the historians' debate in terms of a preset conception of his politics or philosophy. Such a response to Habermas is itself rather leveling and leads one to miss or underplay significant, contextually important features of his interventions, not least of which was his role in triggering the historians' debate itself.

Not addressed in Habermas's critique but bearing on the question of at least limited relations between the Historikerstreit and the general issue of historicization (Historisierung) of the Holocaust is the representation of the Nazi period in and through the social history of everyday life (*Alltagsgeschichte*). Here the exchange of letters between Martin Broszat and Saul Friedlander is particularly illuminating.[12]

Broszat is upset by the fact that for a long time after the war, Germans were able to write German history only by way of extreme distancing, as if they were treating the history of a foreign people. "We wrote about this history only in the third person, and not in the first person plural; we were no longer able to feel that this history was somehow dealing with ourselves, and was 'our thing' " (p. 100). For Broszat, "historicization" contributes to lifting this barrier by putting Germans in touch with their past. As Saul Friedlander notes, however, the problem is the relation between intention and result. Broszat construes historicization in terms of the insertion of the Nazis in the larger context of everyday life, which at times went on relatively

---

[12]"A Controversy about the Historicization of National Socialism," in *New German Critique* 44 (1988), 85–126. My discussion of Broszat does not imply that one may assimilate his views to those of Nolte or even Hillgruber. Nor do I address the problem of Broszat's own historical writing and research in his other publications. My analysis is directed to certain aspects of Broszat's exchange with Friedlander in which the revisionist possibilities of a certain approach to social history are at issue. I nonetheless think it is misleading to go beyond the point of necessary distinction and to dissociate or detach the "theoretical and methodological problems" of "historicization" (Historisierung), as expounded by Broszat, from the "polemics" of the Historikerstreit, as Ian Kershaw attempts to do (*The Nazi Dictatorship: Problems and Perspectives of Interpretation*, 2d ed. [London: Edward Arnold, 1989], p. 150). This gesture "rescues" all of social history and Alltagsgeschichte at the risk of obscuring or downplaying the crucial issues of precisely how they are undertaken and the contextual functions they may be argued to serve.

undisturbed by what was happening in the concentration and death camps. For Friedlander, both leveling comparisons and the integration of events into everyday life may induce "some kind of overall relativization of the moral problems *specifically raised by Nazism*" (p. 104).[13] He elaborates his point in this manner: "For the historian, the widening and nuancing of the picture [i]s of the essence. But the 'historicization' . . . could mean not so much a widening of the picture, as a *shift of focus*. From *that* perspective, the insistence on *Alltag* or on long-range social trends could indeed strongly relativize what I still consider as the decisive historiographical approach to that period, an approach which considers these twelve years as a definable historical unit dominated, first of all, by the 'primacy of politics' " (p. 104).

Friedlander seems to allow for Alltagsgeschichte that would widen the picture without shifting the focus, perhaps one that would stress the tense and complex interaction between the everyday and the role of issues that are of crucial concern to Friedlander.[14] Still, Friedlander's notion of the primacy of politics includes the centrality of Auschwitz—and everything it stands for—in focusing one's picture of the Third Reich. Here I would note that centering in this case need not be conceived as a mere metaphysical residue; it may be understood as a functional necessity that is most responsibly undertaken when it is self-conscious and critically related to an explicit evaluation of priorities in the representation of historical events. Indeed, a central focus is least subject to control when its role and determinants are not posed as an explicit problem and thereby problematized. Any central focus cannot, however, be essentialized or presented as eternal, and the open question is whether and how an account may be justifiably decentered insofar as Auschwitz is indeed "worked through" in an acceptable manner—a question that may arise more for a future generation than for today's. At present it may be enough to observe that Auschwitz as a central focus need not serve to provide

[13]It is noteworthy that Adorno asserts that "for countless people it wasn't all that bad under fascism. Terror's sharp edge was directed only against a few relatively well-defined groups." But he insists that a focus on this side of everyday life aggravates the "diminished faculty of memory" and furthers resistance to working through the problems posed by other aspects of the Nazi regime. See "What Does Coming to Terms with the Past Mean?" pp. 120–21.

[14]On this problem, see Christopher Browning, "German Memory, Judicial Interrogation, and Historical Reconstruction: Writing Perpetrator History from Postwar Testimony," in Saul Friedlander, ed., *Probing the Limits of Representation: Nazism and the "Final Solution"* (Cambridge: Harvard University Press, 1992), pp. 22–36.

the false comfort and unearned security that critics of "centering" contest.

That Broszat's defense of Alltagsgeschichte may indeed involve a dubious shift of focus and even possibly apologetic tendencies is indicated by other features of his argument. For example, he relies on a contrast between "mythical memory" and scientific history. He asserts that the former is not "simply the negative opposite pole to scholarship and scientific method" (p. 101). But he wants to keep the two clear, distinct, and sharply separated, and the very terms he uses convey a negative connotation with respect to what he calls "mythical." He also relegates the mythical to Jews with special needs in representation that are nonetheless beyond the bounds of "authentic" historiography. "Precisely when confronted with the inexpressible events of the Holocaust, many Jews have indeed come to regard as indispensable a ritualized, almost historical theological remembrance, interwoven with other elements of Jewish fundamental world-historical experience, alongside the mere dry historical reconstruction of facts—because the incommensurability of Auschwitz cannot be dealt with in any other way" (p. 101). I shall later touch on the manner in which Broszat's concerns may be related to the problem of "acting-out" in contrast to "working-through." But I have already intimated that acting-out is probably unavoidable as a response to extremely traumatizing events, and one has to be especially careful about possible functions of any seeming critique of it. Indeed, those who criticize acting-out may combine denial with their own form of it. In any case, to oppose "dry historical reconstruction of facts" to "ritualized, almost theological remembrance," is not helpful, for such an opposition repeats in displaced form the seemingly averted opposition between history and "mythical memory." It also avoids the crucial problem of the demands placed on the historical use of language in attempting to account for phenomena such as Auschwitz, and it facilitates a return to conventional if not narrowly positivistic historiography. I have already argued that the basic problem is best posed in terms of transference and the need to work through rather than deny it or act it out. This problem in different ways confronts not only Jews but those in various subject-positions, including Germans, and it is arguable that certain ritualized aspects of language may be essential to processes of mourning that are bound up with working through transference in certain cases. This issue should not be prejudged, and the precise manner in which historiography is or is not compatible with ritualized uses of language is certainly intricate and controversial. Neither should the issue be foreclosed through overly simple oppositions between history and "mythical memory" or between dry reconstruction of facts and ritualization.

The questionable nature of Broszat's argument is even more pronounced when he appeals to the experience of people living under the Third Reich. In a crucial passage, Broszat asserts that

> the liquidation of the Jews was only feasible during the period of time in which it actually was carried out specifically because that liquidation was not in the limelight of events, but rather could largely be concealed and kept quiet. Such concealment was possible because this destruction involved a minority which even many years before had been systematically removed from the field of vision of the surrounding non-Jewish world as a result of social ghettoization. The ease with which the centrality of the "Final Solution" was carried out became a possibility because the fate of the Jews constituted a little-noticed matter of secondary importance for the majority of Germans during the war; and because for the allied enemies of Germany, it was likewise only one among a multitude of problems they had to deal with during the war, and by no means the most important one.
>
> It is evident that the role of Auschwitz in the original historical context of action is one that is significantly different from its subsequent importance in terms of later historical perspective. The German historian too will certainly accept that Auschwitz—due to its singular significance—functions in retrospection as the central event of the Nazi period. Yet qua scientist and scholar, he cannot readily accept that Auschwitz also be made, after the fact, into the cardinal point, the hinge on which the entire factual complex of historical events of the Nazi period turns. He cannot simply accept without further ado that this entire complex of history be moved into the shadow of Auschwitz—yes, that Auschwitz even be made into the decisive measuring-rod for the historical perception of this period. (Pp. 102–3)

Once again the structure of contradiction is apparent: Auschwitz is/is not the central event/cardinal point of the Nazi period. One may express Broszat's point in less paradoxical terms by observing that for him the centrality of Auschwitz is something that appears belatedly. But Broszat's specific construction of this point holds only for certain groups with whom he tends to identify. And even if his point holds for these groups, it does not imply that the understanding of

Auschwitz as central to the Nazi regime is a mere "anachronism" that a scientific history should cut through in order to reach the historical truth about the period. The centrality of Auschwitz could appear simply as an anachronism only for a history that ignores the significance of belated recognition or even immerses itself in the hegemonic perspective of the time and shares its view of victims. Moreover, a policy of systematic ghettoization began in the mid-1930s, and whether "many years" elapsed until the onset of the "Final Solution" is debatable, especially in the case of adult Germans. A significant number of Jews had gone far toward assimilation. More generally, Jews had made important contributions to the German culture from which Nazis and other anti-Semites wanted to exclude them. Indeed, the status of Jews as preferred scapegoats onto whom one's own anxieties could be projected was exacerbated by the fact that they were perceived as blurring boundaries and were attacked for contradictory reasons: as capitalists and communists, carriers of modernity and backward remnants, rootless cosmopolitans and ghettoized separatists, ugly non-Aryans and objects of erotic desire. The force with which the Jews were converted into a separate and distinct "outside" attested to the degree to which they were threatening from within and thereby a source of repressed anxiety and self-doubt.

But even if one accepts all factual and certain interpretive elements of Broszat's account as accurate, his argument may still be seen as faulty. The historian should certainly note whatever corresponds to the experience of the time, although the construction of this experience may be more difficult than Broszat's account intimates. But this experience does not simply dictate the perspective of the historian. The centrality of focus may be determined by a priority in values even if this priority is not shared by participants or, more precisely, by participants exercising — or more or less actively accepting — hegemony. (With regard to Jews and other oppressed groups such as "Gypsies" and homosexuals living under the Nazi regime, it would be a euphemistic understatement to speak of the "centrality" of Auschwitz.) And even if the Nazi period does in some sense move under the shadow of Auschwitz, this does not mean, as Broszat later intimates, that one must "force totally under [Auschwitz's] usurped domination those non-National Socialist German traditions which extended into the Nazi period and, due to their being 'appropriated' by the regime, to a certain extent themselves fell prey to National Socialism" (p. 103). Instead the problem would be to determine how — and precisely to what extent—such traditions fell prey to, or even facilitated the emergence of, national socialism, and the attempt to extricate them from their Nazi uses and abuses would require, as Habermas intimated, an explicit reckoning with the ways they were or were not involved in Auschwitz.

In his response to Broszat, Saul Friedlander provides grounds for questioning the factual premises as well as the formal argumentation of Broszat's account. Relying on such recent studies as Ian Kershaw's revised English edition of The "Hitler Myth": Image and Reality in the Third Reich[15] and H. Obernaus and S. Obernaus's "Schreiben, wie es wirklich war!" Aufzeichnungen Karl Duerkefaeldens aus den Jahren 1933–1945,[16] Friedlander states: "In short, although the destruction of the Jews may have been a minor point in the perceptions and policies of the allies during the war, it seems, more and more, that it loomed as a hidden but perceived fact in many German minds during the war itself. If my point is correct, it has considerable importance in relation to the core thesis of [Broszat's] 'Plea.' Indeed, normal life with the knowledge of ongoing massive crimes committed by one's own nation and one's own society is not so normal after all" (p. 108).

Friedlander's comment of course bears on the issue of suppression and repression rather than simple ignorance. Its force is heightened by another set of observations he makes:

Nobody denies the "banality of evil" at many levels within this annihilation process, but it possibly is not the only explanation at all levels.

In my opinion, part of the leadership and part of the followers, too, had the feeling of accomplishing something truly, historically, metahistorically exceptional. . . . Himmler's Posen speech [was] the expression of a Rausch, the feeling of an almost superhuman enterprise. That is why I would tend to consider some important aspects of the Nazi movement in terms of "political religion" in the sense used by Eric Voegelin, Norman Cohn, Karl Dietrich Bracher, James Rhodes, Uriel Tal and many others. (P. 109)[17]

[15]Oxford: Oxford University Press, 1987.
[16]Hannover: Fackelträger, 1985.
[17]Here it may be useful to cite the most notorious passage of Himmler's 1943 Posen speech to members of the SS: " 'The Jewish people must be exterminated,' say all party comrades, 'obviously, our party programme contains exclusion of the Jews, extermination, and we'll do it.' And then they all come, those honest eighty million Germans, and each and every one has his one decent Jew. Obviously, the other Jews are all swine, but this one is first class. Of all who talk like this not a single one has looked on,

Broszat himself touches on suppression not among Germans under the Third Reich but among historians, and his comment brings out some of the dubious possibilities of the critique of acting-out: "As I see it, the danger of suppressing the period consists not only in the customary practice of forgetting, but rather, in this instance—almost in paradoxical fashion—likewise in the fact that one is too overly 'concerned,' for didactic reasons, about this chapter in history. . . . The gigantic dictatorial and criminal dimension of the Nazi period also harbors within it the danger that the authenticity of this segment of history may end up being buried beneath monumental sites for the Resistance—and indeed perhaps also beneath memorials for the Holocaust" (p. 118).

The reminder that the Holocaust may serve as "symbolic capital" or as a pretext for self-serving monumentalization is apposite. Still, the very concept of "authenticity" is of questionable usefulness, particularly when it is employed as a misleading synonym for accurate reconstruction. And one may well resist the degeneration of concern or even commitment into propaganda and partisan advocacy but nonetheless insist that there are valid didactic purposes in historiography, especially for those who are teachers as well as scholars. There is also a problem in the appeal to normalized methods or balanced accounts in the representation of rather abnormal and unbalanced phenomena

has endured it. Most of you, in contrast, well know what it means when a hundred corpses lie there together, five hundred, a thousand. To have endured *this* and—apart from a few exceptions of human weakness—to have remained decent, this is what has made us hard. This is a glorious page in our history which has never been written and will never be written"; quoted in Emil L. Fackenheim, "Concerning Authentic and Unauthentic Responses to the Holocaust" (first published 1975) in Michael R. Marrus, ed., *The Nazi Holocaust*, vol. 1 (Westport, Conn.: Meckler, 1989), p. 77. Himmler's words point to the relation between fanatical intoxication and the appeal of a radically transgressive sublimity, and his incredible conception of "decency" is itself made possible by an abusive notion of the division of life into discrete spheres. One may further observe that Hitler himself indicated the manner in which the desire for racial purification, facilitated in certain respects by modern technical, analytic, and bureaucratic rationality, was nonetheless bound up with ritual and sexual anxieties: "With satanic joy in his face, the black-haired Jewish youth lurks in wait for the unsuspecting girl whom he defiles with his blood, thus stealing her from her people . . . . It was and it is Jews who bring the Negroes into the Rhineland, always with the same secret thought and clear aim of ruining the hated white race by the necessarily resulting bastardization, throwing it down from its cultural and political height, and himself rising to be its master"; *Mein Kampf*, trans. Ralph Manheim (1925; Boston: Houghton Mifflin, 1971), p. 325. The role of suppressed or repressed anxiety of the constitutive "outside" (that marks the "inside") is attested to by Hitler's own concern about whether he had some Jewish "blood."

that make distinctive demands on the historian. But the most basic point is that the critique of acting-out may, if undertaken in a certain way, facilitate denial or even the inclination to blame the victim. Indeed, it may not be entirely beside the point to observe that a concern for memorials as necessary acts of memory is quite understandable given that the Nazis wanted the destruction of Jews to be total and to include their elimination from memory itself at least in the form of Jewish self-representation. (In this specific context, a Jewish public act of memory might function as an act of resistance.) Hitler planned to substitute Nazi memories of Jews for Jewish ones through monuments that commemorated his acts of destruction and oblivion.[18] The project of total mastery of the past was a goal of the Nazis, and one should not in general confuse either dubious monumentalization or the project of total *Bewältigung* (mastery) with legitimate forms of memory, overcoming, and working-through.

Throughout this chapter, I have insisted that a crucial issue raised by the Historikerstreit is how precisely the emphasis on uniqueness or comparability functions in the historian's own context. I have also suggested that this issue can be illuminated through a nonreductive use of certain psychoanalytic concepts—a use attuned to the relationship between psychoanalysis and sociopolitical issues. I want to conclude with a few brief and inadequate statements about the general requirements of an attempt to work through problems rather than to deny or act them out.

Working-through requires the recognition that we are involved in transferential relations to the past in ways that vary according to the subject-positions we find ourselves in, rework, and invent. It also involves the attempt to counteract the projective reprocessing of the past through which we deny certain of its features and act out our own desires for self-confirming or identity-forming meaning. By contrast, working-through is bound up with the role of problematic but significant distinctions, including that between accurate reconstruction of the past and committed exchange with it. These distinctions should be neither reified into binary oppositions and separate spheres nor collapsed into an indiscriminate will to rewrite the past. In addition, working-through relies on a certain use of memory and judgment—a use that involves the critique of ideology, prominently

---

[18]On these problems, see James E. Young, "Memory and Monument," in Hartman, ed., *Bitburg in Moral and Political Perspective*, pp. 103–13.

including the critique of the scapegoat "mechanism" that had a historically specific and not simply arbitrary or abstract role in the Nazi treatment of the Jews. What is not confronted critically does not disappear; it tends to return as the repressed.[19]

How language is used is a crucial consideration in working through problems, and the historiographical use of language confronts specific difficulties and challenges in the face of limit cases that may reduce one to silence. Auschwitz as reality and as metonym is the extreme limit case that threatens classifications, categories, and comparisons. It may reduce one to silence. Silence that is not a sign of utter defeat is, however, itself a potentially ritual attitude, but in this sense it is a *silence survenu* intricately bound up with certain uses of language.

The attempt to come to terms with extremely traumatizing events involves the work of mourning.[20] This work encompasses a relation between language and silence that is in some sense ritualized. Certain rituals teach us that this work does not exclude forms of humor, and gallows humor has been an important response to extreme situations on the part of victims themselves. Needless to say, the employment of humor is one of the most delicate and complicated issues in the light (or darkness) of certain events.

Historical understanding is not furthered by routine oppositions between "scientific" history and its stereotypical if not scapegoated "other," which often appears in the form of myth, ritual, or memory. Such oppositions serve primarily as mechanisms of defense and denial that signal overreaction to the possibility of acting-out— overreaction prompting a confinement of historiography to self-defeating positivistic protocols that may stimulate a return of the repressed in relatively uncontrolled and uncritical forms. In cases of

---

[19]There is a tragic sense in which Hitler, while losing the war, achieved certain of his goals in his policy of extermination—at least with respect to western and central European Jews whose populations and culture were largely destroyed. Although the actual threat to remaining Jews should not be underestimated, one of the more bizarre aspects of recent events in certain regions of Europe is anti-Semitism in the relative absence of real referents. One may perhaps call this phenomenon imaginary or fetishized anti-Semitism. It reveals in a heightened and almost clinical manner the role of the imaginary in anti-Semitism more generally, a role that can of course be attended by very real effects.

[20]The problem of the work of mourning receives excellent treatment in Eric Santner's *Stranded Objects: Mourning, Memory, and Film in Postwar Germany* (Ithaca: Cornell University Press, 1990).

extreme trauma, certain kinds of acting-out may not be entirely overcome, and working-through may itself require the recognition of loss
that cannot be made good: scars that will not disappear and even
wounds that will not heal. The problem facing historians—a problem
itself inflected by the other subject-positions occupied by given
historians—is how to articulate the relation between the requirements
of scientific expertise and the less easily definable demands placed
upon the use of language by the difficult attempt to work through
transferential relations in a dialogue with the past having implications
for the present and future. This dialogue is not purely personal or
psychological. One of its vital aspects is the exploration of how different approaches relate to the generation of viable institutions of both
discourse and social life that effectively resist the recurrence of anything comparable to the Nazi regime. More generally, in the dialogic
dimension of historical study one seeks not abstracted meaning but
meaningful guides to thought and practice, and one seeks them not in
a hypostatized past or in some teleological master code but in and
through one's very exchange with the past. But to be critical and self-
critical, this undertaking must be sensitive to the problem of the possibilities and limits of meaning, including the threat of finding oneself
at the point of irrecoverable loss and empty silence. The quest for a
"positive" identity or for normalization through denial provides only
illusory meaning and does not further the emergence of an acceptable
future. A reckoning with the past in keeping with democratic values
requires the ability—or at least the attempt—to read scars and to affirm only what deserves affirmation as one turns the lamp of critical
reflection on oneself and one's own.[21]

[21]Since 1989 the Historikerstreit has been eclipsed by the uncertainties as well as the
promise of German reunification in the wider context of the movement for European
integration. The recrudescence of scapegoating tendencies, the hostility toward immi-
grants, and the rise of neo-Nazi groups are the most negative aspects of the recent configuration. Yet the debate over the so-called failure of the intellectuals in responding to
the challenge of reunification—and especially the controversy centering on Christa
Wolf—indicate that problems rehearsed in the historians' debate have not been transcended. The East German past arose to create difficulties not only through the here-
tofore avoided issue of complicity in the Nazi regime but through the more clear and
present dangers to stability created by disclosure of the shockingly unexpected extent
of spying, informing, and intimidation under the former communist government. Indeed, it has been argued that the ultimate goal of both the Historikerstreit and the debate over the "failure of the intellectuals" is similar: "one wants to get away from a past
that is considered either a burden or an embarrassment in order to construct an alternative agenda for the future. While the attempt to overcome the German past in the

name of 'normalization' was not successful in the historians' debate, it may very well end up successful in its more removed and diluted form in the current culture debate''; Andreas Huyssen, "After the Wall: The Failure of German Intellectuals," *New German Critique* 52 (Winter 1991), 126. In any case, whatever the more immediate effects of re-unification, the problems raised in the historians' debate must return in a different way in the new context of a unified German nation-state insofar as the manner in which one comes to terms with the past affects the attempt to construct the present and future.

THREE

∾

Historicizing the Holocaust

I would like to return to certain problems in the light of Arno J. Mayer's *Why Did the Heavens Not Darken?: The "Final Solution" in History*.[1] A close reading and analysis of this important book will permit a more detailed investigation of issues touched on in the previous chapters.

I have asserted that, for many if not most historians, to historicize means to contextualize. Certainly, historical understanding requires contextualization even if the latter is problematized in certain ways and seen as a necessary rather than sufficient condition of a self-critical historiography that acknowledges the importance of self-understanding in the attempt to make one's assumptions explicit and to work critically through a relation to the past. In this respect, Mayer's book presents the reader with a curious asymmetry: it attempts to explain the Holocaust through a superabundance of contextual information in support of a specific explanatory thesis about the past, but it makes no sustained attempt to contextualize itself by situating its argument in the contemporary controversy that reached a provisional climax in the so-called historians' debate (Historikerstreit).

This asymmetry is itself highly significant. Mayer's approach reinforces the view that the historian should write history and engage only in very limited ways in critical self-reflection about the way history is written. Critical self-reflection, especially when it is not restricted to the discrete "think piece" but included within a "proper"

[1] New York: Pantheon, 1988.

history, may be seen as narcissistically self-indulgent or symptomatic of a "descent into discourse."[2] My own view is that one must combine the roles of historian and critical theorist or at least see them as tensely interactive and, in the best of circumstances, mutually supportive. Indeed, this combination should improve the quality of both history and criticism. One debilitating binary opposition that has had widespread currency in professional historiography draws a decisive contrast between those who write history and those who write about writing it. The former are often seen as the "real" or "working" historians. The latter may at times be objects of a litany of aspersions ranging from the charge of succumbing to the dreaded wiles of metahistory to that of perpetrating something analogous to welfare chiseling. This view often assumes a truncated idea of history relying on further extreme oppositions (for example, between events and texts—as if texts were purely manipulable figments of the imagination and not themselves historical events intricately related to other events). It also may induce the charge that those who criticize certain assumptions are all relativists and proponents of the belief that "anything goes"—a charge that may attest to the accuser's "anything goes" proclivity not to read carefully and distinguish between those lumped together and castigated under convenient but misleading labels.[3]

The concentration on past contexts in abstraction from their relation to present problems and debates has the function of enhancing a sense of pure objectivity in the representation and explanation of the past. This deceptive "objectivity-effect" should be distinguished from

[2]See, for example, Bryan D. Palmer's *Descent into Discourse* (Philadelphia: Temple University Press, 1990), which is particularly notable in that Palmer seems to have read almost everything relevant to contemporary debates about historiography but to have understood too little. Although he makes the commendable effort to reassert the importance of social history, he does so in such uncritical terms that he may well do a disservice to an important enterprise that is in need of rearticulation and defense. His spirited polemic may require hyperbole to register, but the polemic is too indiscriminate in the way it is applied to the specific texts and positions of very different theorists and historians.

[3]See, for example, Gertrude Himmelfarb's "Post-modernist History and the Flight from Fact," *Times Literary Supplement*, 16 October 1992, pp. 12–15. Himmelfarb offers an ostensibly pious and reasonable but poorly argued attack on a carelessly associated series of historians (including both Arno Mayer and myself, among many others). An article such as Himmelfarb's is especially objectionable because of its ability to reach a generally educated public that may actually rely on it for knowledge of tendencies it analyzes in a rashly generalized and misleading fashion.

a defensible mode of objectivity achieved in and through an explicit, theoretically alert resistance to projective or wish-fulfilling tendencies and an attempt to engage critically the problem of one's relation to the past. Indeed, an objectivity-effect may accompany a concealed tendency to enact projective or wish-fulfilling tendencies in the very way the past is objectified.

Concentrating on objectified and abstracted (or "split-off") past contexts also confines understanding to a purely interpretive or contemplative role that blocks sustained consideration of the problem of the implication of the interpreter in both the object of interpretation and in contemporary discussions of it. Such dissociated concentration also functions to obviate the need to attend to the issue of the mediated relation between understanding and sociopolitical practice. Moreover, it restricts one's exchange with the past to a monologue in which the "voices" or perspectives of those one studies function at best as mere illustrations or evidence for a thesis but cannot be made to challenge the interpretation or explanation one places on them. Finally, the diminished or virtually nonexistent sense of one's implication in what one studies and in a contemporary context of circumstantial constraints and intellectual controversies obscures the problem of the subject-positions of the historian that relate his or her individual perspective or voice to social problems and possibilities. At most the problem of subjectivity is seen in excessively personal terms, confined to a paratext (for example, a preface or coda), and isolated from the narrative or argument of the principal text that furnishes the substantive account of the past. The result of these one-sided procedures seems so questionable in Mayer's case that it may generate doubts about standard modes of objectivist contextualism in less controversial areas of research. It raises both the problem of the relation between the historian and the object of study and the question of how one should confront that relation in research that is both meticulously documented and responsibly self-critical.[4]

What are some salient components of the largely absent contempo-

[4]The approach that I have, for convenience sake, termed conventional is, however, increasingly contested in historiography. See, for example, Ranajit Guha and Gayatri Chakravorty Spivak, eds., *Selected Subaltern Studies* (New York: Oxford University Press, 1988), and Joan Wallach Scott, *Gender and the Politics of History* (New York: Columbia University Press, 1988). See also Peter Novick, *That Noble Dream: The "Objectivity" Question and the American Historical Profession* (New York: Cambridge University Press, 1988) for a long-term history of the role of the concept of objectivity in American professional historiography.

rary context in Mayer's text? I have addressed dimensions of this context in the preceding chapter, and I shall not repeat here my argument on the historians' debate. I shall simply remind the reader that I tried to raise the issue of how one should negotiate transferential relations to the object of study whereby processes active in it are repeated with more or less significant variations in the account of the historian. I also suggested that the Holocaust presents the historian with transference in the most traumatic and disconcerting form conceivable. Here I need simply reiterate that I am using the concept of transference in a broad and relatively nontechnical sense to refer to the problem of the at times extremely charged or "cathected" implication of the historian in the processes he or she studies. The specific feature of this implication that I insist upon is the tendency to displace—that is, to repeat in variable and often disguised form—aspects of those processes in one's account of them. I think this broad sense of transference may be found in Freud's texts, but in Freud and in subsequent psychoanalytic thinkers it is often overshadowed if not obscured by the restriction of transference to the one-on-one clinical relation of analyst and analysand as well as its explanation in terms of the Oedipal complex. The rethinking of the concept in a broader context and with less assured explanatory mechanisms may enable one to shed new light on historiographic debates that have tended to get bogged down in standard binary oppositions between objectivity and subjectivity, universalism and relativism. But the concept of transference is not in and of itself explanatory; it does not solve problems but indicates their presence, and the processes to which it points either happen blindly (even at times when they are denied) or are confronted with more or less critical vigilance and a measure of responsible control.

That transference and responses to it cannot be seen in narrowly psychological terms but always involve social and political issues is itself dramatically illustrated by recent developments. Indeed, the very understanding of psychoanalysis merely as a psychology of the individual is itself a profound misunderstanding that functions to conceal the interaction between transferential processes and sociopolitical problems. The effort of the early Frankfurt School to forge a link between Freud and Marx should itself be seen not as an idiosyncratic or dated project but as a specific, yet in certain respects paradigmatic, attempt to theorize the bond between psychoanalytic and sociopolitical processes. The disabling effects of not making this necessary attempt are nowhere more blatant than in the views of certain participants in the historians' debate.[5]

Comments made during the Bitburg incident indicate how the historians' debate is part of a broader attempt, especially prominent in neoconservative circles, to accentuate the positive in history or at least to have all parties derive some benefit from a potentially devastating past. Helmut Kohl and Ronald Reagan were at one in attempting to "emancipate" Germany from what they saw as a debilitating memory. In Reagan's case, the notion of emancipation was tantamount to unearned, celebratory forgetting that invited the return of the repressed. It simply ignored the problems of public acknowledgment, mourning, and working-through. As Reagan put it when he tried to justify his initial decision not to visit a concentration camp during his trip to Germany commemorating the fortieth anniversary of the end of the war:

> I feel very strongly that this time, in commemorating the end of that great war, that instead of reawakening the memories and so forth, and the passions of the time, that maybe we should observe this day when, 40 years ago, peace began and friendship, because we now find ourselves allies and friends of the countries that we once fought against, and that we, it'd be almost a celebration of the end of an era and the coming into what has now been some 40 years of peace for us. And I felt that, since the German people have very few alive that remember

[5]Stephen Brockmann's "Politics of German History" (*History and Theory* 29 [1990], 179–89) provides helpful information about both the contemporary political stakes of the Historikerstreit and its implication in a long tradition of debate concerning the "peculiarities" of German history. Its principal drawbacks are its obliviousness to the implications of its own arguments and its insensitivity to the problem of transference. Hence, it provides a strikingly ameliorative analysis of Nolte's views and rather misleadingly stresses the similarities between Nolte's and Habermas's assumptions, as if the differences between them were not of crucial importance. In the process, Brockmann tends to downplay or even trivialize the Historikerstreit through the contradictory strategies of reducing it to an epiphenomenon of both present politics and very long traditions. Brockmann can thus write both that "the real argument was not about history but about the political present" (p. 183) and that "the *Historikerstreit*, which seemed so new to its participants and to outside observers, becomes merely another in a long series of debates whose fixed pole is the concept of the *Sonderweg* [special path in history] (viewed positively or negatively) and of history as the appropriate location for *Sinngebung*—literally, the giving of meaning" (p. 186). What Brockmann sees as the "irony" of being involved in varied rearticulations of the past is not, as he seems to think, confined to participants in the Historikerstreit. Unless one affirms either of the complementary and, I think, illusory extremes of pure continuity with the past or beginning anew ex nihilo, one has to come to terms with the problem of precisely how one negotiates those rearticulations with respect to both norms of historiographical practice and involvement in ideological and political controversy.

even the war, and certainly none of them who were adults and participating in any way, and the, they do, they have a feeling and a guilt feeling that's been imposed upon them. And I just think it's unnecessary. I think they should be recognized for the democracy that they've created and the democratic principles they now espouse.[6]

The grammatical double take in Reagan's statement ("and the, they do, they have") may attest to the enormity of a view that denies not only the existence of wartime participants and, by implication, of former Nazis in Germany but even the prevalence of a memory of events; it may also derive from the curious assumption that no German participants in the war had lived to be as old as Reagan himself and that very few Germans had memories better than his. More important, Reagan misconstrues the process whereby one can achieve a condition that allows one to let bygones be bygones, and he does not address the possibility that a viable and legitimate democracy cannot be based on celebratory oblivion but requires a critical attempt to come to terms with the past.

When news reports disclosed that Bitburg cemetery contained SS graves, Reagan still defended his decision to visit it: "I think that there is nothing wrong with visiting that cemetery where those young men are victims of Nazism also, even though they were fighting in German uniform, drafted into service to carry out the hateful wishes of the Nazis. They were victims, just as surely as the victims in the concentration camps."[7] The indiscriminate generalization of victimhood and the dissociation of the army and even of the SS from Nazism were carried even further by a comment of Reagan at Bergen-Belsen, which he finally decided to visit because of public pressure. Hitler not only became the sole source of all evil but was transformed into an unnamed stock figure who made all the world his victim. Reagan referred to "the awful evil started by one man—an evil that victimized all the world with its destruction. For year after year, until that man and his evil were destroyed, hell yawned forth its awful contents."[8] It is curious that a suspect appeal to demonology came from the great communicator of "positive" messages and the specialist in affirmative recognition scenes. It is even more daunting that a *New York Times*/CBS poll taken after the visit to Bitburg indicated that as

[6]Reported in the *New York Times*, 22 March 1985.
[7]Reported in the *New York Times*, 19 April 1985.
[8]Reported in the *New York Times*, 6 May 1985.

many people in the United States (41 percent) approved of Reagan's actions as disapproved of them.

Another dimension of the contemporary context, which has played a variable role in the historians' debate, at least as a background factor, is the use of the Shoah as "symbolic capital" by Israel as well as the entire Israeli-Palestinian conflict and the marked (at times justified) opposition to Israeli policy, notably on the left and by Arab and other Third World states. Here one of course has an extremely complicated set of issues where one must be attentive to important differences within given groups or categories. There have been and continue to be significant debates over Israeli policy within Israel, and not all of those even on the far left are anti-Israeli. In his Personal Preface (which I discuss more fully later in this chapter), Mayer makes a brief allusion to these problems while commenting on his visit to Israel as a graduate student in 1950: "Without minimizing Israel's security dilemma, both [Ernst] Simon and the far left of democratic Marxists took exception to the unbending policy of postindependence governments toward Israeli Arabs and the Arab states, which could only make Israel's future more and more contingent on its American connection. During my second visit to Israel in 1954 I was struck by the wisdom and the precision of these apprehensions" (pp. xii–xiii).

Mayer does not inform us, even in his Personal Preface, about his views on these problems as they unfolded between 1954 and the publication of his book. Nor does he address directly the role of the Shoah as "symbolic capital." It is difficult to know how to situate, in the recent past, the use of the Shoah to justify or sanction whatever Israel does to others on the grounds that what happened under the Nazis can "never again" be allowed to happen to Jews. At times it seems that this apologetic move is not so much explicitly made by defenders of certain questionable policies as somehow assumed as a diffuse possibility and often introduced by those who would proleptically reject its relevance. Indeed, this move may by now have come to exist as a brooding omnipresence and be so manifestly beside the point in certain cases as to make its explicit use unavailable or at least blatantly farfetched. Pierre Vidal-Naquet, whose expert knowledge in this matter as in other aspects of the revisionist controversy and the study of the Shoah far exceeds my own, has written that in Israel "the Shoah serves as a perpetual self-justification in all domains, in legitimizing the slightest border incident as marking a renewal of the massacre, in assimilating the Palestinians (toward whom the Israelis, all the same, are guilty of undeniable wrongs) to the SS. The result has been effective—even though the great majority of Israel's inhabitants has had no direct experience of Nazi persecution—but some prefer to hear no more of those tragic days, and one can even find here and there in Israel a Faurisson disciple!"[9]

Vidal-Naquet's own book is devoted largely to the more blatant revisionism of figures such as Robert Faurisson, Arthur Butz, and Paul Rassinier, but he also touches on broader issues, including the historians' debate. He discusses, moreover, revisionist tendencies on the far left in France, notably in La Vieille Taupe and its founder (a former militant of Socialisme ou Barbarie) Pierre Guillaume. As Vidal-Naquet puts it: "In the view of La Vieille Taupe, there was no specificity to the Hitler experience among the gallery of modern tyrannies: the concentration camps could only be exploitation camps, in the economic sense of the word, and, as a result, the extermination camps could not have existed since, in all due logic, they should not have existed" (p. 118).

This extreme position is the absurd extension of the more general orthodox Marxist view of the economy and class conflict as the principal motors of history to which everything else must be subordinated. Hence, one has the idea that Nazism and fascism were somehow caused by capitalism (at least "in the last analysis") and the belief that a focus on them, or what may be specific to them and not clearly derivable from capitalism, is diversionary for the revolutionary movement and obscures the truth about history. Moreover, one has the attendant belief that any pronounced attention to the Shoah must function in the present as pro-Israeli propaganda and go against revolutionary interests. Needless to say, a critical response to even these more modulated orthodox Marxist views does not entail a dismissal of the problem of the relation between Nazism and capitalism either structurally or in terms of group alliances. Nor does it imply a lack of concern with ideological uses of the Shoah. On the latter issue,

[9]*Assassins of Memory: Essays on the Denial of the Holocaust*, trans. with a foreword by Jeffrey Mehlman (1987; New York: Columbia University Press, 1992), p. 122. One may nonetheless observe that in a book replete with extensive footnotes that document general propositions, there is no reference that gives examples of recent cases of Israeli use of the Shoah as "perpetual justification in all domains." One may ask whether this is because in Vidal-Naquet's experience—and in fact—this use is so clear and patent as to obviate the need for specific references or because the invocation of the possible Israeli use of the Shoah as "symbolic capital" has itself become something of a required ritual gesture, notably for those who might be suspected of pro-Israeli sympathies.

Vidal-Naquet provides a concise and admirable statement: "The worst crimes that might be committed by Israel would not be justified by Treblinka, but conversely they do not change a single bit the totally criminal nature of Auschwitz and Treblinka" (p. 131).

I shall later allude to Mayer's own leftist sympathies which, in their problematic relation to Jewish identity, may create unthematized and unexamined pressures on his argument. In *The Assassins of Memory* Vidal-Naquet refers appreciatively to Mayer's book, for which he provided a blurb. (On the dust jacket he calls it "the most important effort ever made by a historian to think critically about the unthinkable.") His preface to the French edition of Mayer's book (published in 1990) is mixed, but in it he does rebuke Lucy Dawidowicz because of her criticism of Mayer for revisionist tendencies (in her review in *Commentary*, October 1989). In his interesting foreword to *The Assassins of Memory*, Jeffrey Mehlman brings out some of the complications of Vidal-Naquet's own response to Mayer. He observes that Mayer "in no way denied the Nazi extermination of the Jews" and that Butz in his review of Mayer for the revisionist *Journal of Historical Review* denounced the book as "shoddy" (p. xvii). But he also notes that Mayer's very inclusion of Butz and Rassinier in his bibliography was an "innovation" (p. 145n) in serious scholarship about the Holocaust. I would add that not only did this gesture seem to lend their work a certain standing if not legitimacy but that the indiscriminate character of Mayer's bibliography had a leveling effect. In it hundreds of references simply appear seriatim with no sense of their relative importance or credibility. Mehlman also points out (p. xviii) that Robert Faurisson in his review for the *Journal of Historical Review* took a dig at Vidal-Naquet, who has been his greatest adversary, by "touting" Mayer as "Pierre Vidal-Naquet's friend." Faurisson picked up on passages in Mayer's book that he believed served the revisionist cause. One of these (on p. 362–63 of Mayer) begins: "Sources for the study of gas chambers are at once rare and unreliable." It includes the statement: "There is no denying the many contradictions, ambiguities, and errors in the existing sources." (Mehlman points out that Vidal-Naquet, in his preface to the French edition of Mayer's book, rejected the assertion that sources for the study of gas chambers are "rare and unreliable" [p.145n]). Faurisson also highlighted Mayer's argument that disease and exhaustion caused more deaths among Jews than outright murder.

Mehlman himself uses Vidal-Naquet's complicated response to

Mayer to help explain what he terms "Vidal-Naquet's oddly dispirited pseudo-conclusion" (p. xviii) to his book. Vidal-Naquet ends what he himself calls his "melancholic essay" by quoting with apparent approval a tango by the Argentine poet Enrique Santos Discépolo. This bitterly ironic piece begins: "That the world was and always will be a sty / I know quite well." Its recurrent motif is not only the untenability of oppositions but the leveling of all distinctions—a process presumably happening in the "world" and one that the poet (in the dubious tradition of an indiscriminate kind of "culture critique") seems to assert in his own participatory voice. Thus: "Today it's all the same / whether one's loyal or betrays. / Ignorant, erudite, robber, / generous or a con man. / Everything's the same!" The tango ends: "No one cares if you were born honest. / It's all the same: the guy who slaves / Night and day like an ox, / The one who lives off of his girls, / The one who kills, the one who cures / Or the one who has become an outlaw." Curiously, Vidal-Naquet introduces his full quotation of this piece by stating that it "describe[s] rather well this world of ours, in which, all the same, there sprout every now and then a few flowers of truth that instill hope and whose gardener, along with many others, I do my best to be, without for all that knowing how to set things aright" (p. 140). One might object that Vidal-Naquet goes too far in accepting as self-evident the "yes, but" response the piece may evoke in a benevolent reader without attending to the possibility (indeed the plausibility) of other readings, for example, one that would stress the despairing and somewhat self-pitying tone of the poet's "tough-guy" voice. Vidal-Naquet's elliptical, somewhat vague final words continue in the vein of his questionable interpretation and take a rather wan distance from the poem: "Will truth have the last word? How one would like to be sure of it" (p. 142).

The complexity of Vidal-Naquet's response to some of the questions raised by Mayer's book should nonetheless act as a signal to the reader of the controversial nature of both the issues I address and my arguments about them. Having given these caveats, I now turn directly to Mayer's book to analyze what I think are some of its important and questionable features. As I noted at the outset, the book gives insufficient sense of the contemporary intellectual and political. context that bears on the story it recounts. It seems to be written with little if any awareness of the historiographical and political controversies surrounding the problems it treats. For this reason among others, the book seems to be enmeshed in uncontrolled processes of displacement and denial. There is no reference to Bitburg. And there is no direct and sustained coming to terms with problems raised in the His-torikerstreit. For example, Andreas Hillgruber's *Zweierlei Untergang* also appears in the extensive bibliography with a strange leveling ef-fect. Hillgruber's book is lost in the crowd and not subjected to critical scrutiny. Nor are Mayer's at times emphatic and insufficiently quali-fied arguments compared with Hillgruber's account. Mayer simply seems to tell it like it is and to seek the unmediated truth.

In his largely favorable review of Mayer's book, V. R. Berghahn de-fends Mayer against any attempt to align his views with Ernst Nolte's.[10] In his Personal Preface Mayer himself seems to make an ob-lique allusion to Nolte (without mentioning him or his writings by name) when he discusses his own immediate postwar experience in interrogating German generals and leading scientists who apologeti-cally invoked the argument that the Nazis at least opposed Bolshe-vism: "The Third Reich's defeated generals and scientists anticipated, by forty years, the arguments of retrovisionist [sic] historians in Ger-many who today seek to rationalize the Nazi regime by characterizing it as intrinsically designed and essential for the struggle against the 'greater evil' of Soviet communism" (p. xii). On one level, this com-ment reinforces Berghahn's attempt to dissociate Mayer from Nolte's more extreme claims, such as the idea that the Nazi genocide was a defensive response to a perceived threat from Stalinist Russia or even from the Jews themselves. But this attempt, despite its limited valid-ity, does not reckon with the more uncontrolled and even inconsis-tent dimensions of Mayer's account or with its relation—particularly in its own insistence on the primary role of anti-Marxist ideology and the causal priority of the war against the Russians on the eastern front in determining Nazi policy toward the Jews—to more subtle forms of revisionism. Unfortunately, the latter may serve to make the ten-dency "respectable" among those who would be outraged by direct association with blatantly revisionist theses. In any case, Mayer him-self does not sufficiently situate his argument with respect to politi-cally and ideologically charged controversies of whose existence and nature he was certainly aware. In this sense Mayer does little—or at least not enough—to guard his book against misleading uses and abuses. Not only the manner in which he propounds this thesis but his reticence—or at best his extremely limited and overly general

[10]*New York Times Book Review*, 19 February 1989.

comments—about the relation of his argument to its intertextual analogues and contextual surroundings may even (however unintentionally) invite abuse.

One determinant of Mayer's approach seems to be an overweening desire to employ strictly conventional historical procedures and uses of language in addressing the phenomenon he does not even want to call the Holocaust.[11] In certain ways, the book may be seen as a negative experiment—a case study in how not to write about the Holocaust—not because it is bad conventional history but because in certain ways it strains overmuch, however unsuccessfully at times, to be good conventional history in a case where certain basic procedures of conventional history may well be necessary but not sufficient. Without carefully examining the assumptions, virtues, and limitations of his project, Mayer seeks to provide a seemingly rational and objective explanation for the bewildering combination of instrumental rationality and substantive irrationality that typified the Third Reich. The book in fact resembles in format, mode of argumention, and rhetoric Mayer's *Persistence of the Old Regime: Europe to the Great War*, a work that won considerable praise within the historical profession.[12] *Why Did the Heavens Not Darken?* can perhaps serve didactically as an example of what may occur when one does not heed sufficiently the special demands—at times the impossible choices or aporias and in any event the pressures on the use of language—that confront the historian particularly (but not exclusively) when he or she attempts to account for certain events.

Mayer does, however, depart from conventional historiography in a dubious manner. He does not footnote statements or paragraphs but relies on the bibliography to provide his sources. This procedure makes it difficult to locate the basis of particular assertions and arguments. In the context of Mayer's study, the omission of the standard

[11]Trying to avoid any sacrificial or religious connotation, Mayer, as we shall see, prefers the seemingly more antiseptic neologism "Judeocide." He fails to recognize that his term is close to Nazi bureaucratic jargon.

[12]Insofar as Mayer stresses the role of older elites and structures in bringing about the larger context of crisis and war that serves as the necessary framework for explaining the "Judeocide," *Why Did the Heavens Not Darken?* may even be read as a corollary to *The Persistence of the Old Regime* (New York: Pantheon, 1981). István Deák has criticized Mayer's stress on the role of the old regime in eastern Europe, for it tends to downplay the populist, social-revolutionary element in east European chauvinism and anti-Semitism. See "The Incomprehensible Holocaust," *New York Review of Books*, 28 September 1989.

footnoting apparatus does not function as a thought-provoking "alienation effect" that may call into question the role of standard procedures. It is a lack in an otherwise conventional account, but a lack that may of course itself invite questions about the motivation for it and its effects. For one thing, the omission rather deceptively fosters the sense that one is reading not a controversial account enmeshed, however implicitly or even blindly, in ideological issues but a massively informed synthesis that conveys what may appear to the general reader simply to be the objective statement of a novel thesis.

What is this thesis and what is the past context that serves as an explanation? In what seems by the end of the book to be endless, almost compulsive repetition that is not advanced by argument but in fact undermined by it, Mayer asserts the priority of the German campaign on the eastern front against the Soviet Union and Bolshevism. Auschwitz and "Judeocide" are derivatives of the *Drang nach Osten* motivated by animosity against Bolshevism and the Soviet Union. Strangely enough, what from one vantage point seems to border on sophisticated neoconservative revisionism corroborates what may also be read as orthodox Marxist monocausal explanation conveniently centered on the Soviet Union and Bolshevism. But other, more critical dimensions of a Marxist approach to history that might resist a convergence with neoconservatism have little effective role in Mayer's text. There is, for example, no attempt to relate an analysis of society, politics, and ideology to the problem of the relation between theory and practice, including the question of the implication of the writer in the problems he or she analyzes—an implication that is not purely "personal" or narrowly experiential. Particularly in the absence of such an attempted reckoning, one may wonder to what extent elements of an orthodox Marxist orientation reinforced by an extreme reliance on conventional documentary and positivistic procedures offer too simple a solution to overdetermined relations and obscure the role of a problematic Jewish identity in one's response to the past.

Mayer begins with what is clearly labeled a "personal preface" in which his own involvement in the events he is to recount is indeed briefly noted but in purely personal terms. He tells us, for example, that his maternal "grandparents were transported on April 6, 1943, to Theresienstadt, the concentration camp located in an ancient fortified town with large military barracks not far from Prague[. . .] My grandfather died in Theresienstadt on December 3, 1943. But my

grandmother was among the approximately 17,000 emaciated and ter-
rorized inmates liberated by the Red Army on May 9, 1945, exactly five
years after the invasion of her native country" (pp. ix–x). He also writes:

> As for my own immediate family, it was neither poor nor *grand*
> *bourgeois*, but middle-class. Fully emancipated and largely acculturated
> Luxembourgian Jews, we observed the High Holidays, held the yearly
> Seder, and celebrated Chanukah. My sister and I reluctantly went to
> Sunday school, and I was bar mitzvahed[. . .] By the time he returned
> to Luxembourg in 1924, my father had become an antifascist and a
> Zionist with strong left-democratic leanings[. . .] If we left Luxembourg
> in good time and never stopped to look back, it was because my father
> had long since recognized the innate warlike temper and anti-Semitism
> of the neighboring Nazi regime. (P. xi)

It is difficult to know what to make of the Personal Preface. It
evokes the reader's empathy. Yet stylistically it is close to the rest of
the book in its precise denotative tone and its provision of a superabundance of detailed information that in this instance at times seems
somewhat beside the point. Still, in its "personal" content, it is jar-
ringly different from the chapters that follow it. Its relation to the substantive account is entirely unmediated. Its disclosures may even
seem to disarm criticism in someone who has no comparable authen-
ticating experience in his or her own life. I want simply to make one
point about the textual function of the preface. I think it by and large
delimits and quarantines the questions of subject-position and narrative voice and diverts them in a narrowly subjective direction, thereby
obviating the need to confront in the principal text itself the less easily
confined problem of transference and the way it links individual and
society. And it is premised on an extreme subjective/objective or
private/public dichotomy that functions to obscure the more intricate
issue of how necessary distinctions function and ought to function in
the writing of history. The preface seems to serve as a kind of safety
valve that draws off and releases the forces (such as the problem of a
Jewish background and its relation to a Marxist commitment in one's
self-understanding) that are explicitly prevented from exerting pressure in the principal text. But, as we shall see, the repressed or suppressed tends to return in an account in which the role of uncontrolled displacement and even contradiction is prominent. Mayer
ends the preface with a self-denying comment that is belied by the air
of mastery, confident marshaling of facts and statistics, position of

omniscient narrator or transcendental spectator, monocausal insistence, and unguarded assertion of theses in the rest of the book: "At bottom the Judeocide remains as incomprehensible to me today as five years ago, when I set out to study and rethink it" (p. xv).

Mayer relies on comparison and contextualization to deny the uniqueness of "Judeocide," any particularities of which may be explained by reference to the exigencies of war on the eastern front. The two primary comparisons he invokes are the Thirty Years' War and the First Crusade, but their role is to bring out the nature of the campaign against the Bolsheviks as a holy war. One may agree that the politically "religious" nature of the Nazi animus against both Bolsheviks and Jews was indeed important, but it does not gain in credibility or force from the particular comparisons Mayer invokes. In making his comparisons, moreover, Mayer is concerned primarily with the similarities rather than with significant differences. And though he is almost obsessed with the "religious" nature of Nazi animosity against the Bolsheviks and Russia, he provides little insight into the Nazi victimization of Jews and other oppressed minorities. His own desire is clearly to give a central position to the Nazi animus against the Bolsheviks, and the fulfillment of this desire results either in contradictory statements or in a tendency to downplay if not marginalize Nazi anti-Semitism. It is almost as if the paramount importance of Bolshevism and the Nazi opposition to it functioned to lessen the significance of the merely derivative "Jewish problem."

In addition, Mayer wants to cleanse historiography itself of any ritual admixture and present it as the paradigm of pure secular rationality. Not only does critical history have an adversarial or homeopathic role to play in relation to ideology; it somehow is able to transcend ideological implication and ritual processes toward a purely enlightened realm. Identification with historiography seems to provide the (assimilated?) secular historian with a full identity that excludes the relevance of all other subject-positions.

Mayer explicitly relies on an opposition between myth and history that defines and tends to reify the presumably dichotomous positions of certain Jews and historians. The memory of apparently unenlightened Jews is relegated to myth and acting-out, in sharp and unmediated contrast to the requirements of history.

> But gradually, even if unwittingly, this cult of remembrance has become overly sectarian. More and more, it has helped to disconnect the Jewish

catastrophe from its secular historical setting, while placing it within the providential history of the Jewish people to be commemorated, lamented, and restrictively interpreted. Its reification has found expression and consecration in the religiously freighted word concept "the Holocaust," a term whose standard meaning is a sacrificial offering wholly consumed by fire in exaltation of God. The embryonic creed of "the Holocaust," which has also became [sic] an *idée-force*, has taken the reflective and transparent remembrances of survivors and woven them into a collective prescriptive "memory" unconducive to critical and contextual thinking about the Jewish calamity. A central premise is that the victimization of the Jews at the hands of Nazi Germany and its collaborators is absolutely unprecedented, completely *sui generis*, and thus beyond historical imagining. (Pp. 16–17)

Mayer is convincing in his effort to warn against the excesses of theologization and to stress the need for a critical historiography. But he apparently does not sense the danger in generalizing rashly about what he seems to present as the conspiratorial activity of certain unnamed Jews, and he does not elucidate what he means by "the reflective and transparent remembrances of survivors" in a case where the traumatizing effects of extreme suffering and the role of belated memory are patent. Nor does he see historiography as a process involving the attempt to relate and work critically through highly charged and even traumatizing memories but as somehow simply different and detached from "memory." One need not believe that historiography may be either reduced to memory in the literal sense or simply conflated with myth and ritual in order to observe that Mayer's stark opposition may readily facilitate a movement toward uncritical conventionality, normalization, and even positivism. (It may also prompt the complementary overreaction whereby one vents unchecked subjectivity and may even be moved by outrage and anger to castigate Mayer as a "false witness.") It is also significant that Mayer's rejection of the term "Holocaust," when it does not induce usage of the neologism "Judeocide," ends up in repeated recourse to such exhausted terms as "catastrophe," "calamity," and "disaster."

One may sympathize with Mayer in his attempt to counteract a sacralization of events that seems to be implied in the literal meaning of "holocaust." But one is here in an area where there are no easy, uninvolved, or purely objective choices. Perhaps it is best not to become fixated on any one term but to use various terms while continually indicating their limitations. In addressing limit cases, one inevitably risks repeating processes active in the phenomena one studies, including the tendency to veer in the directions of sacrificial elevation and bureaucratic reduction. The difficulty is to counteract this tendency, and the danger is that the avoidance of certain terms may induce even more dubious choices (such as "Judeocide"). Mayer thinks he has eliminated problems by not using the term "holocaust," but he may have simply displaced them in a manner that masks difficulties and lessens chances of critical control. Thus it is not surprising that he produces his own credo, which he believes expresses the epitome of critical rationality:

> Compared to the Muse of memory, however, the Muse of history is sworn to certain ideas and rules for recording and interpreting the past. Since the Enlightenment, historians have shared certain commonsense notions of causality and accuracy. They have also presumed the past to be accessible by virtue of being profane, not providential. In addition, rather than give free reign to their subjectivity, they are supposed to master it. At a minimum, historians are expected to avow their own prejudices and to probe those of their sources. No less important, they invite critics, both friendly and hostile, to verify the authenticity and reliability of their evidence as well as to debate the logic of their constructions and the coherence of their explanations. Historians must also develop a lateral and wide-angled vision, for they are enjoined to probe for linkages between events that were unclear or unknown to contemporaries. (P. 17)

Is it helpful to oppose in such a stark manner the "Muse" of history and the "Muse" of memory? Are "commonsense" notions of causality and accuracy enough to distinguish a critical historiography? Does historiography really require an assumption about the "nature" of the past—be it providential or profane—or instead a critical and secular understanding of the procedures through which the past is to be recounted, understood, and explained? Can the desire for mastery lead to excesses that undercut the possibility of responsible but limited control? Should not scholarly exchange itself involve the attempt to elicit "prejudices" or assumptions that are not clear to the author? Are these "prejudices" better understood as aspects of a transferential relation to the past which always has a bearing on the role of memory in the present? How does one develop a "lateral and wide-angled vision" without dubiously shifting one's focus or sacrificing careful attention to specifics, details, and countertendencies that may qualify or even contest one's vision? In any case, it is noteworthy that the binary opposition between memory and history is contradicted by Mayer almost as soon as it is put forth, for he criticizes some modern histories that are too close to "memory" in his overly restricted sense, and he praises, as exemplary histories, works that make critical use of memory:

> It is striking that the foremost contemporary chroniclers of the recent Jewish disaster, unlike those of earlier times, recorded their eyewitness observations in the spirit of Enlightenment history. No retrospective memoir, literary work, or historical analysis can match the precision and penetration of Emmanuel Ringelblum's *Notes from the Warsaw Ghetto*, of Adam Czerniaków's *Warsaw Diary*, of the collectively kept *Chronicle of the Lódz Ghetto, 1941–1944*. These three firsthand chronicles, written inside the cities of the dying and the dead, were framed with distinctly modern ideas of facticity, chronology, and context, and also of the dynamics of collaboration and resistance under conditions of extreme powerlessness. More remarkable still, they registered the impact of the course of world history, particularly the war, on the daily life and fate of the ghettos. (P. 17)

In spite of the questionably "progressivist" contrast between the benighted past and the enlightened present, Mayer's own analysis in this passage is enough to indicate that more complex concepts are needed than those provided by the simple opposition between mythical memory and "profane" history, for memory may itself be critical and some secular history uncritical or heavily ideological. Indeed, the role of such an opposition may well be to evacuate the problem of transference and the need to come to terms with it in the writing of history. A bizarre consequence of Mayer's reliance on this binary opposition between mythical memory and history is his tendency to attribute to an artificially purified conception of history the quasi-transcendental and incomparably unique status he denies to the Holocaust. This is one way in which the repressed returns.

The core of Mayer's substantive argument is, as I have intimated, the imputation of causal priority to the eastern campaign and the attempt to ground this priority in comparison and contextualization. Here is but one of the many assertions of the thesis, one that is particularly informative because it confronts a point that Mayer recurrently touches on: that the attacks on Bolsheviks and on Jews were often inextricably interconnected in Nazi propaganda and policy. Mayer nonetheless gratuitously insists on getting putative causal priorities straight and weighting them in a one-sidedly decisive fashion: "The assault upon the Jews was unquestionably intertwined with the assault on bolshevism from the very outset. But this is not to say that it was the dominant strand in the hybrid 'Judeobolshevism' that Barbarossa [Hitler's term for the eastern campaign] targeted for destruction. In fact, the war against the Jews was a graft or a parasite upon the eastern campaign, which always remained its host, even or especially once it became mired deep in Russia" (P. 270).

Mayer relies on the suspect language of parasitology, which he himself tells us was a favorite of the Nazis. Here too is testimony that denial of transference and the need to work critically through it encourages blind repetition and return of the repressed. In the very rhetoric of Mayer's arguments, the use of seeming qualifications such as "unquestionably," "certainly," or "to be sure" invariably leads to "but" or "however" as his thesis is repeatedly pounded home despite its contradictory forms of enunciation and the absence of convincing evidence. In addition, Mayer does at times strike distinctively apologetic notes: "But just as the Wehrmacht did not plan mass murder of Soviet prisoners of war, the SS did not predetermine the genocidal murder of Jews. In the fall and early winter of 1941 the field armies and Einsatzgruppen were driven to their respective but inseparable crimes by the intrinsic enormity and savagery of Barbarossa compounded by its contingent derailment" (p. 271).

In light of the "ample evidence . . . that the *Einsatzgruppen*, the specially formed police battalians of the SS, began the systematic liquidation of Eastern Jewry as soon as circumstances permitted, a few weeks after the invasion of the Soviet Union in June 1941,"[13] Mayer's

[13]Deák, "The Incomprehensible Holocaust," p. 71. In a critical review of recent literature, Christopher R. Browning provides a nuanced account of the complexities in the development of the practices of Einsatzgruppen between June and October 1941. See "Beyond 'Intentionalism' and 'Functionalism': The Decision for the Final Solution Reconsidered," in *The Path to Genocide: Essays on Launching the Final Solution* (Cambridge: Cambridge University Press, 1992), pp. 86–121. Browning argues against the idea that the "Final Solution" was the result of frustration because of the difficulties or defeats of Barbarossa and insists instead that "the chronology suggests a rather consistent pattern between victory and radicalization" (p. 121). He also makes the important argument that the dominant emphasis on Einsatzgruppen may confuse issues because different units of the latter learned of new turns in policy at different times and because Himmler's massive build-up of manpower in the East during the summer of 1941 also involved SS, police battalions, and units of native collaborators (pp. 104–9). In addition,

appeal to contingency, unplanned activity, and the force of circumstance seems exaggerated at best. To overemphasize the role of such factors as contingency does not counter effectively arguments based on extreme intentionalism but compounds their shortcomings by inhibiting more careful and qualified accounts of complex events.

Three specific points are worth making, for they contradict or severely impair Mayer's thesis. First, he emphasizes the movement from a policy of exclusion or resettlement of the Jews to one of mass extermination, and he attributes the latter to the exigencies of the eastern campaign. Without denying the importance of the difference between exclusion and extermination, one may nonetheless note that they are sometimes labile facets of a logic of scapegoating and victimization that was active in Nazi propaganda and policy well before the eastern campaign. Mayer has little to say about the possible workings of a scapegoat "mechanism" that took specific forms—both perversely ritualistic and bureaucratically routine—in the Holocaust. Indeed, what is especially difficult to grasp is the combination of

---

he sees a "close and sympathetic" relation between Hitler and Himmler and argues that "if one wants to know what Hitler was thinking, one should look at what Himmler was doing" (p. 121). Despite the importance of his evidence and arguments, Browning does little to elucidate why there were over time policies of expulsion (or resettlement), ghettoization, and extermination, and like others, he tends to conflate ideology and intention. Ideology need not operate exclusively in terms of explicit intentions and plans. And the "ideological" role of such forces as deranged "sacrificialism," scapegoating, and victimization cannot be reduced to the basic model of instrumental rationality that informs both intentionalism and functionalism. To the extent they played a role, such forces also lessen the importance of whether extermination was the result of the elation of victory or the frustration of defeat, and they help to connect (without leading one to conflate) expulsion (exclusion), ghettoization (localized inclusion), and extermination as aspects of a scapegoat "mechanism." I would also note that explanations of Nazi policy in terms of eugenics, racial hygiene, and the attempt to eliminate all "life unworthy of life" share the virtues and limitations of other emphases on scientific, technological, and bureaucratic rationality. If made to eliminate or downplay the significance of other forces, such emphases overly sanitize and rationalize certain processes. They also avoid the problem of the interaction between pseudoscientific and ritualistic aspects of "race," and they engage in a mode of abstraction that denies the specificity of both perpetrators (by focusing on processes that overarch the Nazi period temporally and in terms of comparable developments elsewhere) and victims (by assimilating Jews and other victims rather than posing the problem of their complex relations and asking, for example, whether and how processes involving "ritual" anxiety, scapegoating, and victimization applied to the "mentally ill," "Gypsies," and homosexuals). For the argument affirming the centrality of eugenics and hygiene, see Detlev Peukert, "The Genesis of the 'Final Solution' from the Spirit of Science," in Thomas Childers and Jane Caplan, eds., *Reevaluating the Third Reich* (New York: Holmes and Meier, 1993), pp. 234–52.

extreme technical or instrumental rationality and distorted aspects of "sacrificialism" in the Nazi regime.

Second, Mayer says very little about the 1939 Hitler-Stalin pact, and when he does refer to it in rather perfunctory terms, it is to address Stalin's motivations rather than Hitler's (pp. 176–77). He does not discuss how the Nazis could have treated the Russians with such instrumental rationality in light of their putative obsession with a ritualistic holy war. Hitler himself sensed a problem, and, in a proclamation of 22 June 1941, he noted that he made the pact only with "extreme difficulty." The fact that Hitler, while always amalgamating Jews and Bolsheviks, distinguished between Jewish Bolshevik leaders and the Russian people did not eliminate the difficulty, but it provided a slender basis for a pact with the Russians. Even Hitler's contortions would indicate that any comparable "pact" with the Jews would be entirely out of the question.

Third, Mayer himself presents evidence that the possibility of extermination appeared before the eastern campaign and was continued after the loss of the campaign was a foregone conclusion. Mayer notes that as early as 30 January 1939, in an open address to the new Reichstag, Hitler had prophesied that another world war would "result not in the Bolshevization of the world and with it the victory of the Jews, but in the annihilation of the Jewish race in Europe" (quoted on p. 295). He also quotes Hilter's proclamation of 2 October 1941 to troops on the eastern front after the fall of Kiev, in which Hitler asserted that the extreme poverty of Russia was "the result of nearly twenty-five years of Jewish rule, with a Bolshevik system that is essentially similar to the capitalist system, the carriers of both systems being the same, namely Jews and only Jews" (quoted on p. 244). And he disarmingly notes something that should be devastating for his thesis: "Seemingly discontinuous with the intrinsic social amalgam and tactical ambiguity of the Nazi project, as well as uninformed by precedent, the extermination sites defy explanation. . . . By the time the four killing centers [Chelmno, Belzec, Sobibór, and Treblinka] were established, however, this advancing tide [of the *Drang nach Osten* and Operation Barbarossa] had crested, which meant that their mission was at best marginally related to military and security operations. . . . The four annihilation sites were intended primarily for the decimation of the Jews of Poland and of certain occupied Soviet territories farther east" (pp. 377–78). The seemingly obvious conclusion is that the eastern campaign may well have been an aggravating factor in the Nazi project of extermination, but it can hardly be seen as its unique cause.

   At this point it may be useful to compare briefly Mayer's attempt to explain the Holocaust with three other recent and rather influential ventures that differ from his approach in that they focus on much less circumstantial or delimited factors and raise broader historical and interpretive questions: Philippe Lacoue-Labarthe's *Heidegger, Art and Politics*,[14] Zygmunt Bauman's *Modernity and the Holocaust*,[15] and Jean-François Lyotard's *Heidegger and "the jews."*[16]

   Lacoue-Labarthe works within a Heideggerian frame of reference even as he criticizes Heidegger's silence about the Holocaust. His sweepingly philosophical approach is quite different from Mayer's, and his quest for the essence of phenomena (Heidegger's thought, fascism, modernity, the West) is dismissive toward the work of historians, which he doubts "will be able to contribute anything really decisive" (p. 39). Nor does he join Mayer in affirming a purified rationality in his own voice. Indeed, in Lacoue-Labarthe a hypertrophic rationality is part of the problem, and, "in the Auschwitz apocalypse, it was nothing less than the West, in its essence, that reveals itself" (p. 25).

   Lacoue-Labarthe at first denies any sacrificial admixture in Nazi practice: "To speak of a 'Holocaust' is a self-serving misinterpretation, as is any reference to an archaic scape-goating mechanism. There was not the least 'sacrificial' aspect in this *operation*, in which what was calculated coldly and with the maximum efficiency and economy (and never for a moment hysterically or deliriously) was a pure and simple *elimination*" (p. 37). This one-sided interpretation is itself overly indebted to Heidegger's notion of the modern technological *Gestell* (framework) as well as to Hannah Arendt's idea of the banality of evil. (It also derives from Lacoue-Labarthe's understandable desire to distance his approach from the specific interpretation and use of the scapegoat mechanism in the work of René Girard.) It is nonetheless significant that Lacoue-Labarthe himself later qualifies his view: "Reconsidering the question, I wonder whether in fact, at quite another level, which would force us at least to re-work the anthropological notion of sacrifice, one should not speak of sacrifice. This is, indeed,

[14]Cambridge, Mass.: Basil Blackwell, 1990.
[15]Ithaca: Cornell University Press, 1989.
[16]Trans. Andreas Michel and Mark S. Roberts with a foreword by David Carroll (1988; Minneapolis: University of Minnesota Press, 1990).

an admission that I am purely and simply at a loss—and I remain so. Or, in other words, in this case too, I reserve my response" (p. 52). I suggest that Nazi scapegoating and victimization may indicate the role of an extremely problematic "sacrificialism" (which took a particularly degraded form in the Nazi quest for purification through the elimination of a putatively contaminating presence) and raise the question of its relation to both a policy of extermination and instrumental or technical rationality. Lacoue-Labarthe's interpretation also relies overmuch on the concept of "national aestheticism," or a totalizing aesthetic ideology, in its explanation of Nazism and underplays not only the role of ritual or sacrificial elements but the appeal of radical transgression and the sublime; he in general remains too much within a Heideggerian manner of posing problems and oscillates, at times wildly, between an interpretive reliance on Heidegger and critiques of Heidegger's shortcomings with respect to his Nazi involvement.

In certain ways Zygmunt Bauman provides a useful corrective to Lacoue-Labarthe. For Lacoue-Labarthe, the Holocaust is the essence—or at least the quintessentially characteristic product—of the Western tradition that takes the modern form of a technological *Gestell*. Bauman sees the Holocaust as "a characteristically modern phenomenon" (p. xiii) not in the sense of "the *truth* of modernity" but as "a *possibility* that modernity contains" (p. 6). Yet at times in Bauman this possibility seems to turn into a probability, at least once "the modern drive to a fully designed, fully controlled world . . . [gets] out of control and run[s] wild" (p. 92). Even more broadly, Bauman, while acknowledging that he focuses on one factor, asserts that it is "arguably the most crucial among the constituent factors of the Holocaust: the typically modern, technological-bureaucratic patterns of action and the mentality they institutionalize, generate, sustain and reproduce" (p. 95). Thus Bauman in more measured fashion converges with the emphasis of Lacoue-Labarthe and sees modern rationality quite differently from Mayer. Like Lacoue-Labarthe, he also stresses the meeting of technical rationality with an aesthetics of the beautiful: "Invariably, there is an aesthetic dimension to the design: the ideal world about to be built conforms to the standards of superior beauty. . . . This is a gardener's vision, projected upon a world-size screen." Some gardeners "hate the weeds that spoil their design— that ugliness in the midst of beauty, litter in the midst of serene order" (p. 91). But others are unemotional about them. "Not that it makes a difference to the weeds; both gardeners exterminate them" (p. 92).

Bauman's tendency to focus on bureaucratization and technical rationality may be abetted by a Weberian notion that the sociologist should concentrate on distinctive features of a historical constellation or period, in this case, modernity. He adds to this view a thesis about the way society does not create morality but "adiaphorizes," or renders it indifferent, thereby redeploying morality as a bureaucratic ethos and permitting extreme cruelty (at times perpetrated without emotion) in collective action. He asserts: "It was the combination of growing potency of means and the unconstrained determination to use it in the service of an artificial, designed order, that gave human cruelty its distinctively *modern* touch and made the Gulag, Auschwitz and Hiroshima possible, perhaps even unavoidable" (p. 219).

Bauman is no doubt correct in stressing the superficiality of a pure binary opposition between a positively valorized, quasi-mythical modern rationality or enlightenment (which Mayer at times seems to affirm) and presumably anomalous or regressive "barbarism," and he explores certain factors that were indeed important in the Holocaust. In addition, one may agree with his argument that the Holocaust has tended to be denied or marginalized and that it should not be seen solely as a phenomenon relevant to Jewish or German history and to the work of specialists in those areas. Equally convincing is his insistence that ordinary people, who in different circumstances are morally decent, can perform reprehensible acts when placed in certain roles that are structured in an authoritative, self-certain, impersonal hierarchy. His critique of a value-neutral social science and his call for both a greater concern with normativity and an ethics up to the level of modern problems are also apposite.

One may, however, doubt whether Bauman provides an adequate basis for a morality that he sees as social (in the primary sense of intersubjective) but not societal (or produced by social agencies and structures). He rightly rejects what he takes to be the standard sociological position that derives morality from nonmoral social conditions and construes immoral behavior as a return to presocial individuality that is tantamount to animality. He is also suggestive in his turn to Emmanuel Levinas and the idea that responsibility is the primary structure of subjectivity (p. 183). Yet he tends to remain within a very general, if not essentializing or ontologizing, frame of reference that may inhibit one from posing the issue of morality or normative judgment in more specific terms with reference to the variable modes of interaction of social individuals and the elucidation of how certain institutions and practices might abet desirable interactions. He even reverses sociologistic reductionism by deriving morality from subjective, "primeval moral drives" (p. 188). I want to stress here that Bauman understands the way the Holocaust represents a modern possibility too much in terms of the role of instrumental rationality and bureaucratization (maximal distance from the other). Also, despite his probing discussion of boundary-maintenance that became more insecure with Jewish assimilation (pp. 56–60) and his occasional references to such phenomena as "salvation-inspired and salvation-seeking genocide" (p. 219), he does not sufficiently address the relationship between instrumental rationality and ritual anxiety over boundary-transgression or the seemingly purifying, redemptive role of sacrificialism—forces that legitimate cruelty and, in their more "sublime" variants, may help to account for its apparently "transcendent," emotionless modes. He even tends to dismiss the significance of ideology in the Holocaust (p. 176). Thus he tends to ignore or downplay what "modernity" and its analysts, including Bauman himself, may repress not as a mere "barbaric" or "archaic" (much less presocial) anomaly but as modernity's constitutive outside, to wit, secularized and often distorted religious forces that may accompany disenchantment, a bureaucratic ethos, and "the death of God."

Committed Nazis were ready to sacrifice themselves for the Führer (who assumed a quasi-divine position), and they joined at times fanatical self-sacrifice with an ideological devotion to victimization and scapegoating that seemed to have "sacrificial" dimensions (at least in the projective construction of the other as the source of contamination that engendered excessive, at times ambivalent, "ritual" and erotic anxiety). Self-sacrifice took on a "heroic" cast in a military ethos that stressed hardness (or iron will) and involved devotion to a supreme leader, and it might go to unheard-of extremes or be associated with unspeakable deeds in a context in which secular transcendence merged with radical transgression. One might even suggest that Jews were sacrificed for (or to) Hitler because it was known that "getting rid" of them (*Entfernung*) was the Führer's will. In an obvious sense victims were innocent of the contradictory "crimes" of which they were made the projective vehicles, although Nazis repressed or denied this innocence by the manifest opprobrium heaped on victims. Still, one may ask whether the very deceptions of perpetrators vis-à-vis victims could be seen as motivated in part by the desire to produce at least the illusion that the victim was willing.

Whether or to what extent victims were themselves induced to participate in a sacrificial "logic" is moot and extremely controversial in more ways than one. The possibility is raised by the "sheep-to-slaughter" metaphor (favored by Raul Hilberg despite his interpretive orientation centered on bureaucratization). In addition, the one-for-many "logic" of Jewish councils ("sacrificing" one or some to save many more) might conceivably have had a sacrificial dimension as part of its rationale (or counterrationality). But, to be more than speculative, these possibilities in particular would require substantiation through research—research that might be offensive and not worth undertaking to the extent that it required posing insensitive or intrusively misleading questions to survivors. In any case, one aspect of the term "Holocaust" (as Mayer warns) is a retrospective acceptance or perhaps appropriation of a sacrificial "logic" in an attempt to make religious sense of traumatic events. Moreover, the fact that the German term "Opfer" means both "victim" and "sacrifice" makes the elision to a sacrificial frame of reference almost invisible when one refers to victims—a point that underscores the need to pose problems as carefully and critically as possible. Difficulties are only compounded by the fact that a "sacrificial" logic is itself potentially excessive and difficult to control, and even raising the question of its possible role may lead the analyst into unintended discursive movements or unwanted connotations.

One may nonetheless argue that the goal of historically informed analysis is not to focus on what may be distinctive in modernity. It is rather to elucidate the intricate conjunction of distinctively modern features (such as the seemingly dominant role of instrumental rationality, bureaucratization, and massive technical resources) with the recurrence of often repressed forces, such as scapegoating with "sacrificial" dimensions. Indeed, the latter, as elements of a returning repressed, may be particularly distorted because of their imbrication or combination with more distinctively modern factors that seem to leave no room for them. (To the extent that the Shoah itself has been repressed—at times through its very canonization—one might even refer to a repression of repression.) Bauman himself at times acknowledges (for example, on p. 94) that the Holocaust was the result of a convergence of factors including radical anti-Semitism of "the Nazi type"; the command by the state of a huge bureaucratic apparatus; a

wartime state of emergency that allowed the government and bureaucracy to do things that might have faced more serious obstacles in
peacetime; and the noninterference or passive acceptance of those
things by the population at large. The "Nazi type" of anti-Semitism,
at least for Hitler and an elite of committed party members, involved
scapegoating, and one should at least entertain the possibility of a
Nazi sublime that, in a fascination for radical transgression, complicated the desire for a "beautiful" and rational totality that would exclude Jews—although (as Himmler's 1943 Posen speech indicates) a
quest for the sublime could also legitimate extermination. In general,
Bauman's main line of argument has much greater applicability to bystanders, functionaries, and technocrats (such as Eichmann) than to
figures such as Hitler or Himmler. And in the case of victims, his account (notably chapter 5, "Soliciting the Co-operation of the Victim")
is more pertinent to members of Jewish councils (*Judenräte*) and unin-
terned Jewish elites than to people in the camps whose conditions of
existence Bauman's categories (such as "a situation that does not contain a good choice" [p. 206]) do not enable one to address with any
degree of adequacy. Even with respect to Jewish councils, moreover,
Bauman's account is misleading insofar as it focuses excessively on
the responses of victims in relative isolation from the actions of perpetrators, refers only in passing to acts of noncooperation or resistance, employs a rather ill-defined if not situationally inappropriate
concept of rationality, and applies this concept to members of Jewish
councils without providing a sufficient analysis of the impossible conditions created for them by Nazis. In general, Bauman relies too uncritically on the work of such scholars as Hannah Arendt and Raul
Hilberg, repeating the former's one-sided account of Jewish councils
and the latter's stress on bureaucratization and predominant reliance
on the documentation left by perpetrators to discuss the behavior of
victims.[17]

[17]See Hannah Arendt, *Eichmann in Jerusalem: A Report on the Banality of Evil* (1963; London: Penguin, 1977); Raul Hilberg, *The Destruction of the European Jews* (New York:
Homes and Meier, 1985). Dan Diner contests the application of the concept of rationality to the behavior of the Jewish councils and argues instead that "such an assumed
rationality is negated, fractured by the reality the Nazis created"; "Historical Understanding and Counterrationality: the *Judenrat* as Epistemological Vantage," in Saul
Friedlander, ed., *Probing the Limits of Representation: Nazism and the "Final Solution"*
(Cambridge: Harvard University Press, 1992), p. 142. Jeffrey Herf provides a wealth of
important material in arguing against the idea that the Nazi regime was based solely or
even primarily on instrumental or bureaucratic rationality. He contends that ideology

In *Heidegger and "the jews,"* Jean-François Lyotard does stress the role of the sublime, and he offers some telling criticisms of Lacoue-Labarthe. In one sense, he provides a provocative discursive elaboration of the 1968 French chant: "We are all German Jews." And he

---

was indeed crucial to the regime and that its defense of technology, far from being narrowly technical or bureaucratic in nature, was bound up with reactionary, romantic, and irrational ideas of spirit, soul, and will.

Herf helps to show how "leading members of the Nazi regime actually came to believe that German technology was in fact the expression of an Aryan racial soul" (p. 222), especially with respect to Goebbels's "steely romanticism." But he does not sufficiently illuminate the nature of that "soul" or of Nazi ideology, particularly with reference to racism and anti-Semitism whose centrality he recognizes. Romantic technologism provides at most one rationale (if not rationalization) for anti-Semitism, for example, through the idea that the Jews were carriers of abstraction and finance capitalism that inhibited technology as the emanation of an Aryan, Faustian soul. But this is hardly a sufficient account of the bases of anti-Semitism, and figures such as Hitler and Himmler are not adequately understood as romantic technologists. Herf lends too much credence to the notion that modern anti-Semitism was a "translation" of a revolt against commodity fetishism into biological terms (p. 132) or a biologization of capitalist social relations (p. 138)—a circular interpretation that authorizes any "translation" or transcoding, makes anti-Semitism too direct a result or even expression of capitalism, and begs many questions (for example, animus against Jews on "concrete" grounds such as "blood" and putative sexual traits). Moreover, anti-Semitism was not, as Herf admits, central to the thought of key "reactionary modernists" such as Ernst Jünger and Oswald Spengler. Indeed, the basic concepts of Herf's study—reaction, modernism, irrationalism, and romaticism, for example—tend to remain uncritical if not ideological, and Herf remains too much on the level of conceptualization of the figures he studies, adding the memorable label "reactionary modernism" to account for their thought. The inadequate theoretical elaboration of his own basic concepts may be one reason for his tendency to rely excessively on the German *Sonderweg* rather than consistently and carefully to weigh the importance of distinctive features of German history in trying to account for the "Final Solution." See *Reactionary Modernism: Technology, Culture, and Politics in Weimar and the Third Reich* (New York: Cambridge University Press, 1984).

On an interpretive level that could be argued to better illuminate phenomena, I suggest that what Herf sees as reaction should be understood as a return of the repressed, which marks "modernity" not as some vague updated romanticism but as a constitutive outside. Such an "outside" marks the "inside" (the self seeking identity as well as the collectivity seeking solidarity) in a manner whose recognition is resisted and hence less subject to a responsible measure of critical control. A significant feature of Nazi racist and anti-Semitic ideology was that instead of attempting to resist or control certain processes (such as hostility or opposition to others perceived as threatening and even polluting), it gave active state support and legitimation to them, thereby publicly authorizing people to act them out and/or bureaucratically implement them. In this sense, a phenomenon such as scapegoating, far from being a simple utilitarian device to abet social integration, might be seen as a state-sanctioned practice, involving compulsive anxiety over "ritual" contamination and projection onto the other of anxiety-producing forces (however contradictory)—a practice that might well go to wildly destructive and self-defeating extremes. Nazi "solidarity" was thus inherently unstable.

returns to his convincing view of the "excess" of the Holocaust whereby one is recurrently confronted by the need to put into language what cannot as yet be acceptably "phrased." He thus brings out the extent to which all of us in the postwar world are, in one way or another, implicated in—indeed fractured and dispossessed by—the events of the Holocaust and under the obligation to come to terms with them in a manner that does not simply deny or repress their radically disorienting import.

In this particular book, however, Lyotard also intensifies Lacoue-Labarthe's tendency to "trope" away from specificity and evacuate history by construing the caesura of the Holocaust as a total trauma that is un(re)presentable and reduces everyone (victims, witnesses, perpetrators, revisionists, those born later) to an ultimately homogenizing yet sublime silence. In his own voice Lyotard excessively valorizes the role of the sublime and does not provide a more nuanced examination or evaluation of its various modalities and possibilities. He even tends to identity "the [lowercase] jews" with a hyperbolic "anaesthetics" of the sublime and his own "postmodern" understanding of its analogues or accompaniments: trauma, *écriture*, alterity, nomadism, the un(re)presentable, *Nachträglichkeit*, not-forgetting-that-there-is-the-Forgotten, and so forth. Here, for example, is one of his breathless characterizations (or noncharacterizations) of "the jews":

It seems to me, to be brief, that "the jews" are within the "spirit" of the Occident that is so preoccupied with foundational thinking, what resists this spirit; within this will, the will to want, what gets in the way of this will; within its accomplishments, projects, and progress, what never ceases to reopen the wound of the unaccomplished. "The jews" are the irremissible in the West's movement of remission and pardon. They are what cannot be domesticated in the obsession to domesticate.[. . .] They are always away from home when they are at home, in their so-called own tradition, because it includes exodus as its beginning, excision, impropriety, and respect for the forgotten. [. . .] [Their] thought ignores dialectics and dialogues. [. . .] Heidegger-Hölderlin's god is merely pagan-Christian, the god of bread, wine, earth and blood. He is not the god of the unreadable book, which only demands respect and does not tolerate that one liberate oneself from respect and disrespect (of good and evil) through the sublation of sacrifice, the old mainstay of the dialectic. There is nothing to offer this god in exchange. (Pp. 21–23)

One is tempted to add that for Lyotard, Christians (even Jews) are at best merely modern whereas "jews" are postmodern. To the extent that Jews are at issue in the account, it is through an unargued and ideologically tendentious focus on the diaspora that does not adequately address such issues as solidaristic communal traditions, dialogic modes of exchange, the role of representation in storytelling, the quest for a homeland, the role of Zionism, and the place of presumably "jewish" features in other traditions (for example, radical transcendentalism in Christianity). Lyotard's histrionically allegorized appropriation of "the jews" as dispossessed and abstract markers of postmodern motifs obliterates both the specificity of the Jews as a complex historical people and the problem of their actual and formal relations to other peoples or traditions. What Lyotard seems to "enact" is a massive metalepsis whereby the Shoah is transcoded into postmodernism. This "enactment" tends to obscure the historical and interpretive issue of the extent to which postmodernism should itself be understood—indeed worked through and not simply celebrated—as a displacement, disguise, and at times distortion of aspects of the Shoah. It also threatens to induce Lyotard to blindly act out certain problems that are not explicitly formulated and critically framed.

Not only does Lyotard ignore the manner in which the Nazis may have sought their own distorted vision of sublimity; he even runs the risk of repeating in his own voice the Nazi project of purveying stereotypes of the Jews as antiaesthetic, ugly, nomadic, rootless, and so forth—indeed, of memorializing the forgetting of the Jews as anything other than pretexts for acting out one's own contemporary obsessions and appropriative preoccupations. But now valorizations are reversed so that what was negative becomes positive or at least affirmative as the sublime. Lyotard does not cogently address the problem of the relation of the sublime to desirable normative limits, and "Auschwitz" is converted into a decathected paradigm of the "differend" that subverts speculative dialectics and representational aesthetics.

Lyotard's influential version of postmodernism may be most dubious with respect to his engagement with the Shoah in *Heidegger and "the jews,"* for he does not elaborate a mutually questioning relation between history and theory or provide a different perspective on his often cogent critiques of totalization or defenses of experimentalism. Instead, theory not only displaces history in favor of its putative conditions of possibility (as in Lacoue-Labarthe); it tends to become an extreme theoreticism that sacrifices history and forecloses inquiry into the latter's bearing on contemporary questions. It is difficult to see what is gained by renaming or rebaptizing alterity and *différance* as "the jews," thereby obscuring or even obviating the problems of both critically coming to terms with postmodernism and posing in more explicit, careful, and problematic terms the relation of alterity and *différance* to the Jews as a historical people. Lyotard's account is too restricted, particularly insofar as it is not conjoined with an attempt both to situate ideologies historically and to elaborate an approach wherein ideological distortions may be criticized and worked through rather than simply reversed, repeated, and acted out. Let me add what should go without saying: a critical investigation of sacrificialism, the scapegoat mechanism, and the Nazi sublime should in no way condone them or sanction the idea that what happened to the Jews was indeed providential or an act of divine justice. On the contrary, it is only by investigating the character and operation of certain phenomena that one can be in a position to engage in an altogether necessary and potentially effective critique of them and to counteract unjustifiable inferences or interpretations.

Even a brief look at the books of two important philosophers and a foremost sociologist further heightens the question of how precisely the emphasis on uniqueness or comparability functions in one's own context. A related issue is how the concepts of uniqueness (or better: distinctiveness) and comparability may be taken from an absolute status and combined or mediated without giving way either to an extreme historicist particularism (that would relegate the Shoah exclusively to Jewish or German history) or to universalism (that would identify the Holocaust with history or modernity)—both of which would border on denial. I have intimated that these issues can be illuminated through a careful use of certain psychoanalytic concepts. An appeal to such concepts does not eliminate the necessary and legitimate role of standard or conventional historiographical techniques, but it may help to indicate their limitations and the need critically to scrutinize or supplement them, especially in the attempt to account for extreme phenomena. Such phenomena seem to invite dubious responses and pose particularly marked challenges for historical and critical understanding. Mayer's book, unfortunately, provides relatively little guidance in the attempt to work through problems rather than to deny or act them out. Mayer is rightfully concerned about self-interested and indulgent uses of the Holocaust to legitimate current political interests or to bolster religious fundamentalism. But the oppositional tactic he employs lends itself too easily to the complementary desire to forget or to deny aspects of the past in ways that also further dubious political interests and ideological imperatives.

My comments about Mayer's book (and about Lacoue-Labarthe's, Bauman's, and Lyotard's) should not be interpreted to imply that I am in possession of some formula that would allow one to write or speak about events in a nonproblematic manner. I do not think there is such a formula. And any approach, however resistant to formulaic reduction, will harbor problems. One may nonetheless attempt to point out certain pressures, possibilities, and pitfalls that would have to be confronted in any more acceptable way of addressing problems. Mayer's book would have benefited significantly from a self-critical effort to situate its procedures and arguments (notably with reference to the Historikerstreit) and explicitly to avert dubious uses of them. One may even agree with Mayer that the Holocaust should in certain ways be historicized but disagree with him in the manner in which he historicizes it and insist that any such project take special precautions in view of the prevalent abuses of a certain kind of historicization in the recent past.

In concluding this discussion, I believe it may be useful to supplement my critique of Mayer and others with an attempt, however provisional, to offer a "model" of the Nazi regime that delineates in starkest outline some of its crucial ideological and operating principles. In so doing, I shall try to render explicit (hence make more available for examination and criticism) certain points that appear in circumstantial fashion elsewhere in this book. Here I want to enter a strong caveat concerning an important aspect of my own argument. I refer to the role of scapegoating and victimization that involved a secularized "ritual" or even distorted "sacrificial" component. And I intimate that this role was significant, at least for certain figures such as Hitler, Himmler, and their more fanatical followers—figures who arguably were prime movers in the Nazi *Bewegung*. This component plays an important role in the "model" I am about to propose. But I would insist that its status be kept hypothetical or even explicitly speculative and not promoted into one's own hobbyhorse or converted into a basis for dogmatic assertions about the "essence" of the regime. I am insisting on this component because I think it has recently been underemphasized and, more important, that its problematic combination with more obvious and easily documentable features, such as the role of bureaucracy or hygienic considerations, has tended to be ignored. Yet there is a sense in which the insistence on sacrificialism involving a scapegoat mechanism may itself get out of control and become compulsive, all-consuming, and conducive to overinterpretation. This tendency may exist even if one insists that one is attempting to elaborate a basis for a critique of scapegoating and attendant forms of victimization and that one also is trying to propose a better framework for coming to terms with the problem of secular displacements in contemporary (and at times occulted) forms.

There are of course many modalities of ritual, and sacrifice—or, more specifically, modern secularized and distorted sacrificialism—does not exhaust them. There is also a sense in which the very concept of ritual may be poorly understood at present and open to excessive expansion (in this sense becoming the dubious complement to an excessively encompassing, increasingly porous concept of rationality, such as one finds in Bauman). Hence, there may be good reasons for pointing to what appear to be a secularized anxiety about "ritual" contamination, a "sacrificial" desire for purification, and a tendency to "scapegoat" and victimize those who are made projectively to embody what one represses in oneself, especially when these aspects of Nazi responses to Jews are not adequately taken into account. But there are also good reasons to be on one's guard against excessive claims and cautious in putting forth or entertaining contentions.

One might see the Nazis as an "in-group" based on two types of relationship: the bureaucratic machine (investigated at length by Bauman and by the historian Raul Hilberg in his analysis of the "machinery of destruction") and the total community with scapegoating dimensions and charismatic leadership. In the Nazis one finds brought together in a distorted unity or *Gleichschaltung* (synchronization) modes that Max Weber saw in terms of analytically distinct or even opposed ideal types. (One might, however, also note that technical or bureaucratic rationality might itself be seen to involve evacuated rituals and interpreted in terms of processes involving the analytic purification of categories and the elimination of problematic residues or remainders.)

The bureaucratic machine, involving technical rationality and organization, could function either as the means to the end of total community or as a parallel system of integration. In the bureaucratic machine individuals performed functions or jobs in technically rational ways, and the other as the target of bureaucratic activity was radically objectified. Both the limits to, and the attempt to reinstitute, this process of objectification are shown in the fact that members of killing squads in the East were psychologically affected by their deeds, especially the shooting of women and children, and gassing was "invented" as a more objectifying or neutralizing procedure to counteract the suffering and demoralization of the perpetrators. One may also mention Adolf Eichmann's well-known defense that in the camps he was simply doing his job or performing his duty as a good, obedient bureaucrat—a defense that routinized the Kantian categorical imperative. Bureaucratic organizations might generate competing centers of power and authority in "polycratic" fashion, but they might nonetheless keep individuals atomized and thus directly or indirectly further—or at least not contest—the ideal of solidarity under the dominant auspices of the totalizing community.

The second type of solidarity was the desired end or higher goal of collective life. This was the community having displaced sacrificial dimensions: the *Volksgemeinschaft*, or total community of the people. At the limit there was to be an undifferentiated unity or even identity of the German people or nation in a common will. An immediate bond was to be established between the willful leader and the self-sacrificing masses who followed the leader. In a sense, one had a narcissistic fusion of Führer and *Volk* in a specular relationship. This immediate bond, undisturbed by criticism, was affirmed in shared symbols and gestures, for example, the swastika and the Hitler salute. Symbols were celebrated in emotional yet orchestrated secular rituals such as the Nuremberg rallies, where large masses might have a largely spectator role but were to be given an elated feeling of participation. One's very identity as a German was to be generated and regenerated through identification with the leader, and this identity was solidified by a racial ideology that represented Germans as members of a superior people. Within the Volk the SS formed an elite that represented to the highest degree the virtues of the Nazi, and to some extent a tension existed between a volkish ideology and the elitism of the SS—a tension that was mitigated somewhat by the purge of the SA.

Alfred Rosenberg, a principal ideologist of the movement, declined in influence after 1935 and fell out of favor with the Hitler-Stalin pact of 1939, which he opposed. He was criticized by key figures, notably Goebbels, and he criticized Goebbels, Himmler, and others—even

Hitler toward the end—for betraying the true idea and ideals of national socialism (as Rosenberg himself envisioned them). But his star rose somewhat after Germany unilaterally broke the pact with Russia in June of 1941, and he was appointed Reich Minister for the Eastern Occupied Territories. Moreover, his sense of the movement did have an important early influence on Hitler, and he may in certain respects be seen as a foremost exponent of the warped "idealism" or "spirituality" that motivated anti-Semitism even when it proved counterproductive for the economy and the war effort. In Rosenberg's vision:

> The state is no longer an entity which, be it close to the party and the movement or be it a mechanical apparatus, is a ruling instrument; rather it is an instrument of the National Socialist *Weltanschauung*. On the surface, this would appear to be merely a trifling difference in emphasis between state-political and perception-critical forms of thought. And yet, clarification of the intellectual presuppositions is of great importance, because a false conceptual picture will yield—if not right away, then most certainly in the course of time—practical consequences for political action. If we continue to speak of the total state, younger National Socialists and coming generations will gradually shift the state concept into the centre of things, and the activities of state officials will be felt to be the primary ones. If, however, we emphasize with all clarity today that it is a certain political ideology and movement that demands the right of totality, the gaze of generations will be directed upon the movement, and the relationship between state and N.S.D.A.P. will be seen in a totally different light than if one were to designate statishness itself as primary. The National Socialist Movement is the moulded strength of twentieth-century thought; moulded for the security of the collective German *Volk* and of its blood and character. The state, as a most powerful and virile instrument, is placed at the disposal of the movement, and its life-strengths and powers are continuously renewed by the movement in order that it remain flexible and capable of resistance while avoiding the dangers of bureaucratization, petrification and estrangement from the *Volk*.[18]

Whatever one may make of Rosenberg's specific formulation, this notion of totality reinforces the idea of the regime as ideally a whole, both organic and spiritual, in accordance with an "aesthetic" of beauty. But this idea is complicated by the relation of the regime to

[18]"The Ideal State" (first published in 1936 as "Totaler Staat?"), in *Alfred Rosenberg: Selected Writings*, ed. Robert Pois (London: Jonathan Cape, 1970), pp. 191–92.

out-groups that are at least metaphorically within the nation, notably Jews, homosexuals, and "Gypsies." Groups outside the nation, such as foreign nations, might be either potential allies (if Aryan) or enemies against whom martial virtues—underwritten by a "spiritual" celebration of iron will and a Social Darwinist ethos of struggle and survival of the fittest—might be manifested. But out-groups inside the nation posed a special threat. In one sense, these groups disturbed the beautiful whole and so had to be eliminated. They were radically objectified in neutralizing, bureaucratic terms, for example, as a "problem" that had to be "solved." But as outsiders within the nation, they were also destabilizing sources of phobic anxiety and quasi-ritual contamination.

Nazi ideology could not tolerate an inmixture of otherness in the self—a hybridization to which the fundamental contributions of Jews to German culture attested and which had to be exorcised through racial essentialism or hypostatization that made the other "within" into a localized entity fully discrete and separate from the self. Hence the Jews formed a constitutive outside for the Nazi (one marking the inside in a way that is denied and repressed), thus becoming a phantasmatic cause of all evil and the projective carrier of the anxieties and ills of the modern world. The Jews were both a hygienic and a ritual threat to a "pure" Nazi identity, and concepts such as "germ"—indeed "race" itself—functioned in different registers: pseudoscientific and ritualistic. (The notion of an "emasculating germ" encapsulates the overdetermined status of a seemingly biological concept.) The imaginary dimension of phobic anxiety may help to understand Hitler's plans for a museum in Prague devoted to an extinct Jewish race. These plans looked forward to the time when the "Final Solution" would be totally successful in empirical fact, yet they also anticipated both the elimination of Jewish self-representation or memory and the retention of the Jew as a phantasm within the Nazi imaginary that was in some sense necessary for a paranoid, narcissistic, radically exclusionary, and inherently insecure type of internal solidarity. Moreover, the phobic anxiety surrounding the Jew had an erotic dimension.

The representation of Jews as vermin is a forceful example of the imbrication of hygienic, ritualistic, and erotic anxieties. The rat is the stereotypical, unsanitary bearer of filth and disease. As denizen of the sewer, it is a figure of the lower world and a typically demonized, dirty mediator between it and the ideally sanitized world above-ground. Among other pieces of empirical and fictional evidence, Freud's study of the "Rat Man" brings out the role of the rat in homophobic fantasy. The obsessive fear of the "Rat Man" was set off by a story about the punishment of a criminal in the East which involved a pot turned upside down over his buttocks with some rats in it that bored their way into his anus.[19] (This phobia is of course active in Poe's "Pit and the Pendulum.") A facet of Ernst Nolte's own paranoid speculations during the Historikerstreit also attests to the homophobic, projective anxiety aroused by the rat. For Nolte, Hitler knew of tortures inflicted on opponents by the Russian secret police soon after the revolution, tortures involving a "rat cage" that had earlier been used by the Chinese, thereby attesting to the "Asiatic" nature of the atrocities to which Hitler was presumably reacting.[20]

One may observe that characteristics ascribed to Jews were attributed to homosexuals and "Gypsies," who were also in some sense others within the Volksgemeinschaft posing ritualistic and phobic threats. The Jews, like homosexuals, were coded culturally as feminine as well as "dirty," and like "Gypsies" they were nomadic, rootless, and devoid of a sense of the homeland. This interpenetration of "alien" — or actively alienated — traits may help account for the similar treatment of the three groups.

I have indicated that there may have been a negatively "sublime" aspect in the Nazi reaction to aliens within — one that further complicates without denying the role of an "aesthetic" ideology of totalization and "beauty." It is of interest that Alfred Rosenberg, early in his career, wrote a book on the sublime (or *das Erhabene*) titled *Longinus in England bis zum Ende des 18.Jahrhunderts*.[21] The book is a learned disquisition on the challenge posed by Longinus to the more classical theories of Aristotle, Horace, and Quintilian, and (as the title indicates) it traces the influence of Longinus in England up to the end of

---

[19]See "Notes upon a Case of Obsessional Neurosis," *The Standard Edition of the Complete Psychological Works of Sigmund Freud* 10, trans. James Strachey (London: Hogarth, 1955), pp. 153–249.

[20]"Vergangenheit, die nicht vergehen will," *Frankfurter Allgemeine Zeitung*, 6 June 1986. Charles Maier argues that Hitler's references to the "rat cage" in conversation, after his original mention of it in 1943 to which Nolte refers, "seem clearly to confirm that [Hitler] was referring to Lubianka prison, not to exotic tortures": *The Unmasterable Past: History, Holocaust, and German National Identity* (Cambridge: Harvard University Press, 1988), p. 179. I am not sure whether this specification accounts fully for Hitler's own phobic anxieties.

[21]Berlin: Mayer and Müller, 1917.

the eighteenth century. One cannot draw any direct inferences from this text to Nazi ideology.[22] But one obvious difficulty in speculating about the motivations of the "Final Solution" is the silence with which the policy was covered, not only with respect to the Volk and the outside world but among elite perpetrators themselves. Yet, while having obvious utilitarian rationales, silence is presumably also the "appropriate" response in the face of the sublime. I have already referred to one instance where extermination or annihilation (separated by a mere comma from exclusion or evacuation) was discussed: Himmler's Posen speech to SS officers, and it may be informative to return to it, this time in the more colloquial translation provided in the collection of documents edited by Lucy Dawidowicz.[23] The paragraph I

[22]See also Rosenberg's discussion of the sublime in the context of the aesthetic will in *The Myth of the Twentieth Century* (1930; Torrance, Calif.: Noontide Press, 1982). After discussing Kant's and Schiller's conceptions of the sublime, Rosenberg criticizes them for "only hesitatingly [. . .] allow[ing] sublimity to be held as valid in art" and for wanting "to continually return to their conclusions as to 'harmony of mental powers,' instead of recognizing the spiritual-willed experience and the awakening of the active spiritual power as the essence of the aesthetic condition" (p. 258). He praises Nietzsche's description of "the hour of birth of a great work" and quotes a passage that ends: "All occurs in the highest degree involuntarily, but as in a storm of feeling, of unconditionality, of godliness." Among other references, he alludes to "the greatest poet among the Germans": Hölderlin. After discussing Hyperion's encounter with "only piecework [beings] without unity of soul, without inner drive, without life-totality," he exclaims: "Today [Hölderlin's] work would be the sole cry of despair—or of attack—even more the outpourings of a glowing innermost torment of will. But the beauty which Holderlin [sic] felt as religion was not the 'contemplative' satiety of our philosophizing doctors, but the highest enhanced life-totality; a bundle of all elevations of soul tied together for a brief moment; of all longings of the heart; of all sinew-cords of the will." Then Rosenberg refers to the complaint of "modern aesthetes" that "there exists an unmoralistic or amoralistic spirit" in "this deep willed artistic power" and discerns in that complaint "a feature of the impure Mediterranean race which is spread particularly by the Jewish literary guild." But "Nordic-Germanic art attacks, from the beginning, this assertion as a lie"—a lie that may be countered by reading "Wagner's letters to Liszt in order to measure how deeply true race separates itself from asphalt intellectualism" (pp. 261–62). Rosenberg observes that "the cultural work of Bayreuth remains forever beyond question" (p. 262), although he finds that in Wagner's drama, language and message are at times overwhelmed by the music (pp. 263–64). Still, "Wagner's soul life coincides with the deepest undertones of great European men," and "what is shown in an unleashing of will among the greatest is also the essential commandment for all other true artists of the West" (pp. 265–66). Moreover, "the eternally searching and active Nordic man seeks repose and is often inclined to value it higher than everything else. But once he has gained it by struggle he does not allow it to capture him. He seeks, researches, and shapes further" (p. 266).

[23]*A Holocaust Reader* (West Orange, N.J.: Behrman House, 1976). See also the analysis of Himmler's Posen speech in Peter Haidu, "The Dialectics of Unspeakability: Language, Silence, and the Narratives of Desubjectification," in Friedlander, ed., *Probing*

quoted earlier (see pp. 62–63) is itself framed by the question of silence, for immediately before it Himmler asserts:

> I also want to make reference before you here, in complete frankness, to a really grave matter. Among ourselves, this once, it shall be uttered quite frankly; but in public we will never speak of it. Just as we did not hesitate on June 30, 1934, to do our duty as ordered, to stand up against the wall comrades who had transgressed, and shoot them, also we have never talked about this and never will. It was the tact which I am glad to say is a matter of course to us that made us never discuss it among ourselves, never talk about it. Each of us shuddered, and yet each one knew that he would do it again if it were ordered and if it were necessary. (Pp. 132–33)

Himmler compares the extermination of the Jews to the purge of Ernst Röhm and the SA, a step that eliminated both an extremely volkish element and a site reputed to favor homoerotic relations. He refers to tact and to the duty to obey orders in shooting transgressors, but he also refers to the shudder that bespeaks an aesthetics of shock. And he mentions the knowledge that one would do the deed again if it were ordered and necessary. His words imply that in his very act of speaking about what is (except this once) kept under a veil of silence, he is himself transgressing Nazi taboos—a transgression permissible only "among us," the elite of high-ranking SS officers. Then, in a kind of heightening contagion of transgression, of seeming antidotes that are supposed to fight fire with fire but run wild and not only become worse than the putative disease but actually construct it in paranoid fashion, he refers to an extreme act that may itself be ordered and necessary:

> I am referring to the evacuation of the Jews, the annihilation of the Jewish people. This is one of those things that are easily said. "The

---

the Limits of Representation: Nazism and the "Final Solution," pp. 277–99. Haidu notes that for Himmler "orders are sacred (heilig): 'Orders must be sacred. When generals obey, armies obey automatically. This sacredness of orders [diese Heiligkeit des Befehls] applies the more, the larger our territory grows.' The duty to exterminate the Jews is one of these orders, falling into the category of the sacred" (p. 288). On anti-Semitism, the aestheticization of politics, and the role of quasi-religious symbols in mass mobilization, see the important works of George Mosse, especially The Nationalization of the Masses: Political Symbolism and Mass Movements in Germany from the Napoleonic Wars through the Third Reich (New York: Howard Fertig, 1975), and Masses and Man. Nationalist and Fascist Perceptions of Reality (New York: Howard Fertig, 1980).

Jewish people is going to be annihilated," says every party member. "Sure, it's in our program, elimination of the Jews, annihilation — we'll take care of it." And then they all come trudging, 80 million worthy Germans, and each of them has his one decent Jew. Sure, the others are swine, but this one is an A-1 Jew. Of all those who talk this way, not one has seen it happen, not one has been through it. Most of you must know what it means to see a hundred corpses lie side by side, or five hundred, or a thousand. To have stuck this out and — excepting cases of human weakness — to have kept our integrity, that is what has made us hard. In our history this is an unwritten and never-to-be-written page of glory, for we know how difficult we would have made it for ourselves if today — amid the bombing raids, the hardships and the deprivations of war — we still had the Jews in every city as secret saboteurs, agitators, and demagogues. If the Jews were still ensconced in the body of the German nation, we probably would have reached the 1916–17 stage by now. (P. 133)

This passage is not homogeneous in terms of the motivations or the "aesthetics" on which it relies. The quick, almost imperceptible passage from evacuation to annihilation does attest to the lability of ways of getting rid of the alien other in terms of a quasi-sacrificial response involving a scapegoat mechanism. And Himmler stresses the role of excess as he insists on the marked contrast between the 80 million Germans who are willing to qualify their anti-Semitism with at least one exception that may weaken resolve and the uncompromising absolutism of a fanatical, sectarian elite. This elite has perpetrated, beheld, and endured a certain unspeakable "spectacle" — a spectacle evoked in terms of a numerically increasing series reminiscent of the Kantian mathematical sublime, a series that can always go on to infinity, at least in the imaginary with its infinite desire that no material analogon or concrete image can satisfy. (This series may perhaps evoke the Miltonic phrase that haunted Burke and Wordsworth, a phrase to which no concrete example or image could adequately correspond: a universe of death.) Himmler also appeals to writing: a forever absent, abysmally silent inscription commemorates this ne plus ultra of "our history" in "an unwritten, never-to-be-written page of glory."

For Himmler, to have stuck out the impossible spectacle and to have kept one's integrity or decency is what makes one hard. There may be an incommensurable distance between sticking out the unspeakable, unrepresentable "scene" of mass death and keeping one's integrity, for the former would seem to refer to a negatively sublime moment that beggars the imagination and the latter to ordinary morality or normativity. Perhaps it is this ability to live incommensurables or to hold together in oneself the antinomies of existence—and to resist being affected by trauma—that makes one hard. Hardness was of course one of the foremost, adamantly gendered yet also machinelike virtues of the SS man, a virtue that represented a less bureaucratic, more genuinely ascetic and "heroic" version of the Kantian categorical imperative. After what may be a point of negative sublimity, Himmler turns to utilitarian yet also paranoid and phantasmatic reasons for expulsion and extermination in terms of the imagined difficulties and putative dangers posed by Jews "ensconced in the body of the German nation."

In the next paragraph, in a prototypical case of displacement in the technical psychoanalytic sense of movement to the small and relatively insignificant object, Himmler seems to give an example of what keeping one's integrity or remaining decent means, an example that differentiates SS men from stereotypical Jews and again invokes punishment for transgression. The SS will take none of Jewish wealth for themselves, and those SS—"not very many"—who have "transgressed" (by acting like stereotypically greedy Jews) will themselves "die, without mercy." Himmler adds: "We had the moral right, we had the duty toward our people, to kill this people which wanted to kill us. But we do not have the right to enrich ourselves with so much as a fur, a watch, a mark, or a cigarette or anything else." Then, after brutally expelling the inner temptation and hypostatizing or essentializing it in the phobic figure of the Jew, Himmler comes full circle by invoking the ambivalent logic of contamination: "Having exterminated a germ, we do not want, in the end, to be infected by the germ, and die of it" (p. 135).

These passages bring out the complexity of any attempt to understand the "Final Solution" or the Nazi regime in terms of a given "aesthetic" or "ethos," for one seems to have various elements in overdetermined combinations. There are even indications of the grotesque, for example, in Hitler's speeches with their hypnotic, compulsive, mechanically repetitive power and their excessively histrionic, almost ludicrous and infantile pathos. For Himmler, moreover, the SS would be a true brotherhood that reincarnated antibureaucratic, traditional, "spiritual" values of self-sacrifice, honor, loyalty, obedience, bravery, and truthfulness—values that proved one was "worthy to live in the time of Adolf Hitler" (p. 136). Himmler ends his Posen speech with a prognostication, an appeal to destiny, and a prayerlike, utopian invocation to the leader that approaches a quasi-religious *Rausch*:

> Woe betide if the Germanic people were not to prevail! It would be the end of beauty and civilization, of the creative power of this earth. That is the distant future. It is for this that we fight, pledged to hand down the heritage of our ancestors.
>
> We look into the distance because we know what it will be. That is why we are doing our duty more fanatically than ever, more devoutly than ever, more bravely, obediently, and honorably than ever. We want to be worthy of having been permitted to be the first SS men of the Führer, Adolf Hitler, in the long history of the Germanic people which stretches before us.
>
> We now direct our thought to the Führer, our Führer, Adolf Hitler, who will create the Germanic Reich and will lead us into the Germanic future.
>
> To our Führer Adolf Hitler
Sieg Heil!
Sieg Heil!
Sieg Heil!

At this point it is difficult for the commentator to know where to direct his thought. In seeking an acceptable way of representing and responding to the Holocaust, one may well recognize the special demands placed on language and the need to account critically for the contemporary contextual implications of one's views. But it is perhaps best not to enter into a rhetorical competition with Himmler or strive for a strikingly unheard-of level of discourse that somehow is up to the level of the events in which he took part. One thing that may be derived from the foregoing analysis is the contention that in one's own attempt to address issues, one cannot simply celebrate transgression, abstractly affirm limits, or confide in one aesthetic or another. One is rather confronted with the problem of the actual and desirable interaction between normative limits (whose contestable nature always remains to be specified) and "transgressive" challenges to them—a problem made particularly difficult in the light of the extremity and distortions of the Nazi "experience."

FOUR

❧

Paul de Man as
Object of Transference

I would like to address the problem of the complicated interaction of the personal, the political, and the textual through an examination of one dimension of the controversy over the World War II journalistic writings of Paul de Man. There are at least three dimensions to this controversy, and the one on which I focus here has received relatively little attention. The first two dimensions are (1) the early writings themselves, their meaning, their context, and their relation to the other activities of the young de Man; and (2) the relation of the later to the early de Man on textual, personal, and political levels. My focus is on the nature of certain contemporary responses to the first two dimensions, particularly insofar as they involve an exchange between past and present that is best approached through the problem of transference and the manner in which one negotiates it. This transferential dimension has, I think, been largely ignored, denied, repressed, or acted out rather than thematized in the attempt to work it through.

Transference is itself at the intersection of the personal, political, and textual, and it encompasses at least two related issues: the way in which problems and processes active in the texts or artifacts we study are repeated in displaced and often disguised or distorted form in our very accounts of them; and the more interpersonal dimension of involvement made familiar by psychoanalysis. One may begin with the assumption that it is unjustifiable to reduce texts to mere symptoms of a life or to hypostatize texts in a purely formalistic manner; but with reference to de Man it is particularly difficult to determine precisely how to articulate ways in which text and life interact by posing questions to each other.

It is commonplace to observe that de Man "gets under your skin." On a personal level, this is clearly true for those who worked with him as graduate students or as colleagues. The responses of former students are never neutral or even mildly affective, but always highly charged or "cathected" in positive, negative, or strongly ambivalent ways. De Man marked those with whom he worked, and this impact is only strengthened by the role of mimetic rivalry among his students. It may not be too much of an exaggeration to say that a student of de Man has always had one ideal reader in mind, and positive recognition by that reader was the highest mark of affirmation. One should not, however, see mimetic rivalry in a narrowly competitive sense, for among those who retained a largely positive relation to de Man there was and still is a strong sense of solidarity and mutual aid. Needless to add, there is also a strong mutual animosity between those who have in some sense been able to "stick by" de Man and those who have "turned against" him, especially in the wake of the discovery of his World War II articles. The very use of loaded terms such as "stick by" and "turn against" itself bears witness to the problematic and at times disorienting interaction between the personal and the textual. Indeed, in the general reputation of de Man it is very difficult to distinguish clearly between the contribution of his written texts and that of his pedagogical practice, reinforced, of course, by his other professional activities and his personal aura.

De Man also "impressed" in various ways those who were not his students or who became students only by adoption. Colleagues have attested to their friendship and special relation to him, and after de Man's death Jacques Derrida was moved to reflect on the nature of friendship. Even those who barely knew de Man (such as myself) or never met him have an often unacknowledged affective response to his texts. Indeed, these reactions to reading de Man of like or dislike—perhaps love, hate, or (as in my case) ambivalence—are rather exceptional as responses to theoretical writings. Here there is an apparent paradox. De Man's writings themselves convey little manifest affect and even engage in a critique of pathos in a defense of theoretical rigor. Yet conceptual purism and self-effacing analysis provoke intense affective responses in the reader and make the textual de Man an object of desire, unease, and mimetic rivalry.

Thus far what I have said should provoke little disagreement even if one might want to qualify or elaborate certain of my observations in a different fashion. But what is, I think, significant is that the transferential relation to de Man and to his texts has been the subject of such little reflection. What is equally significant is that what appears to be the trauma caused (at least for some) by the discovery of the World War II journalism has not been confronted in its full import—a trauma aggravated by the intensely transferential relations to de Man and by the fact that these relations often remained suppressed or repressed. It may be more precise to refer to the effects of trauma in responses to the discovery, for it is difficult to specify the exact nature of the trauma, which seems bound up with both personal and textual issues, involving, but not reducible to, questions of authorship and authority—issues that are difficult to sort out. Indeed, the limited reflection about these issues has itself furthered the tendency to manifest seemingly posttraumatic reactions without an attempt to specify the nature of possible trauma. Nor has the self-serving hyperbole, tendentiousness, and *Schadenfreude* of opponents assisted in posing and exploring problems in a fruitful manner.

In addition, when de Man died he was, in certain circles, on the verge of apotheosis. Among his admirers there was little sign of the *Angstbereitschaft* (readiness to feel anxiety) that Freud saw as necessary to avoid traumatization. For example, the praise of his work in certain essays in *Reading de Man Reading* (where only an appended section of Geoffrey Hartman's essay registered and tried to address the "shock" of the newly discovered early articles)[1]—or the very nature of the often awe-inspired references to de Man in *The Lesson of Paul de Man*[2]—as well as the tenor of the session at the Modern Language Association annual convention just after his death, during which former students and colleagues testified to the importance of his work, was quite extraordinary. Viewed in retrospect, the scene almost seemed set for a classical tragedy. Wlad Godzich—who titled his 1983 introduction to a new edition of *Blindness and Insight* "Caution! Reader at Work!"—asserted that de Man harbored no illusion about leaving "the realm of representation" and residing in that of reason, but that, "having brought the understanding to a point of paralysis,

[1]Lindsay Waters and Wlad Godzich, eds., *Reading de Man Reading* (Minneapolis: University of Minnesota Press, 1989). Hartman's reference to "shock" is on p. 14.
[2]*Yale French Studies*, no. 69 (1985).

and reached the point of the inscription of the 'simulacrity' of the simulacrum, he stands at the very edge of human finitude, knowing such knowledge as there is within the compass of that finitude."[3] Godzich's analysis seemed to be corroborated in Werner Hamacher's essay "Lectio: De Man's Imperative" in which, after listing what he found to be the crucial questions confronting the student of literature at the present time, Hamacher asserted: "These questions can be posed with the prospect of an answer in terms of only a single contemporary literary theorist. Only Paul de Man has exposed himself in his works to the demands of these questions."[4]

At the time of his death de Man had a very special status indeed. For some—perhaps for many—he was almost sacred, whether sacred pure or impure, and with the ambivalence and labile possibilities of sudden reversal that come with this status. Indeed, the sense of trauma was intensified by the very status de Man had attained by the time of his death. Yet what was largely missing between this point of ascension and the reactions to the "fall" were attempts to acknowledge, come to terms with, and work through transferential relations as well as the traumatic reactions that the discovery of the World War II articles, coming so close upon de Man's death and near apotheosis, at times caused.

De Man's very understanding of language in his later works made dispossession, trauma, and mourning constitutive features of the linguistic process itself, and his continual critique of an "aesthetic ideology" of totalization, organicism, full rootedness, and the elimination of difference—in brief, the illusory realization of the imaginary—may in certain limited and problematic ways be read as applicable to the assumptions of the Nazi movement. I would also note that the undoing of the binary oppositions, while perhaps more marked and sustained in Derrida than in de Man, has been a crucial aspect of deconstruction in general and is very important for the critique of a scapegoat mechanism that resists internal alterity, is intolerant of mixed or hybridized forms, and requires a fixed, pure, and decisive divide between the integral self and the other. But, although they are certainly not irrelevant to the investigation of historicity—indeed, they may well be necessary to understand its conditions of

---

[3]Paul de Man, *Blindness and Insight: Essays in the Rhetoric of Contemporary Criticism*, intro. Wlad Godzich (1971; Minneapolis: University of Minnesota Press, 1983), p. xxix.
[4]In *Reading de Man Reading*, p. 172.

possibility—these valuable initiatives do not sufficiently address specific historical traumas such as the Shoah or, in a more minor key, the contemporary effects on at least some people of the discovery of de Man's own unacknowledged early writings.

Eric Santner has argued that the minimal role of affectivity in the texts of de Man is related to the role of melancholy and arrested mourning in them.[5] Melancholy may be necessary for mourning, but it blocks *Trauerarbeit* (the work of mourning) insofar as the melancholic disavows loss, remains narcissistically identified with the loved other, and is unable to affirm, empathize with, and, in certain respects, take leave of the other as other. It is only through mourning that melancholy can be countered by laughter and carnivalesque forces in general. I suggest that, at least on a textual level, the absence in the later de Man of an acknowledgment of his early writings and an attempt to come to terms with—and take explicit leave of—them and the past to which they were related may be read as a sign of resistance to mourning in specific terms. I think it is deceptive to conflate this resistance with a refusal of excuse making or even of confession. Indeed, no one was in a better position than de Man to thematize the temptations of excuse making and to prevent its conflation with a critical and self-critical attempt to come to terms with the past. But here it is important not to undercut or disavow one's own capacity for empathy, and it may well be the case that de Man was caught up in a harrowingly intricate interaction between willing suppression and unwilling inability to remember with respect to his past—an interaction about which one can only speculate. In any case, the point I want to stress is that de Man's textual resistance to remembering, mourning, and working through trauma in an open reckoning with specific events is to some extent repeated in those who resist coming explicitly to terms with transference and possible trauma in their responses to de Man.

In de Man's texts mourning takes place in an extremely attenuated, abstract, and oblique manner that is equivocal and not countered by more direct forms of communication and specific modes of implication or self-contextualization. Some of those who comment on de Man have a tendency to repeat his gesture in a more or less allegorizing and apologetic vein, to exaggerate traces of self-contestation in the

---

[5]*Stranded Objects: Mourning, Memory, and Film in Postwar Germany* (Ithaca: Cornell University Press, 1990), pp. 26–30.

early writings, to rewrite the past in a manner that underwrites a more "positive" identity in the present, and to overinterpret the role of self-criticism in the relation of the later to the earlier unacknowledged writings. This is perhaps one massive way in which transference is acted out rather than thematized in the difficult and perhaps never fully successful attempt to work through it. It is also a way in which one is—however unintentionally and perhaps in contradiction to one's explicit, strongly held political views—insufficiently attentive to an important public context for the controversy over de Man: revisionist interpretations of the Holocaust. Acting out and even extreme resistance or denial may be necessary prerequisites of working through traumatic events, and, in considering the responses of those who were close to de Man, empathy is clearly warranted. But criticism may also be called for both to facilitate "working-through" and to address the public consequences of reading and interpretation, notably with respect to revisionism. Indeed, what may be acceptable as private acts of friendship or love may be questionable as interventions in a politically fraught field of public discourse.

I now turn to what I see as three very problematic responses to de Man in thinkers whose work I respect and admire: Shoshana Felman, Jacques Derrida, and Fredric Jameson.

Felman has written with remarkable insight on the problem of transference in reading and interpretation.[6] But in her "Paul de Man's Silence" this problem is itself passed over in silence.[7] Instead, her article attempts to explicate and to justify de Man's silence with respect to his World War II articles. She adopts two important strategies in making her argument. First, she contends that de Man's later writings said all that could or need be said about his own silence and that there was no need for an explicit reckoning with the early articles. Thus she

[6]See, for example, Shoshana Felman, "Turning the Screw of Interpretation," *Yale French Studies*, no. 55/56 (1977) (Literature and Psychoanalysis: The Question of Reading: Otherwise), 94–207. I would simply note that my own treatment of problems in negotiating transference may help to illuminate one crucial issue: how can such brilliant figures as Felman, Derrida, and Jameson, who have done such important and justifiably influential work, also in certain contexts make very questionable arguments?

[7]*Critical Inquiry* 15 (1989), 704–44. Reprinted as "After the Apocalypse: Paul de Man and the Fall to Silence," in Shoshana Felman and Dori Laub, M.D., *Testimony: Crises of Witnessing in Literature, Psychoanalysis, and History* (New York: Routledge, 1992), pp. 120–64. References are to the version printed in *Critical Inquiry*; page numbers are cited parenthetically in the text.

writes: "It is no longer possible to distinguish between heroes and knaves, regeneration and destruction, deliverance and entanglement, speeches and acts, history and faith, idealistic faith and (self-)deception, justice and totalitarianism, utmost barbarism and utmost civilized refinement, freedom of will and radical enslavement to historical manipulations and ideological coercions. Indeed, in his afterlife as Ishmael [in Melville's *Moby-Dick*], in his later writings and his teaching, de Man, I suggest, does nothing other than testify to the complexity and ambiguity of history as Holocaust" (pp. 719–20). Felman adds:

> History as Holocaust is mutely omnipresent in the theoretical endeavor of de Man's mature work. The war's disastrous historical and political effects are what is implicitly at stake in the text's insistent focus on, and tracking of, an ever-lurking blindness it underscores as the primary human (and historical) condition. De Man's entire writing effort is a silent trace of the reality of an event whose very historicity, borne out by the author's own catastrophic experience, has occurred precisely as the event of the preclusion—the event of the impossibility—of its own witnessing; an event that could thus name the very namelessness, the very magnitude, the very materiality of what de Man will constantly refer to as the ever-threatening *impossibility of reading*. (P. 722)

One may agree with the view that de Man's later work in some sense implicitly inscribes historicity and the Holocaust and yet take issue with Felman's reading of the manner and relative adequacy with which this inscription takes place. But even if one fully agrees with Felman about the nature of the silent inscription of historicity and the Holocaust in de Man's later texts, one may yet argue that this procedure is not sufficient to explain the absence of an explicit attempt to come to terms with the early articles. (One may also object to a reduction of alternatives to an extreme binary opposition between silence and a finalized, "totalizing overview" [p.720]). A conception of the workings of the later texts in terms of silent traces, mute omnipresences, and allegorical allusions is too general to account for a specific lack, notably when the conception is prompted by a manifest desire to justify that lack. Indeed, if de Man believed that silence was the only acceptable response to the Holocaust or his own relation to it, he might at the very least have said as much, however paradoxical or aporetic the gesture would have been. The idea that "the war's disastrous historical and political effects are what is implicitly at stake in the text's insistent focus on, and tracking of, an ever-lurking blindness it underscores as the primary human (and historical) condition" lends itself to the interpretation Felman ostensibly attempts to counter: the view that de Man evasively essentialized a problem he was unwilling or unable to confront in specific terms.

Although she contends that de Man's silence said all that can or need be said, Felman nonetheless engages in an extremely speculative form of contextualizing ascription by filling in de Man's silences with views explicitly elaborated by others, be they contemporary figures (such as Michel Leiris) or an author such as Melville. In one of the most dubious instances of this tendency, with reference to a review by de Man that appeared in *Le Soir* on 1 September 1942, titled " 'Le Massacre des Innocents' —poème de Hubert Dubois," she comments: "The poem de Man chose to review, written by a Belgian author, is a barely masked allegory of the Nazi extermination of the Jews" (p. 714). Felman does not observe that this construction of the poem is her own and is not mentioned by de Man, who in fact provides an extremely formal, overly generalized, and essentializing analysis. De Man writes in this review that the poem "unite[s] . . . the laws of truth with those of poetry" and shows that "suffering is salutary because it enables one to expiate repeated crimes against the human person."[8] Felman herself quotes another essentializing and vague comment de Man makes without exploring its relation to her exegesis: "One could easily call 'The Massacre of the Innocents' a meditation on the guilt which has led humanity to the awful state in which it is plunged at the present moment" (p. 715). From de Man's statements it is difficult to see whose guilt is at issue, and one could easily interpret these statements to mean that the Jews themselves participate in—or even bear the primary burden of—this putative guilt. Indeed, one of the more curious features of Felman's mode of contextualizing is that, in its pointillist attempt to trace chronologies or situate events, it often ignores some blatant historical matters, notably everything that the Nazis had said about and done to the Jews before 4 March 1941 (the date of de Man's most manifestly dubious article, "Les Juifs dans la Littérature actuelle").

Felman's second strategy may be necessary to lend credence to her

<hr />

[8] *Wartime Journalism, 1939–1943, by Paul de Man*, ed. Werner Hamacher, Neil Hertz, and Thomas Keenan (Lincoln: University of Nebraska Press, 1988), pp. 265–66 (hereafter *Wartime Journalism*).

first, but it is even less convincing in nature. She assimilates de Man's silence to the silence of Holocaust victims and survivors in general and to that of Primo Levi in particular. This strategy helps to explain her earlier-quoted reference to the "event of the preclusion"—a hyperbolic rendition of de Man's putatively "catastrophic experience" that accords with the specious attempt to equate it with the extremely traumatic experiences of victims and survivors. In a note she thanks "Dori Laub, M.D., who helped [her] to articulate this perspective on the basis of his clinical experience with survivors" (p. 708). And she quotes Primo Levi, who "from a different position" writes in *The Drowned and the Saved*:

> We, the survivors, are not the true witnesses. This is an uncomfortable notion of which I have become conscious little by little, reading the memoirs of others and reading mine at a distance of years. . . . Those who . . . have not returned to tell about it or have returned mute, . . . they are . . . the submerged, the complete witnesses, the ones whose depositions would have a general significance. (Quoted on p. 721)

Felman adds in her own voice:

> Incorporating the silence of the witness who has returned mute into his very writing, de Man's entire work and his later theories bear implicit witness to the Holocaust, not as its (impossible and failed) narrator (a narrator-journalist whom the war had dispossessed of his own voice) but as a witness to the very blindness of his own, and others', witness, a firsthand witness to the Holocaust's historical disintegration of the witness. (P. 721)

It is, however, important to note that in the passage Felman quotes and, I think, misappropriates, Levi is referring to Holocaust victims whose experience was even more extreme than this own—those who "drowned" or were struck speechless. He is unwilling even to compare himself to these "true witnesses," and in the process he effects a telling reversal by raising up the lowly and desperate who were generally despised by other inmates themselves. The so-called Muslims who could not go on were for Levi "the submerged, the complete witnesses, the ones whose depositions would have a general significance." In words elided by Felman, Levi asserts: "We survivors are not only an exiguous but also an anomalous minority: we are those who by their prevarications or abilities or good luck did not touch bottom."[9] To compare these nonsurviving victims or even Levi to de Man—who was neither a nonsurvivor nor a survivor in any comparable sense—is to elide the very significance of the difference in position between Levi and de Man through an unfortunate lapse of judgment. It verges on the idea (quite important at Bitburg) that all those involved in the Holocaust were victims—a view which Levi, despite his sensitivity to the existence of a "gray zone" and to the effects of the Nazi policy of trying to turn victims into accomplices, adamantly rejects in *The Drowned and the Saved*: "I know that the murderers existed, not only in Germany, and still exist, retired or on active duty, and that to confuse them with their victims is a moral disease or an aesthetic affectation or a sinister sign of complicity; above all, it is precious service rendered (intentionally or not) to the negators of truth" (pp. 48–49). De Man was not a murderer, but he was clearly not a victim or a survivor in the sense Felman attempts to make him out as being. In fact, Felman is so intent on establishing de Man's status as a victim and survivor that she pays little, if any, attention to those who were the manifest victims and survivors of the Holocaust.

It may also be useful to quote Levi on silence, for his remarks are instructive despite their dubious indebtedness to a largely unexamined tradition of high culture, overly analytic rationality, teleological assumptions, and restrictive humanism:

> According to a theory fashionable during those years, which to me
> seems frivolous and irritating, "incommunicability" supposedly was an
> inevitable ingredient, a life sentence inherent to the human condition,
> particularly the life style of industrial society; we are monads, incapable
> of reciprocal messages, or capable only of truncated messages, false at
> their departure, misunderstood on their arrival. Discourse is fictitious,
> pure noise, a painted veil, that conceals existential silence; we are alone,
> even (or especially) if we live in pairs. It seems to me that this lament
> originates in and points to mental laziness; certainly it encourages it, in a
> dangerous vicious circle. Except for cases of pathological incapacity, one
> can and must communicate, and thereby contribute in a useful and easy
> way to the peace of others and oneself, because silence, the absence of
> signals, is itself a signal, but an ambiguous one, and ambiguity
> generates anxiety and suspicion. To say that it is impossible to
> communicate is false; one always can. To refuse to communicate is a
> failing; we are biologically and socially predisposed to communication,

[9]*The Drowned and the Saved* (1986; New York: Vintage Books, 1988), p. 83.

and in particular to its highly evolved and noble form, which is language. All members of the human species speak, no nonhuman species knows how to speak. (Pp. 88–89)

Even more apposite is this comment of Kierkegaard's, which was written from a general philosophical position much closer to de Man's:

It is not true that direct communication is superior to indirect communication. No, no. But the fact is that no man has ever been born who could use the indirect method even fairly well, to say nothing of using it all his life. For we human beings need each other, and in that there is already directness.

Only the God-man is in every respect indirect communication from first to last. He did not need men, but they infinitely needed him; he loves men, but according to his conception of what love is; therefore he does not change in the slightest toward their conception, does not speak directly in such a way that he also surrenders the possibility of offense— which his existence (*Existents*) in the guise of servant is.[10]

Felman would not seem to be presenting de Man in terms of "pathological incapacity" (although one may perhaps argue this point),[11] but at times she tends to read him in terms that Kierkegaard

[10]*Søren Kierkegaard's Journals and Papers*, ed. and trans. Howard V. Hong and Edna H. Hong (Bloomington: Indiana University Press, 1970), p. 384.

[11]At times Felman seems to be positioning both the Holocaust and de Man's relation to it in terms of foreclosure—but foreclosure that is paradoxically an object of conscious choice. Foreclosure seems to be at issue in her reference to the "event of the preclusion" or in a formulation such as the following: "I take [de Man's silence] to be (among other things) his consequent refusal of a discursive relation to the past that might have any shadow of resemblance to his past relation to the past" (p. 710). The foreclosed for Lacan is not integrated into the subject's unconscious and is not symbolized at all; it is situated in the Real and reemerges "from the outside" (rather than as the repressed), particularly through hallucination. Felman's conception of silence as the only appropriate response to the Holocaust (as the putative "event of the preclusion") seems to make foreclosure a strategy, although its relation to psychosis or extreme pathology in general is not discussed in her article. As I indicate elsewhere, I think this positioning of the Holocaust is dubious insofar as it remains exclusive, displaces a more intricate and differential understanding of the interaction between language and its limits, and obviates all representation and symbolization other than the indirect and allegorical, which, in the case of Felman's treatment of de Man, remain extremely associative and speculative. Foreclosure may be a pertinent category in the case of survivors who had extremely traumatic experiences. But with respect to the limited issue of de Man's relation to his past as writer of the World War II articles, I find it implausible to appeal to such an extreme response as foreclosure; I find it more plausible to infer that de Man's response fell in the variable range between suppression and repression. In any event, if Felman is postulating foreclosure as de Man's response, this postulation would re-

sees as appropriate only for the God-man. Indeed, one feature of the quasi-divine position in which Felman places de Man is that, through a remarkable act of faith, seeming defects are transfigured into attestations of transcendent virtue and superhuman resolve.

There are complexities in Felman's analysis that my treatment does not address. Her readings of de Man's later writings (such as those on Rousseau and Benjamin) and of their possible relations to the early journalistic pieces are subtle and suggestive. They often reinforce the two strategies I have discussed, but they also introduce complications in the argument that bear on what may in one sense be its most thought provoking and contestable dimensions. The notion that silence was the only way to confront the traumatic past and that de Man in his later work said (or wrote) all that could or need be said about his own silence is reinforced by the view that confession, excuse making, and apology were impossible solutions for de Man. Thus Felman writes: "In deconstructing, in his rigorous commitment to the truth of history, the conceptual system of all apologetic discourses and their very claim to restore an ethical balance—to be 'epistemologically as well as ethically grounded and therefore available as meaning, in the mode of understanding' . . . —de Man keeps reiterating, and demands that we keep facing, the historical *impossibility of reading* (or the Holocaust) as an unredeemable scandal of injustice and of injury." She further contends:

> In the testimony of a work that performs actively an exercise of silence not as simple silence but as the absolute refusal of any trivializing or legitimizing discourse (of apology, of narrative, or of psychologizing explanation of recent history), de Man articulates, thus, neither—as some have argued—an empirical (or psychological) hidden confession nor—as other have suggested—an empirical (or psychological) refusal to confess, but the incapacity of apologetic discourse to account for history as Holocaust, the ethical impossibility of *a confession that, historically and philosophically, cannot take place.* This complex articulation of the impossibility of confession embodies, paradoxically enough, not a denial of the author's guilt but, on the contrary, the most radical and irrevocable assumption of historical responsibility. (P. 733)

There is a sense in which silence may indeed be the only way to confront a traumatic past, but I have tried to argue that this conten-

---

quire argument and substantiation of a sort that her article does not provide, especially if the move is not to appear extremely speculative and apologetic.

tion does not justify a specific silence concerning something that can be said or with respect to the problem of attempting to say what can be said in the face of the risk that language may break down in a more or less telling manner. One difficulty in Felman's approach is a tendency to conflate any possible use of language de Man might have made in relation to his past—any attempt to say anything at all—with confession, excuse making, and apology. This conflation is dubious, although one may indeed argue that any use of language would confront problems posed by confession, excuse making, and apology. Still, the type of sensitivity de Man had about the self-deceptive and paradoxical nature of language does not imply the necessity of only indirect, oblique, or "silent" approaches to problems. It may also be taken to imply the need to break silence and to become involved in the complexities and paradoxes of language even when they involve (but cannot be reduced to) the temptation (or indeed the inevitability) of confession, excuse making, and apology—tendencies no one is above, but which may be resisted in various ways. I have intimated that Felman's line of argument tends to situate de Man outside the range of sociality, for it is only in this quasi-divine, transcendent position that one would be above and beyond such social practices as excuse making, confession, and apology. The "absolute refusal of any trivializing or legitimizing discourse" meets up with "the most radical and irrevocable assumption of historical responsibility" in a realm of absolutes outside society—a realm where history is displaced rather than informed by its conditions of possibility, the Holocaust is equated with the impossibility of reading, and the mechanical, impersonal workings of language paradoxically coincide with ultimate responsibility.

Of course, it is paradoxical in a more trivial and legitimizing sense that Felman's recapitulation of de Man's critique of apology itself functions apologetically in the context of her own argument insofar as it furnishes a rationale for de Man's not publicly and directly addressing his past. It provides alibis through allegorical interpretations that make silence speak and presumably show how what was not explicitly said in one place was really addressed in others. It also focuses, if not fixates, attention on the general trauma of history and language in de Man at the price of displacing, avoiding, or denying both the specific nature of the Holocaust and the difficulties presented by the discovery of de Man's early writings. To make this observation is not to defend a total particularization of phenomena that would detach them from oneself or establish one's superiority or innocence, but it is to question the manner in which Felman avoids the problem of specificity and occludes the relation between general conditions of historicity or language and specific events. In fact, it is Felman's absolutizing notion of an exercise of silence as the only acceptable response to the Holocaust that accords with extreme sacralization (or its secular analogue in a theory of the sublime), which would constitute events not only as distinctive (which they may well be) but as altogether unique and incomparable. Of course, the generalizability of the traumatizing linguistic predicament that reduces all acts of reading to silence and translation to failure would "paradoxically" make the uniqueness of the Holocaust itself as unspecific as the uniqueness of a fingerprint. Specificity is lost between the extremes of particularization and generality, and a one-sided stress on discontinuous breaks and silent responses obviates a notion of the tense and problematic relation between repetition and trauma as well as between representation and its limits. It also leads to a compulsively repeated double bind in which the seemingly impossible demand to say something recurrently eventuates in the fact that one says an often inordinate amount about allegorically associated issues but little, if anything, specific about the Holocaust.

In Felman's account it is, moreover, unclear who or what does the assuming with respect to "the most radical and irrevocable assumption of historical responsibility," for she does not pose the question of the relation between agency (requiring at least the possibility of limited liability and control) and the mechanical, impersonal workings of language. Indeed, this problem seems averted, if not foreclosed, by her exegetical strategy in glossing de Man's silence. A further question (no doubt the most difficult) is whether the notion of a seemingly sublime, "absolute refusal" of certain discourses also implies the refusal of two further possibilities: that of the efficacy of mourning in allowing for any homeopathic or healing process whatsoever and that of an attempt to begin again in history. (These possibilities should not be collapsed into the binary opposite of "absolute refusal," to wit, redemptive totalization and full mastery.) Felman may well be right in concluding that translation is the most suitable "metaphor for the historical necessity of bearing witness" (p. 734). What is open to question is the nature of translation: should it simply be identified with a notion of an utterly fragmented, discontinuous history "devoid of pathos" (p. 742)—a testimony to all "history as Holocaust" (p. 740)—or should it be seen in terms of a more complicated, differential economy of losses and gains? Equally open to question is the precise status of the extreme yet inevitable possibility of silent witnessing in the face of unrepresentable trauma—a possibility that should not be fixated upon, indiscriminately generalized, or made to underwrite the dubious argumentative strategies.

The second text I shall discuss is Jacques Derrida's "Like the Sound of the Sea Deep within a Shell: Paul de Man's War."[12] Written in the heat of the moment and in an obvious state of agitation, this tortuous essay is hardly the best place to understand or evaluate the relations among deconstruction, politics, and history. In it Derrida effectively rebuts slipshod attempts to discredit de Man and deconstruction on the basis of superficial readings and false inferences from the wartime journalism. But he does not effectively resume the reflections on mourning and its role in de Man that he began in his earlier *Mémoires*

---

[12]Trans. Peggy Kamuf, *Critical Inquiry* 14 (1988), 590–652. References are to this version; page numbers are cited parenthetically in the text. Derrida himself apparently believed that he had to move quickly to counteract the effect of misleading newspaper reports (p. 591). Yet he also felt (more contestably) that his approach was not marked by "journalistic haste." He did, however, have the clear sense that his early intervention had a special status: "The fact is there: at the point at which I take the risk of writing on this subject, I have the sense of being the first, thus far the only one to do so, still too quickly to be sure, but without journalistic haste, which is to say without the excuses it sometimes gives the journalist but should not give the academic. It is a formidable privilege, one not designed to alleviate the feeling of responsibility" (p. 592). For reasons that are not altogether clear, Derrida read only a subset of de Man's wartime articles sent to him by Ortwin de Graef—twenty-five from *Le Soir* and four from *Het Vlaamsche Land*. He states: "I have still not understood why and how this selection was made from a set of about 125 [in *Le Soir*]." He also quotes from a letter from de Graef in which the latter refers to the "not altogether arbitrary selection of these texts (it is difficult, for practical reasons, to send you all the articles now, but if you wish to see them, I will try to find a way—in any case, the present selection can give an impression of the general content of the first writings of Paul de Man as concerns the events of the war" (quoted on p. 598). Despite his sense of the importance and nature of his intervention, Derrida does not illuminate further the question of whether he made an effort to obtain all the articles from de Graef. Derrida's article is republished in a slightly revised form in *Responses: On Paul de Man's Wartime Journalism*, ed. Werner Hamacher, Neil Hertz, and Thomas Keenan (Lincoln: University of Nebraska Press, 1989) (hereafter *Responses*). This volume provides a range of responses to de Man's journalism. For an extended discussion and critique of Derrida's treatment of "Les Juifs dans la Littérature actuelle," see David Carroll, "The Temptation of Fascism and the Question of Literature: Justice, Sorrow, and Political Error (An Open Letter to Jacques Derrida)," *Cultural Critique*, no. 15 (Spring 1990), 39–81.

for Paul de Man[13] and take them in a direction that would address the specific issues raised by the early World War II articles. At certain crucial points he even seems almost unconsciously to lend credence to the claim that deconstruction can be used to prove virtually anything by rewriting the past in the light of present interests and desires. Derrida in effect reads the early journalistic writings of de Man—particularly the anti-Semitic article "Les Juifs dans la Littérature actuelle" (published in *Le Soir* of 4 March 1941)[14]—as if they were as intricate and self-questioning as the texts of the later de Man often are.

Derrida acknowledges the proximity of the early articles to what he somewhat vaguely terms "the worst." He also states quite explicitly with respect to what appeared to him to be "the most unbearable" article, "Les Juifs dans la Littérature actuelle": "Nothing in what I am about to say, analyzing the article as closely as possible, will heal over the wound I right away felt when, my breath taken away, I perceived in it what the newspapers have most frequently singled out as recognized antisemitism that would come close to urging exclusions, even the most sinister deportations" (p. 621). It is unclear whether the wound is prematurely healed; at least it seems to be too rapidly covered over. The dismissive reference to newspapers signals the tack Derrida will take. He goes on to employ a pseudo-deconstructive strategy of "on the one hand . . . on the other hand," whereby what is conceded with one hand is countered, if not in good part retracted, with the other. Derrida strains to find mitigating elements in de Man's article in a feat of close reading that approaches projective reprocessing. What is not taken seriously enough is the likelihood that the one hand—that of collaborationist propaganda—is large enough to dwarf the other hand—that of critical distance, if not resistance—to such an extent that at times one seems to have but one hand clapping.

Derrida enumerates aspects of collaborationist propaganda with reference to the question: "Is not what we have here the most unquestionable manifestation of an antisemitism as violent as it is stereotyped?" (p. 621). Yet when he turns to the analysis of what would seem at first glance to be the most incriminating article, this question tends to become rhetorical in the ordinary sense, and his account is punctuated by similarly rhetorical questions. For example, after list-

[13]Trans. Cecile Lindsay, Jonathan Culler, and Eduardo Cadava (New York: Columbia University Press, 1986).
[14]*Wartime Journalism*, p. 45.

ing a number of stereotypical notions of Jewishness and the Jewish contamination of European life in de Man's "Les Juifs," he quotes this passage from the end of the article:

> The observation is, moreover, comforting for Western intellectuals. That they have been able to safeguard themselves from Jewish influence in a domain as representative of culture as literature proves their vitality. If our civilization had let itself be invaded by a foreign force, then we would have to give up much hope for its future. By keeping, in spite of semitic interference in all aspects of European life, an intact originality and character, it has shown that its basic nature is healthy. What is more, one sees that a solution of the Jewish problem that would aim at the creation of a Jewish colony isolated from Europe would not entail, for the literary life of the West, deplorable consequences. The latter would lose, in all, a few personalities of mediocre value and would continue, as in the past, to develop according to its great evolutive laws. (Quoted and translated on p. 623)

Derrida adds: "Will I dare say 'on the other hand' in the face of the *unpardonable* violence and confusion of these sentences?" After two more such questions, he enunciates a fourth: "In the *dominant* context in which they were read in 1941, did not their [de Man's "conclu-sions" in the quoted paragraph] *dominant* effect go unquestionably in the direction of the worst? Or what we now know to have been the worst?" Derrida will indeed "dare" to say "on the other hand," and the question about the dominant effect of the article's "conclusions" tends to dissipate and even fade out given the nature of Derrida's analysis. Derrida will in piecemeal fashion quote and extensively comment on (voice-over?) all of de Man's article, beginning with the end, moving to the beginning, turning to the middle, and then re-turning to the end. This disarticulating and glossing procedure has the effect of obscuring the flow and rhetorical force of de Man's argu-ment.

After quoting the above passage, Derrida asserts that "although one has to condemn these sentences, which I have just done [largely in the form of rhetorical questions], one ought not to do it without examining everything that remains readable in a text one can judge to be disastrous." Although I recognize the possible validity of Derrida's protocol of reading, I shall not try to examine everything in his own long text but focus on a few of the things he finds readable in de Man's, especially with respect to the "other hand." His first major point is that "the *whole* article is organized as an indictment of 'vulgar antisemitism' " (p. 623). One may object that the indictment of vulgar anti-Semitism is not the organizing principle of the whole of de Man's article but a rhetorical strategy that gets it off the ground. Derrida himself focuses insistently on what he sees as "the uncompromising critique of 'vulgar antisemitism'," (p.624), and he even hears "some mockery" in the beginning statements of the article where de Man scoffs at vulgar anti-Semitism and the "myth" that Jews have been "the leaders of literary movements that characterize our age." But de Man asserts that "the Jews have themselves contributed to spreading this myth." The implication, I think, is that the "myth" acquired plausibility from the realization that "the Jews have, in fact, played an important role in the phony and disordered existence of Europe since 1920." De Man in "Les Juifs" is manifestly more concerned about the good name and the fate of culture, literature, and "our civilization" than about the Jews, and his brand of anti-Semitism might be construed as a correlate of an irresponsible and cavalier aestheticism. In any case, Derrida does not observe that what one finds here is the tendency to blame the victim. Instead he states:

> To condemn vulgar antisemitism may leave one to understand that there is a distinguished antisemitism in whose name the vulgar variety is put down. De Man never says such a thing, even though one may condemn his silence. But the phrase can also mean something else, and this reading can always contaminate the other in a clandestine fashion: to condemn "vulgar antisemitism," *especially if one makes no mention of the other kind*, is to condemn antisemitism itself *inasmuch as* it is vulgar, always and essentially vulgar. De Man does not say that either. (P. 625)

The difference between Derrida's responses to the two silences is that the understanding of the first seems to follow from the logic of de Man's argument, whereas the reading of the second seems purely gratuitous. Indeed, part of refinement is not to mention "the other kind." Derrida tries to lend credibility to the idea that a condemnation of vulgar anti-Semitism implies a condemnation of all anti-Semitism by averring that de Man, like his uncle, was "nonconformist," and so was his article. But it was (and is) hardly nonconformist to attempt to distinguish between a vulgar and a refined anti-Semitism and thereby to make anti-Semitism respectable among those who consider themselves refined and would be shocked by association with vulgarity or its trappings. In her contribution to *Responses*, Alice Yaeger Kaplan traces the resonances of de Man's articles—including their inconsistencies—in anti-Semitic and fascist literature of the day, and she notes that the multiplicity of approaches to anti-Semitism "might in their very disagreements . . . give the appearance of respectable 'debate.' What is more, all of them draw in some way on a critique of an 'incorrect' form of racist thinking that is beneath their dignity," with the role of extremist other often being played by Céline.[15]

Derrida also discusses de Man's conception of "very powerful laws" of "esthetic evolution" without observing that this conception can itself posit these laws as a protective shield that functions to reinforce anti-Semitism by situating Jewishness as a contaminating "foreign force" (as de Man clearly does), but assuring that it was unable to infect the sound and healthy nature of "our civilization" in any truly essential way. Nor is such an assurance incompatible with the idea that a rigorous vigilance—even a policy of ghettoization or deportation—is the price of purity in the face of the danger of decadence and contamination. Derrida instead notes that a seemingly "formalist" or "estheticist" thesis at the time went "rather against the current" and that "one can at least read it as an anticonformist attack." He goes on to assert that the "examples" of novelists and movements chosen by de Man (Gide, Kafka, Lawrence, Hemingway, surrealism, futurism) are "troubling": "curious and insolent because there are no others, because there is no German example, because the French example is Gide, the American Hemingway, the English Lawrence, and because Kafka is Jewish, but especially because they represent everything that Nazism or the right wing revolutions would have liked to extirpate from history and the great tradition" (p. 628). As many commentators have noted, the list of authors was not original to de Man but, minus the name of Proust, was borrowed from Aldous Huxley. (This list, which "could be extended indefinitely," is invoked by de Man to bolster the case concerning "very powerful laws" of "esthetic evolution" by showing that novelists since Stendhal have not broken with all past traditions but are "mere continuers" who pursue further a realist aesthetic that plumbs "the secrets of interior life.") Whether de Man knew that Kafka was Jewish is debatable, but that he knew that Proust was Jewish is highly probable. In

[15]See Alice Yaeger Kaplan, "Paul de Man, *Le Soir*, and the Francophone Collaboration (1940–1942)," in *Responses*, pp. 266–84.

her contribution to *Responses*, Kaplan does maintain that "readers of the period would have recognized Kafka as a Jewish writer. Works by Kafka had been withdrawn from sale in France and Germany and acquired a large underground following. In France, Gerhard Heller censored the chapter on Kafka in Camus' *Mythe de Sisyphe*" (p. 283n). Nazism and right-wing revolutions might, however, have found things to admire in Hemingway and Lawrence (the cult of virility, dynamism, and masculinity, for example). And the record of futurism with respect to fascism is hardly sterling, or does the absence of Marinetti's name from the list prove something? In any case, the list is heterogeneous, and one cannot tell clearly why de Man selected it. Elsewhere the early de Man does make positive references to Proust. But his predilection for Proust and his diverse judgments in other respects were not atypical of commentators who expressed anti-Semitic and even fascistic views, such as Robert Brasillach and Drieu la Rochelle.[16]

Toward the end of his discussion of "Les Juifs" Derrida returns to the passage where de Man refers to a "solution of the Jewish problem." He asserts:

> If I persist in wondering how, in what conditions he wrote this, it is because even in the sum total of the articles from that period that I have

[16]On these and related issues, see not only Kaplan's contribution to *Responses* but also her *Reproductions of Banality: Fascism, Literature, and French Intellectual Life* (Minneapolis: University of Minnesota Press, 1986).

One may note that Derrida's strategy of "on the one hand . . . on the other hand" sets up a seemingly judicious balance even if the two hands are in fact of quite different size and weight. The manner in which Derrida frames his discussion of "Les Juifs" is also noteworthy. It is presented in terms of a "third series of examples" after extensive discussion of two other series that are considerably less charged in nature. This positioning tends to lessen the impact of "Les Juifs," and the interpretation of the earlier "examples" (concerning German hegemony and the issue of nationalism), where there is probably more internal qualification and even contradiction in de Man, tends to have a carry-over effect when the reader comes to "Les Juifs." In the discussion of "Les Juifs" itself, the impression of judicious balance is rhetorically reinforced by contestable practices. The rhetorical questions are piled on the "hand" of collaboration, while the "hand" of putative resistance is treated in predominantly declarative terms (it is . . . it is not). The effect of the numerous rhetorical questions is to create doubt and confusion in the reader, for any more "decisive" reading would seem tantamount to intolerance, injustice, and oversimplification. Thus, the latter characteristics, which are blatant in de Man's article, tend to be displaced onto the reader who would point them out and resist Derrida's exegesis. Moreover, the large size of the collaborationist "hand" is itself obscured and compensated for by the fact that it receives relatively little space (pp. 621–23) and—aside from rhetorical questions—is treated in clipped, even abrupt fashion (pp. 622–23), whereas the small "hand" of resistance is discussed at great length (pp. 623–32) and thus discursively magnified.

been able to read, I have found no remark analogous to this one. I did not even find any allusion to the Jews or to some "Jewish problem." Or rather, yes: in May 1941, some remarkable and emphatic praise for Péguy the Dreyfusard. How is one to explain that? (P. 631)

Derrida's univocal interpretation of de Man's view of Charles Péguy is surprising, for one cannot infer from the article that de Man is praising Péguy in his very early role as Dreyfusard—a role that had been overlaid, if not submerged, by Péguy's later identifications as Catholic, conservative, and nationalist. In his article, de Man seems most attracted to the Péguy who is "grand pour son âme, qui ne transige jamais"[17]—Péguy as the genuine nonconformist who indeed went his own way and never compromised with established political authority. In this gesture, de Man would seem to identify with the other who did what de Man himself ostensibly did not do but may have wished he could have done. Derrida in his interpretation goes a bit too far in retrospectively realizing that wish. In addition, one may note the role of blatant anti-Semitism in an article Derrida did not read at the time he wrote his essay—an article published in *Het Vlaamsche Land* on 20 August 1942. This article is, if anything, more questionable than "Les Juifs" because it appeared after deportations of Jews from Belgium had begun.[18] In it de Man contrasts two groups of German writers, a first group that constituted "the aberrant carriers of foreign norms" and a second that "remained true to the proper norms of the country." With reference to the former's values, he writes, "one can legitimately speak of degeneration." And he continues:

The first of these groups celebrates an art with a strongly cerebral position, founded upon some abstract principles and very remote from all naturalness. The theses of expressionism, though very remarkable in themselves, were used here as tricks, as skillful artifices aimed at easy effects. The very legitimate basic rule of artistic transformation, inspired by the personal vision of the creator, served here as a pretext for a forced, caricatured representation of reality. Thus, [the artists of this group] came into open conflict with the proper traditions of German art

[17]De Man, "Notre Chronique Littéraire: Charles Péguy," in *Wartime Journalism*, p. 86.
[18]According to Nora Levin, a transit camp was established in June 1942 in Malines, and the first group of Jews, all foreign-born, were sent to Auschwitz on 4 August. See *The Holocaust: The Destruction of European Jewry 1933–1945* (New York: Schocken, 1968), p. 421.

which had always and before everything clung to a deep spiritual sincerity. Small wonder, then, that it was mainly non-Germans, and specifically jews, who went in this direction.[19]

The last of Derrida's interpretations of "Les Juifs" I want to mention is one wherein Derrida does a double take and "can hardly believe [his] eyes." His response is prompted by the following passage from de Man's article:

> One might have expected that, given the specific characteristics of the Jewish spirit, the latter would have played a more brilliant role in this artistic production. Their cerebralness, their capacity to assimilate doctrines while maintaining a certain coldness in the face of them, would seem to be very precious qualities for the work of lucid analysis that the novel demands. (Quoted on p. 630)

[19]"People and Books. A View on Contemporary German Fiction," trans. Ortwin de Graef, in *Wartime Journalism*, p. 325. Felman's brief discussion of "Les Juifs" resembles Derrida's in certain respects, for example, in noting the importance of the reference to Kafka, in stressing de Man's rejection of "vulgar anti-Semitism," and in its own re-peated use of rhetorical questions. But it differs from Derrida's in others. Felman rele-gates to a footnote de Man's statement about the "creation of a Jewish colony isolated from Europe." She argues that it would be anachronistic to read this statement, printed in March 1941, as condoning deportation of the Jews to extermination camps, because Nazi plans for deportation of Belgian Jews were put into operation only in the summer of 1942. Her rejection of this extreme interpretation is, however, complemented by an opposite extreme when she asserts: "It seems rather, that what de Man's statement is alluding to is the political solution that had been debated since the beginning of the century in Jewish intellectual circles, that of a resettlement of Jews outside of Europe—in Palestine or in Madagascar (a colony the West would give to the Jews)" (pp. 712–13n). There is no indication in "Les Juifs" that de Man is alluding to Zionism in particular or to debates in Jewish circles in general, and Felman's inference here is extremely implausible, especially in view of de Man's formulations. "The creation of a Jewish colony isolated from Europe" that would "not entail any deplorable conse-quences for the literary life of the West" would hardly seem to be a formulation one would initially locate in "Jewish intellectual circles," despite the role of so-called Jewish self-hatred. Moreover, although one may agree with Felman's objection to interpreting de Man's statement as a reference to the "Final Solution," one may nonetheless note the lability between exclusion and extermination within a logic of scapegoating—a logic whose role in de Man's article Felman does seem to acknowledge in her principal text. In the body of her text, however, she levelingly amalgamates "the Christian and Nazi ideologies" with respect to anti-Semitism and anxiety about "the foreign and contam-inating Other," and, in an obvious attempt to isolate and downplay the significance of "Les Juifs," she asserts that "in no other circumstance of his life did de Man propound—or consent to—anti-Semitism" (pp. 712–13). She does not discuss the rela-tion between "Les Juifs" and other early articles of de Man, including the one cited at the beginning of this note.

Derrida asks: "What is coiled up and resonating deep within this sentence? Did one hear that correctly? . . . [De Man] clearly describes what were in his eyes 'precious qualities.' " Whatever its other echo effects, this passage resonates with the later one of 20 August 1942 that I quoted above. And one may observe that de Man does not clearly describe what were in his eyes precious qualities; he refers to what "would seem to be very precious qualities." He does so in a counterfactual move that rhetorically reinforces an account stressing Jewish failure in novelistic production. Moreover, the "qualities" he refers to are extremely equivocal characteristics in what Derrida himself earlier terms "the stereotypical description of the 'Jewish spirit' " (p. 622).

Derrida's early, perhaps premature and preemptive, response unfortunately became a template for some others (for example, Andrzej Warminski's and Samuel Weber's in *Responses*) and authorized apologetic tendencies that might have confronted greater forces of inhibition had Derrida's own analyses been more sensitive to certain issues, including the difficulties posed by transferential relations between him and de Man on both the personal and the intellectual levels. Since de Man's death Derrida has tended to lend credence to the belief that there is a basic similarity or at least convergence between his thought and de Man's. I would in no sense maintain that there is a clear-cut opposition between Derrida's initiatives and de Man's, but an approach more explicitly attuned to problems of transference might abet a more discriminating and critical investigation of the intricate relations—including the differences—between his thought and de Man's.

The third and final instance I treat is somewhat puzzling, for it comes from a rather surprising direction. In an otherwise impressive essay, Fredric Jameson's approach to de Man's wartime journalism is, strangely enough, even less qualified than Derrida's. Indeed, in a curious feat of intertextual one-upmanship, he seems to be responding more to Derrida's essay than to de Man's wartime journalism. Jameson asserts that de Man's "notorious 'anti-Semitic' [Jameson's quotes] article . . . strikes [him] as the ingenious effort at resistance of a young man altogether too smart for his own good." For Jameson, the article was actually telling "garden-variety anti-Semites" that they would "be better advised to stop talking about the Jews altogether and to cultivate [their] own garden."[20] But one may object that this is

[20]"Immanence and Nominalism in Postmodern Theoretical Discourse," in *Postmod-*

precisely and blatantly what the article does not do, although Jameson may express one's profound wish about what the article should have done. Jameson's interpretation is even more questionable when it locates in "Les Juifs dans la Littérature actuelle" an irony that even de Manians have presumably missed. (One may wonder whether Jameson's consistent misspelling of de Man as DeMan is also an "ironic" sign of the projective and appropriative dimension of his account.) In his article de Man is indeed aestheticist, as Jameson claims, but the function of his aestheticism is manifestly anti-Semitic, for the relative autonomy of literary evolution is invoked to defend the relative purity and health of Western literature and civilization in the face of anxiety about Jewish contamination. The logic at play is scapegoating.

In what seem to be its textually unfounded interpolations, Jameson's gloss does not address, and indeed tends to obliterate, the effect and even the existence of passages that he, unlike Derrida, does not even deign to quote. To return to Jameson's metaphor, one might note that garden-variety anti-Semites could well argue that to tend their own garden would be precisely to weed out Jews. Their difference from de Man of "Les Juifs" would be not whether removal is desirable but why: for them, Jews ruin the garden, whereas for de Man, the garden is basically in fine shape and would not miss the Jews.

It is difficult to elicit all the ideological motivations of Jameson's own interpretation. But one of them is the belief, expressed in his essay, that the "exclusive emphasis on anti-Semitism ignores and politically neutralizes its other constitutive feature in the Nazi period: namely, anticommunism. That the very possibility of the Judeocide was absolutely at one with and inseparable from the anticommunist and radical right-wing mission of national socialism is the burden of Arno J. Mayer's conclusive history, *Why Did the Heavens Not Darken?"* (p. 256). But one may observe that an emphasis on the role of anti-Semitism need not be exclusive or serve to downplay the anticommunist impetus of the Nazi regime, although in revisionist circles the stress on Nazi anticommunism may well serve to downplay the importance of anti-Semitism and even (as in the case of Ernst Nolte) to relativize Nazi crimes. Here Jameson misreads Mayer, for it is the manifest burden of the latter's far from conclusive book that anti-

---

ernism, or the Cultural Logic of Late Capitalism (Durham, N.C.: Duke University Press, 1991), p. 258.

Semitism was subordinate to anti-Bolshevism and that the "Judeo-cide" was a derivative or "parasite" of the war on the eastern front.[21]

The reasons for Jameson's transferential investment in de Man may involve a desire to conceptualize a possible alliance between deconstruction and Marxism in terms that Jameson would set. More generally, they may be related to the need for any major theorist to appropriate de Man—and to address the problem posed by his early writings—if his or her own work is to have as broad a resonance as possible in the field of critical theory. Yet these factors, while not irrelevant, are inadequate because de Man seems genuinely to have gotten under Jameson's skin and to have demanded an *Auseinandersetzung* (coming-to-terms). The difficulty is that the transferential problem plays itself out without being thematized, and in Jameson's case the unexamined issue of revisionism in Holocaust studies may be particularly pressing to the extent that there has at times been at least a limited convergence between leftists (such as Arno Mayer) and neo-conservatives on revisionist themes or tendencies.

To confront the question of transference more explicitly may not in itself serve as an effective antidote to revisionism or ensure a better understanding of de Man, early or late, but it may well make such undertakings more possible as well as indicate their bearing on contemporary stakes in interpretation. One justifiable motivation in countering condemnations of de Man is to rebut the indiscriminate idea that de Man's early journalism somehow proves that deconstruction is politically dubious. Indeed, in the recent past the widespread belief that communism has failed and is no longer a serious threat to the West has induced a tendency to seek a stereotypical enemy and scapegoat elsewhere. Preposterous as the gesture may seem, deconstruction has itself at times been cast in this role as the homogeneous, anxiety-producing, politically and socially dangerous other. But the early de Man was not a deconstructionist, however that protean term may be defined, and any attempt to relate his early writings to his later work must rely on more than guilt by association or even the reductive understanding of a general theoretical orientation in terms of a particular series of biographical events. Still, the strained attempt to

[21]See Arno J. Mayer, *Why Did the Heavens Not Darken?: The "Final Solution" in History* (New York: Pantheon, 1988), p. 270 and passim. See also my discussion of this book in Chapter 3.

show that the early journalistic articles were occasions for admirable silence, powerful scenes of self-deconstruction, or even acts of resistance itself unconsciously tends to lend credence to the charge that deconstruction can be used to justify or rewrite anything—a charge that at most applies, in my judgment, to abuses of deconstruction from which no one is altogether immune. The limited argument I have made here is that the types of account provided by Felman, Derrida, and (to some extent) Jameson in their different but related ways tend to deny or excessively mitigate the possible role of trauma and loss, at least with respect to de Man as identificatory object of empowerment; they go too far in their insistence that the desired object remains substantially intact—that de Man (as well as those of us who identify with him) was even in his early articles critical or resisting with respect to Nazism or anti-Semitism and that in any case, his later writings, when properly read (or, in Jameson's case, appropriated), essentially said (or can be made to say) all that needs to be said about his own past, the Holocaust, history, politics, or whatever. What this quasi-theological, fetishistic type of response does is to foreclose the possibility of learning from trauma by acknowledging and mourning the specific losses it involves, thereby at least creating the possibility of elaborating a necessarily problematic and self-questioning post-traumatic "identity"—one wherein one would, for example, attempt to pose in somewhat different and insistently specific terms the question of the actual and desirable relations between deconstruction, politics, and history.

FIVE

 ⤳

Heidegger's Nazi Turn

Martin Heidegger's affiliation with the Nazis has been known since 1933. But until recently it was understood as having been brief in duration, and it was frequently not seen as posing a serious problem for the interpretation of his thought. More widespread concern was, however, caused by Heidegger's postwar silence about the Shoah, a silence broken only by a few comments that were equivocal at best.[1] More recently the research of Hugo Ott and Victor Farías has brought out the depth and duration of Heidegger's engagement as well as the existence of some reprehensible acts he committed in the name of the party.[2] Ott does not attempt an interpretation of Heidegger's

---

[1]In his 1953 republication of the *Introduction to Metaphysics*, which had originally been given as a lecture course in 1935, Heidegger included the following remark: "What, today, finally, is being passed around as the philosophy of National Socialism, but has not the least to do with the inner truth and greatness of the movement (namely the encounter of planetarily determined technology and modern man) goes fishing in these murky waters of 'values and wholes' " (*Einführung in die Metaphysik* [Tübingen: Niemeyer, 1953], p. 152). There is a debate about whether the parenthesis was added in 1953 or existed in the earlier version. In a lecture comment he did not publish, Heidegger is reported to have said: "Agriculture is now a motorized food industry: in its essence it is the same thing as the manufacture of corpses in gas chambers, the same thing as blockades and the reduction of a region to hunger, the same as the manufacture of hydrogen bombs"; cited by Wolfgang Schirmacher, *Technik und Gelassenheit* (Freiburg: Alber, 1983), p. 25, from a typescript of a lecture given by Heidegger before the Bremen Club in December 1949.

[2]Hugo Ott, *Martin Heidegger: Unterwegs zu seiner Biographie* (Frankfurt: Campus, 1988); Victor Farías, *Heidegger et le Nazisme*, trans. Myriam Benarroch and Jean-Baptiste

thought, and Farías's interpretation is very crude and reductive. But even Farías's initiative has had the effect of raising the problem of interpretation for others, and, as Thomas Sheehan has observed,[3] it is no longer possible to read Heidegger as if his relation to the Nazis and his texts of 1933–34 could simply be bracketed in the interest of a discussion of his thought.

French poststructuralists have been heavily indebted to Heidegger (as well as to Nietzsche) and in good part responsible for a renaissance of interest in Heidegger's thought. This is true not only of Jacques Derrida and those close to him, such as Philippe Lacoue-Labarthe and Jean-Luc Nancy, but also of Michel Foucault and Jacques Lacan. Indeed, one could read Derrida in terms of a rewriting or creative "repetition" of Heidegger, at times with significant deconstructive effects. Derrida has been one of the most convincing and influential thinkers in indicating what is still worthy of thought as well as questionable in Heidegger. But his treatment of the political dimension of Heidegger's writings has been, in my judgment, less successful than other aspects of his intervention.

In an essay titled "Heidegger's Silence," Derrida observes:

> For those who understand how to read, there can be no doubt that these readings [his own as well as those of Lacoue-Labarthe and Nancy], in different ways, also express an interest in the political dimension of the text; they attest to an early concern without limiting themselves to non-philosophical documents, which we had, of course, already had at our disposition since 1960–62. We were attempting to understand the way in which Heidegger's difficult work could fit together with what we know of his political engagement.[4]

Yet, until recently, Derrida's interest in the political dimension of Heidegger's work tended to be indirect and allusory, and it was not difficult to read him—and Heidegger through his readings—in a manner that bracketed the political issue, at least with regard to the specific question of Heidegger and the Nazis. In any case, this question was not in the forefront of deconstructive thought or of

Grasset (Lagrasse: Editions Verdier, 1987).

[3] "Heidegger and the Nazis," *New York Review of Books*, 15 June 1988, pp. 38–47.

[4] In *Martin Heidegger and National Socialism*, ed. Günther Neske and Emil Kettering, intro. Karsten Harries, trans. Lisa Harries (1988; New York: Paragon House, 1990), p. 146.

poststructuralism (including the work of Foucault and Lacan) in general. More recently, Derrida attempted to turn to the political issue in a more manifest manner in "Heidegger's Silence" as well as in the book *Of Spirit: Heidegger and the Question*.[5]

In "Heidegger's Silence" Derrida poses a question to those in France who "are suddenly interested in Heidegger's National Socialism":

> Have you read *Being and Time*? For anyone (like some of us) who has begun to read *Being and Time*, anyone who has examined in a questioning and critical, not an orthodox manner, knows very well that this book (like many others) is still waiting to be really read. There are still enormous reserves in Heidegger's text left for further interpretations. It is therefore justified to demand of those who want to draw hasty conclusions from Heidegger's political conduct about his philosophical work that they should at least begin to read. (P. 146)

Later in this chapter I begin in a limited fashion to read or at least to interpret *Being and Time* by noting certain points and entertaining or even putting forth certain contentions about its relation to the pro-Nazi texts of 1933–34. I try to single out in *Being and Time* what I think are particularly important factors that facilitated Heidegger's turn to the Nazis as well as dimensions of the text that may be argued to place this turn in question. I also allude to the vast problem of Heidegger's so-called post-*Kehre* writings in relation to *Being and Time* and the texts of 1933–34.

A provocative but somewhat reductive attempt to contextualize Heidegger's thought was made by Pierre Bourdieu, who had the merit of stressing the affinities between Heidegger and conservative revolutionaries such as Carl Schmitt, Moeller van den Bruck, Oswald Spengler, Ernst Jünger, and Ernst Niekisch.[6] The contextual approach has been aptly epitomized and carried forward by Richard Wolin in his important book *The Politics of Being: The Political Thought of Martin Heidegger*.[7] In Wolin, as in Bourdieu, contextualization is made to serve an emphatic, decisive interpretation of the integral relations between Heidegger's turn to the Nazis and his philosophy in a text such

[5]Trans. Geoffrey Bennington and Rachel Bowlby (1987; Chicago: University of Chicago Press, 1989).

[6]*L'Ontologie politique de Martin Heidegger* (Paris: Editions de Minuit, 1988).

[7]New York: Columbia University Press, 1990.

as *Being and Time* as well as in his post-Kehre writings. Wolin has also collected the relevant texts of 1933–34 as well as related writings from a variety of figures in *The Heidegger Controversy: A Critical Reader*.[8] This collection contains more compromising material than does the collection edited by Günther Neske and Emil Kettering, which tends to leave the reader with a less damaging impression of Heidegger. But both collections are well worth reading. My own problem in interpretation is that I tend to believe two somewhat incompatible things: I share with Derrida the conviction that there is much in Heidegger worthy of thought. I also tend to agree with much in Wolin, although I find his politically oriented, contextualizing interpretation excessively one-dimensional.

Wolin provides pertinent material as well as arguments that are worth taking seriously. He has the special merit of bringing out the importance of Jünger for Heidegger's understanding of modernity, particularly in the 1930s, and his collection includes Jünger's important essay "Total Mobilization."[9] Yet despite some qualifications, Wolin's interpretation of *Being and Time* is narrowly teleological with respect to the Nazi engagement, and his reading of the post-Kehre work sees it by and large as symptomatic of that engagement. Wolin does not argue that *Being and Time* was simply proto-Nazi or that the post-Kehre work should be branded as Nazism by any other name. But he does see strong and meaningful relations between Heidegger's Nazi commitment and his philosophical thought, although the precise nature of these relations is never formulated with the precision and consistency one might desire. *Being and Time* was in some sense programmed to lead to the decision in favor of the Nazis—an interpretation epitomized in Wolin's overly decisive translation of the key term "Entschlossenheit" (generally translated as "resoluteness") as "resolute decision," "resolve," or "decisiveness"—terms that signal what is for Wolin the decisionist, conservative-revolutionary philosophy behind *Being and Time*.[10] Indeed, to make his own case, Wolin

---

[8]New York: Columbia University Press, 1991. My references to the relevant writings of Heidegger are given parenthetically in the text, cited as either "W" (Wolin, ed.) or "N and K" (Neske and Kettering, eds.) followed by the page number.

[9]As Wolin notes on p. 121 of *The Heidegger Controversy*, Heidegger himself mentioned Jünger's significance in his 1945 essay "The Rectorship 1933/34: Facts and Thoughts," which can be found in Neske and Kettering, pp. 15–32. *The Heidegger Controversy* (pp. 61–66) contains a translation of Heidegger's letter to the rector of Freiburg University, 4 November 1945, in which Heidegger requests reinstatement in his professorial duties.

[10]Wolin does recognize in passing (*The Politics of Being*, p. 51) the relation of *Entschlo-*

may be led to repeat what he sees as one of the most dubious aspects of Heidegger's thought—its decisionism.

Wolin also maintains that Derrida in *Of Spirit* "is seduced by the *philosophical veneer* of Heidegger's Rectoral Address—the perfunctory allusions to 'spirit,' the glory of the 'Greek beginning,' and so on; as if this veneer itself could explain the philosopher's Nazism better than the rhetorical-ideological core of the speech, which Derrida strangely refuses to analyze. In truth, what is unique about Heidegger's speech...is that one finds for the first time in his work the awkward and unabashed attempt to fuse traditional philosophical motifs with the Nazi discourse of *Sturm* and *Kampf*" (p. 157).[11] Wolin does not do full justice to the argument of Derrida's *Of Spirit*. The book is brilliant in delineating the role of the concept of spirit in Heidegger and in Western thought more generally, and it is suggestive in tracing the relation between spirit and fire (although perhaps too reticent in not explicitly exploring the seemingly obvious implication of this correlation for "the question"). Moreover, Nazi ideologists, such as Alfred Rosenberg, did make an important attempt to represent Nazism as a "spiritual" movement that counteracted the materialism of both Marxism and capitalism. Thus, it is not beside the point to analyze closely, as Derrida does, Heidegger's varying uses over time of the concept of spirit. The invocation of "spirit" also made the Rectoral Address more palatable to traditional conservatives and humanists and in this sense served a significant rhetorical function in legitimating Nazism. But, as Derrida himself realizes, others might appeal to "spirit" in the critique of Nazism as a corruption of "spirit." In 1933–34 there was for Heidegger sufficient congruence between the actuality of the Nazi movement and his idealized view of its potential to warrant active commitment, whereas after this time the two presumably diverged for him, and an analysis of his uses of spirit may illuminate this movement in his thought. Still, the reliance on the concept of spirit does not fully explain Heidegger's behavior. Its role in the Rectoral Address may tell us as much about his attempt to situate himself vis-à-vis other theorists as about the bases of his affiliation.

It is also noteworthy that appeals to spirit are important in

---

ssenheit to *Erschlossenheit* ("disclosedness") as well as the fact that the former term as "unclosedness" "literally signifies Dasein's 'openness for Being.' " But this recognition has little effect on his interpretation.

[11] The Rectoral Address, or "The Self-Assertion of the German University," is translated in both W, pp. 29–38, and N and K, pp. 5–13.

Heidegger's own letter to the rector of the University of Freiburg dated 4 November 1945, where he sought reinstatement in his professorial duties. In stressing the role of "spirit," Derrida to some extent follows Heidegger's self-interpretation, which in the context of the latter's letter had manifestly apologetic functions. Heidegger asserts that, in accepting the rectorship "reluctantly and in the interest of the university alone," he was "nevertheless absolutely convinced that an autonomous alliance of intellectuals [*der Geistigen*] could deepen and transform a number of essential elements of the 'National Socialist movement' and thereby contribute in its own way to overcoming Europe's disarray and the crisis of the Western Spirit" (W, pp. 62–63). In a rather frank and naive admission of his desire to play philosophical tutor to the Führer and to lead the leader, he goes on to claim that it was "precisely because in the realm of the sciences of spirit so-called 'impossible' persons strove to assert their power and influence on the 'movement' that it seemed to me necessary to emphasize essentially spiritual goals and horizons and to try, on the basis of Western responsibility, to further their influence and reality" (W, p. 62). He also argues that in the first semester of teaching following his resignation from the rectorship, he "sought to show that language was not the biological-racial essence of man, but conversely, that the essence of man was based in language as a basic reality of spirit" (W, p. 64). Moreover, he presents his series of lectures and courses on Nietzsche, beginning in 1936, as "a declaration of spiritual resistance" (W, p. 65). He concludes his letter in this way:

> There was nothing special about my spiritual resistance during the last eleven years [that is, 1934–45]. However, if crude claims continue to be advanced that numerous students had been 'enticed' toward 'National Socialism' by my year as rector, justice requires that one at least recognize that between 1934 and 1944 thousands of students were trained to reflect on the metaphysical basis of our age and that I opened their eyes to the world of spirit and its great traditions in the history of the West. (W, p. 66)

Even if one agrees with aspects of Heidegger's self-interpretation, the fact remains that it is extremely misleading in creating the impression that his affiliation with the Nazis was a passing, even ephemeral, event and that from 1934 on, his acts were to be seen unequivocally as modes of spiritual resistance. Indeed, the very linkage of "spirit" and "resistance" in Heidegger's self-interpretation should make one especially wary in invoking the concept of "spirit" in trying to account for his turn to the Nazis. Here it should be noted that although Derrida in a sense follows Heidegger in stressing the concept of spirit and its role in Heidegger's opposition to racial biologism, his reading tends to go against Heidegger's use of the concept, for Derrida creates the impression that Heidegger's engagement had something to do with his uncritical, undeconstructive invocation of the concept of spirit in his own voice—a concept that in this usage was if anything an inadequate force of resistance.

Heidegger in turning to the Nazis was clearly concerned about a crisis in the Western spirit as an element in a general crisis, but it is important to try to see more fully how he understood this crisis and the needed response to it. Heidegger envisioned this crisis as essential and almost all-consuming—something of apocalyptic proportions. And the response to it had to be a movement that promised a radical if not total breakthrough to an essentially transformed mode of being—in a sense a response to an encompassing trauma in civilization and culture through a traumatic "repetition" of a promise that arose for the West in Greece. In 1933–34, Heidegger saw the Nazis as the bearers of this promise in spite of the extremely objectionable aspects of their movement, to which he was not altogether blind. As he put it in 1945 in "The Rectorate 1933/34: Facts and Thoughts": "At the time, I saw in the movement that had come to power the possibility of an inner self-collection and of a renewal of the people [*Volk*], and a path toward the discovery of its historical-Western purpose. I believed that the university, renewing itself, might also be called to significantly participate in the inner self-correction of the people" (N and K, p. 17). Or again: "The rectorate was an attempt to see something in the movement that had come to power, beyond all its failings and crudeness, that was much more far-reaching and that could perhaps one day bring a concentration on the Germans' Western historical essence" (N and K, p. 29). In the *Spiegel* interview ("Only a God Can Save Us")—an interview given in 1966 but published only after his death in 1976—Heidegger responds to a question that points out that in 1933 he had "the feeling that here is something new, here is a new dawn." Heidegger states: "That is right. It's not that I had spoken only for the sake of appearances; I also saw such a possibility" (W, p. 97).[12]

[12]The *Spiegel* interview is also translated in N and K, pp. 41–66.

It is noteworthy that neither in his letter to the rector of the University of Freiburg nor in his *Spiegel* interview did Heidegger discuss the Shoah. In "Heidegger's Silence," Derrida puts forth what he terms a "hypothesis" in response to a question he poses: "What would have happened if Heidegger had said something [about Auschwitz], and what could he have said?" (N and K, p. 147). Derrida continues:

> Let us assume that Heidegger had not only said about 1933 "I have made a very stupid mistake" but also "Auschwitz is the absolute horror; it is what I fundamentally condemn." Such a statement is familiar to all of us. What would have happened then? He would probably have immediately received an absolution. The files on Heidegger, on the connection between his thought and the events of so-called National Socialism, would have been closed. (N and K, p. 147)

The result would presumably have been that "it would not be necessary for us to ask today what affinities, synchronisms of thinking, and common roots Heidegger's thinking could have with National Socialism, which is still an 'unthought' phenomenon." For Derrida, "Heidegger's horrible, perhaps inexcusable silence . . . leaves us the commandment to think what he himself did not think" (N and K, p. 147). Karsten Harries, in his generally insightful introduction to the volume edited by Neske and Kettering, reinforces Derrida's questions:

> What could he have said? What should he have said? That he abhorred the horror of Auschwitz and felt profoundly ashamed for once having aligned himself with those responsible? Derrida may well be right to suggest that, had he done so, we probably would no longer be occupying ourselves with the question of the significance of Heidegger's involvement with the Nazis. Would this constitute a more adequate response to the challenge of his thought? To the challenge of the Holocaust? Heidegger's silence leaves us the task of thinking what he himself could not or would not think. (Pp. xxxi-xxxii)

Heidegger may well leave us with a task—in certain ways an impossible task—but this fact does not imply that he should not have taken part in it himself. The difficulty with Derrida's "hypothesis" and the conclusions he draws from it is that they easily function apologetically as a way of excusing Heidegger's "perhaps inexcusable" silence. Of crucial importance would be precisely how Heidegger addressed Auschwitz and the problem of silence with respect to it, as well as the relation of both to what he saw as the "new dawn" promised by the Nazi movement. A perfunctory, conventionalized statement of the sort Derrida postulates would indeed have been suspicious, but it is not the only kind of statement one can envision. And a statement from Heidegger would have closed the book on the issue only for those who would take it as the last word by placing Heidegger in a quasi-divine position. Everything in Derrida's own work would lead one to argue that a statement by Heidegger would have constituted a supplementary, not a conclusive, text, perhaps of special interest given its source but in no sense eliminating the need for further discussion.

Through what may be a process of projective identification, Derrida makes another contestable statement about why Heidegger kept silent: "Perhaps Heidegger thought: I can only voice a condemnation of National Socialism if it is possible for me to do so in a language not only at the peak of what I have already said, but also at the peak of what has happened here. He was incapable of doing this. And perhaps his silence is an honest form of admitting he was incapable of it" (N and K, p. 148). In response to this perhaps overly generous speculation, one may remark that one would have preferred Heidegger rather than Derrida to have said at least this much. But one may also suggest that it is questionable to contend, however speculatively, that all comments must satisfy the criterion of being at a rarely attained level of achievement or even of sublimity. Postulating such a criterion might be taken to imply that no one could conceivably be in a position to say anything, and it might even be seen as invoking inappropriate aesthetic or intellectual criteria in a case where ethical and ethicopolitical considerations should be primary. In any event, it would excessively narrow the range of discourse and perhaps relegate certain crucial areas, such as society and politics, to silence or at best to indirect, allusory, and extremely limited commentary that could conceivably attain a certain poetic and/or philosophical "peak." Derrida's stricture may indeed help to explain why eminent thinkers have said so little of interest or note about certain crucial problems—why meta-metaphysical thought, even when it is preoccupied with deconstructing metaphysics, tends to remain within a relatively restricted orbit that is at times sublime but at other times extremely involuted and convoluted as well as out of touch with certain problems. Here one might insist that the views of a Heidegger (or a Derrida) are of interest even—

perhaps particularly—if they are not at the "peak" of their "philosophical" work precisely insofar as they clarify certain issues, engender a livable rhythm in thought (one does not think or live on peaks alone), and underscore the importance of sociopolitical and ethical issues, although the treatment of such issues may not, and in certain ways should not, achieve effects of sublimity. Moreover, in the case of Heidegger, silence may lead to a hypothesis entertaining less noble motives than those about which Derrida speculates—for example, a tendency to deny, repress, and distort unflattering aspects of the past; an inability to admit mistakes; an insensitivity to the fate of the Jews and other victims of the Shoah in the face of a superordinate commitment to Germany, of a certain idea of the West, and of lingering romantic-apocalyptic illusions about salvation and the unrealized potential of the Nazi movement. (These speculations may be reinforced by certain evasive, distorting, and dubious aspects of Heidegger's self-commentaries, notably in "The Rectorate 1933/34: Facts and Thoughts" and the *Spiegel* interview.) Silence is always open to multiple interpretations, and a partial way of controlling or limiting them is to frame silence by trying to say why it may be necessary or desirable.

Derrida also observes:

> Anyone who wants to find something in [Heidegger's] texts on the basis of which one could condemn not only the inner truth of this powerful movement [national socialism] but also its fall and its ruin will be able to find it. He was unable to say anything more about it. It is up to us to say more than "Auschwitz is the absolute horror, one of the absolute horrors in the history of humanity." If we are able to say more, then we should say more. The commandment is, I believe, inscribed in the most horrible and yet perhaps most valuable chance in Heidegger's legacy. (N and K, p. 148)

Unable or unwilling?—that question is difficult to answer with reference to Heidegger's silence. I cannot follow Derrida's "commandment" here or live up to what seems to be the expectation his comments create about saying more. I do want, however, to address the issue of Heidegger's writings and speeches of 1933–34 and then turn, however inadequately, to *Being and Time*. My thesis is that *Being and Time* in significant ways laid itself open to the uses Heidegger made of it in the writings and speeches of 1933–34 but that, as Derrida intimates, it also harbored important tendencies that enable one to place those uses in question. The specific reading and use of *Being and Time* that took place in the texts of 1933–34 was not merely possible; it happened, and it happened on the part of a rather competent reader who was also the author of *Being and Time*. In one sense, the texts of 1933–34 present a veritable "witches' brew" in which concepts and themes of the 1927 work were read in extremely "decisive" fashion and mixed with Nazi ideology and propaganda. The combination of jargons is very powerful in effect. But the combination as well as the tendencies in *Being and Time* that allowed or even invited it may also be contested on the basis of *Being and Time* itself. The latter provides material for the critique of certain of its own tendencies as well as for the "decisive," relatively one-dimensional use made of them in 1933–34. To put my argument in overly simple terms (which I qualify later): *Being and Time* was written for thinkers and especially for philosophers. The writings and speeches of 1933–34 were addressed to Nazis and to philosophers who wanted to justify a commitment to the Nazis.

Let us look briefly at the writings and speeches of 1933–34, which are by now relatively well known, and quote certain passages from them. These texts invoke and at times redefine the concept of spirit, but they do so in the interest of placing it—and the university as well—within the program of *Gleichschaltung* (synchronization or coordination) under the Volk, the Nazi party, and its Führer. In these texts Heidegger hardly appears "reluctant" in his role as rector and would seem to be making a bid to orient the movement in the philosophico-redemptive direction he thought it should take. In a speech of 30 June 1933, given as part of a series of political lectures organized by the Heidelberg Student Association, he even invokes the concept of race in the general sense of *Geschlecht* but without tying it to anti-Semitism:

> The student is forced out into the uncertainty of all things, in which the necessity of engagement [*Einsatz*] is grounded. *University study must again become a risk* [*Wagnis*], not a refuge for the cowardly. Whoever does not survive the battle, lies where he falls. The new courage must accustom itself to steadfastness, for the battle for the institutions where our leaders are educated will continue for a long time. It will be fought out of the strengths of the new Reich that Chancellor Hitler will bring to reality. A hard race [*Geschlecht*] with no thought of self must fight this battle, a race that lives from constant testing and that remains directed towards the goal to which it has committed itself. It is a battle to

determine who shall be the *teachers* and *leaders* at the university [*ein Kampf um die Gestalt des Lehrers und des Führers an der Universität*]. (W, p. 45)

Heidegger made several appeals to Germans to support the plebiscite of 12 November 1933 called by Hitler to sanction (after the fact) Germany's withdrawal from the League of Nations. In one of them Heidegger states quite simply: "The Führer alone *is* the present and future German reality and its law. Learn to know ever more deeply: from now on every single thing demands decision, and every action responsibility. Heil Hitler!" (W, p. 47). A particularly ominous passage occurs in an address Heidegger gave at an election rally held by German university professors in Leipzig to support the upcoming plebiscite:

> We have declared our independence from the idol of thought that is without foundation and power. We see the end of the philosophy that serves such thought. We are certain that the clear hardness and the sure, steady competency [*werkgerechte Sicherheit*] of unyielding, simple questioning about the essence of Being are returning. For a *völkische* Wissenschaft [sic], the courage either to grow or to be destroyed in confrontation with Being [*dem Seienden*] which is the first form of courage, is the innermost motive for questioning. For courage lures one forward; courage frees itself from what has been up to now; courage risks the unaccustomed and the incalculable. For us, questioning is not the unconstrained play of curiosity. Nor is questioning the stubborn insistence on doubt at any price. For us, questioning means: exposing oneself to the sublimity of things and their laws; it means: not closing oneself off to the terror of the untamed and to the confusion of darkness. To be sure, it is for the sake of this questioning that we question, and *not* to serve those who have grown tired and their complacent yearning for comfortable answers. We know: the courage to question, to experience the abysses of existence and to endure the abysses of existence, is in itself already a *higher* answer than any of the all-too-cheap answers afforded by artificial systems of thought. (W, p. 51)

This passage is especially disturbing in its narrowly political coding of a radical questioning of Being that is seen explicitly in terms of self-exposure to sublimity and the "abysses of existence," "not closing oneself off to the terror of the untamed and to the confusion of darkness." I shall return to the point that Heidegger, while by and large silent about the Holocaust, did not in his public addresses or writing (including his most militantly pro-Nazi texts) defend anti-Semitism and that his philosophical thought is in certain ways incompatible with a logic of scapegoating, which is essential for anti-Semitism and related forms of victimization and persecution. But in a passage such as the one just quoted, Heidegger is close to the most dubious ideological application of a philosophy stressing the sublime, the uncanny, the abysss, the untamed, and darkness—one that could well appeal to the perpetrators of the most extreme Nazi crimes. This application or even its possibility may be enough to place in question any such philosophy that is not extremely careful to qualify its openness to the sublime or the abyss both with specific guards against abuses and with an insistence on the countervailing role of normative limits.

Of all his writings and speeches of 1933–34, the Rectoral Address ("The Self-Assertion of the German University") has the greatest claim to philosophical status, and it contained elements that Heidegger never renounced. But it would be deceptive to follow Heidegger in his inclination to give a special status to the Rectoral Address and to isolate it from his other speeches and writings of 1933–34. Indeed, it existed on the cusp between philosophy and propaganda and for this very reason may have been especially effective in legitimating a pro-Nazi commitment. It employs a technique familiar from Heidegger's more philosophical works: his tendency to take up and rework a prevalent term (such as "spirit") until it acquires a distinctively Heideggerian meaning. Yet in important ways the Rectoral Address resonates with other, more manifestly propagandistic pieces of 1933–34, and it combines seemingly philosophical techniques with many dubious gestures, including an affirmative understanding of the new Student Law (intended to organize university students in accordance with the *Führerprinzip*) as a self-placement and initial definition of the students' "essence" (W, p. 34); a linkage of "the will to be a spiritual Volk" with an exposure to "the extreme questionableness of its own existence" (p. 35); a pervasive, chauvinistic idea of Germany's chosen status as heir of the Greeks and vehicle of a redemptive world-historical mission; and an apocalyptic sense of the need for salvation at a time "when the spiritual strength of the West fails and the West starts to come apart at the seams, when this moribund pseudocivilization collapses into itself, pulling all forces into confusion and allowing them to suffocate in madness" (p. 38). But along with further dubious elements that I note later, one of the most questionable moves comes in a passage the second sentence of which Heidegger himself quoted with approval in his 1935 *Introduction to Metaphysics* (*Einführung in die Metaphysik*):

> If we will the essence of science in the sense of *the questioning, unsheltered standing firm in the midst of the uncertainty of the totality of being,* then *this* will to essence will create for our Volk a world of the innermost and most extreme danger, i.e., a truly *spiritual* world. For "spirit" is neither empty acumen nor the noncommittal play of wit nor the busy practice of never-ending rational analysis nor even world reason; rather, spirit is the determined resolve to the essence of Being, a resolve that is attuned to origins and knowing [*wissende Entschlossenheit zum Wesen des Seins*]. And the *spiritual world* of a Volk is not its cultural superstructure, just as little as it is its arsenal of useful knowledge [*Kentnisse*] and values; rather, it is the power that comes from preserving at the most profound level the forces that are rooted in the soil and blood of a Volk, the power to arouse most inwardly and to shake most extensively the Volk's existence. A spiritual world alone will guarantee our Volk greatness. For it will make the constant decision between the will to greatness and the toleration of decline the law that establishes the pace for the march upon which our Volk has embarked on the way to its future history. (W, pp. 33–34)

This passage resonates in obvious ways with the one quoted above from the address at the Leipzig election rally. And although he does not explicitly defend anti-Semitism, Heidegger contrasts profound, volkish German "spirit," as a knowing resolve or openness (Entschlossenheit) to the essence of Being, with traits ("empty acumen," "the noncommittal play of wit," "the busy practice of never-ending rational analysis") culturally coded as Jewish and as characteristics of the shallow intellectual or of French civilization. Moreover, "spirit" in this passage hardly seems to be a force of resistance. It is explicitly defined in terms of a conception of essence and greatness that is referred to blood and soil as well as to the march of the Volk on the way to its future history. "Spirit" here seems to be thoroughly *gleichgeschaltet* (coordinated). And the opposition of "spirit" to "cultural superstructure," "useful knowledge," and "values" aligns it with an insistent, politically charged inclination to essentialize and mythologize.

In his *Spiegel* interview, Heidegger takes his distance from a statement that the interviewer quotes: "The Führer himself and he alone *is* the present and future German reality and its rule." He insists that "these sentences are not found in the rectoral address, but only in the local *Freiburg Students* [sic] *Newspaper*," and he asserts: "I would today no longer write the sentences which you cite. Even by 1934 I no longer said such things" (W, p. 96). In a passage included in the Neske and Kettering but not in the Wolin edition, Heidegger follows these words with the comments: "But today, and today more resolutely than ever, I would repeat the speech on the 'Self-Assertion of the German University,' though admittedly without referring to nationalism. Society has taken the place of the nation [*Volk*]. However, the speech would be just as much of a waste of breath today as it was then" (N and K, p. 46). "Nation" is of course an inadequate translation of "Volk." But the pertinent point is that the *Volk* is essential to the Rectoral Address as to other of Heidegger's texts of 1933–34, and it is difficult to see how one could strike out references to it without further ado. In any event, Heidegger does continue to affirm certain aspects of the Rectoral Address, although he often interprets it in contestable if not downright misleading and self-serving ways. For example, he maintains that the self-assertion of the university "goes against the so-called 'political science' " in the sense of politicized science (W, p. 95). Yet although Heidegger did oppose certain politicizations of science, most notably the biological-racial view of figures such as Ernst Kriek and Alfred Rosenberg, his conception of science and the university in the Rectoral Address was highly politicized and not inconsistent with the overall Nazi project of Gleichschaltung, which Heidegger, like other theorists, wanted to take in his own rather vaguely conceived direction. He also refers to the three "services" he enumerates in the address—labor, the military, and science—and quite gratuitously asserts: "If you read it [the Rectoral Address] carefully, you will see that the 'service of knowledge' does, to be sure, stand in the third place in the enumeration, but in terms of its meaning it is first. One ought to remember that work and the military, like every human activity, are grounded in knowledge and are enlightened by it" (W, p. 96).

In "The Rectorate 1933/34: Facts and Thoughts," Heidegger glosses another dubious aspect of the Rectoral Address in a questionable manner. He maintains that "the attitude of reflection and questioning is oriented toward 'battle' " but that "battle" [*Kampf*] must be understood as *polemos* in the sense of Heraclitus, fragment 53 (N and K, pp. 21–22). In the Rectoral Address, there are indeed allusions to the Greeks, but the insistent and rather militant references to Kampf are explicitly linked to the name of Karl von Clausewitz, not to Heraclitus (W, p. 37). It is nonetheless the case that even in the *Spiegel* interview, Heidegger is willing to stand behind the statement in the Rectoral Address that "the much-sung 'academic freedom' is driven out of the German university. This freedom was false because it was only negative" (W, p. 94). He fails to note that the elimination of academic freedom was part and parcel of the project of Gleichschaltung. In the *Spiegel* interview, Heidegger is also willing to assert that he is not "convinced" that democracy is the political system best "accommodate[d]" to "the global movement of modern technology" (W, p. 104).

A final point may be made about the Rectoral Address. One of the most outlandish and politically tendentious translations and interpretations occurs at the very end of the address. Heidegger does not comment on it in his later reflections. It involves a reference to "the ancient wisdom of the Greeks, " specifically to a statement in Plato's *Republic* (497d, 9). In Paul Shorey's translation, this statement reads: "For all great things are precarious."[13] Heidegger translates it to mean: "All that is great stands in the storm." Through the transparent allusion, Heidegger positions the Nazis as the agents of the longed-for "repetition" of the Greek origin.

It is nonetheless important to stress the point that even in his extremely tendentious texts of 1933–34, Heidegger did not explicitly defend anti-Semitism or racism, although he did use concepts and oppositions that had dubious cultural codings. His philosophical thought, although it occasionally contains some uncontrolled connotations (notably in the indictment of the everyday, the "they," and idle chatter [*Gerede*]), may be argued to place the assumptions of anti-Semitism and racism in radical doubt other than through a suspect use of the concept of spirit. These points are significant insofar as racism was a crucial basis of the Nazi state. In their important book *The Racial State: Germany 1933–1945*, Michael Burleigh and Wolfgang Wippermann argue that Nazi social policy "was designed to achieve a global remodelling of society in accordance with racial criteria."[14] They assert:

[13]*The Collected Dialogues of Plato*, ed. Edith Hamilton and Huntington Cairns (Princeton: Princeton University Press, 1973), p. 733.

[14]New York: Cambridge University Press, 1991. It is noteworthy that Burleigh and

Racialism became the official doctrine of the Nazi state. Notwithstanding marked differences in the theoretical content of the racism avowed by the regime's individual agencies, the object was to create a utopian society organized in accordance with the principles of race.

A key concern in this endeavor was the 'purification of the body of the nation' from 'alien,' 'hereditarily ill,' or 'asocial' 'elements'. Racial 'purification' was an integral part of wider 'social' policies designed to create a 'healthy' performance-oriented 'Aryan' 'national community'. (P. 3)

I would extend Burleigh and Wippermann's argument to make the point that the importance of race—underwritten by pseudoscience and coordinated with scapegoating, victimization, and ritualistic "purification"—brings out the limitation of the understanding of Nazism in terms of an aesthetic ideology (or national aestheticism and the aestheticization of politics). Aestheticization played a problematic role in the Nazi regime, and it could well be conjoined with racism and aspects of a secular religiosity that seemed to involve distorted sacrificialism. But the latter phenomena cannot simply be reduced to aesthetic ideology or seen as mere accidents subordinated to its "essential" status. Indeed, to employ the concept of aesthetic ideology (or its analogues) as one's essential category in interpreting Nazism itself bespeaks an excessively aestheticizing perspective, for it imposes a false unity on complex phenomena and begs the question of the relations among aesthetics, politics, and secularized religion in Nazi ideology and practice. In addition, Heidegger was himself never aware of the extent to which his attempt to extricate what he saw as the promise of national socialism from the "failings and crudeness" of the regime was illusory, at least insofar as the "failings and crudeness" referred to racism and attendant forms of scapegoating and victimization. One could not simply subtract the latter and affirm the remainder because racism and what came with it were crucial if not essential to the regime and intimately bound up with its ultimately genocidal ideology and policies. Nor did Heidegger himself see clearly how his own thought, to the extent that it undermined the bases of racism and scapegoating, also undermined not only his early hopes but also his lingering illusions about the promise of the Nazis.

Let us turn to *Being and Time* (1927).[15] I begin by noting that the text

---

Wippermann do not mention Heidegger although they do criticize Hegel.

[15]Trans. John Macquarrie and Edward Robinson (New York: Harper and Row, 1962).

left itself open to, if it did not invite, the uses Heidegger made of it in 1933–34 in at least two major ways. First, it elaborates a philosophy of process, possibility, and openness to the future, and one may ask whether there is a sufficient stress on the differential need for normative limits in different areas of society and culture. There is also an unsituated, almost numbing tendency to dwell on the crucial problems of the uncanny, anxiety, and Being-toward-death. Second, the text suffers from inadequate self-contextualization and an underspecification of arguments that make it liable to the blind, unthematized assimilation of ideologically coded motifs. At times its discourse even falls prey to a portentous vagueness that is one of Heidegger's most dubious legacies.

Inadequate self-contextualization is particularly pronounced in the text's relation to the thought of conservative-revolutionaries, notably in its jeremiad against the everyday, the "they," and idle chatter—indeed, against every homogeneously perceived aspect of the practice of everyday life.[16] Here the discourse of *Being and Time* resonates with the conservative-revolutionary indictment of modernity, mass society, and mass culture as well as with the ill-defined longing for a redemptive utopia of greater authenticity that would "repeat" the possibilities of a lost golden age. In addition, this indiscriminate form of "culture critique" is reinforced or doubled by the uncritical role of secularized and displaced Christian motifs whose provenance and precise nature are not thematized as a problem—motifs such as fallenness, originary guilt, the call of conscience, and the everyday as the locus of divertissement. In this respect the text often reads like an evacuated secular version of extreme world-negating, ascetic, tran-

---

[16]It would be interesting to compare and contrast Heidegger's treatment of the everyday with that of Michel de Certeau in *The Practice of Everyday Life* (Berkeley: University of California Press, 1984). De Certeau at times goes to the opposite extreme of a rather uncritical celebration of putative tactics of resistance to dominant culture as they appear in everyday life. It should be noted that one relatively specific aspect of Heidegger's critique is of averageness (*Durchschnittlichkeit*) as a particular modality of everydayness in which the statistical average becomes the regulative norm and exceptions are ruled out or pathologized. In averageness, one has "an animus against the exceptional," a "levelling down of possibilities," and a "tendency to take things easy and make them easy" (p. 165). Here Heidegger looks back to Kierkegaard and forward to Foucault. Indeed, Heidegger's animus against the diversions of the everyday in mass society (as well as other aspects of his account) may owe as much or more to Kierkegaard as to contemporary conservative-revolutionaries. This duality of unthematized reference complicates the problem of interpretation insofar as Kierkegaard would be mischaracterized if one were to see him as a conservative-revolutionary ideologist.

scendental Christianity in the Augustinian (if not the Gnostic) tradition.

One may well argue that the reading of *Being and Time* in terms of either conservative-revolutionary ideology or unthematized, displaced Christian motifs is partial and even contestable. (Heidegger himself argued against the latter interpretation in his "Letter on Humanism" [1947].)[17] But the very fact that Heidegger did not explicitly thematize the problem of the relation of his argument to prevalent ideologies did nothing to avoid—and may even have actively invited—such a reading. *Being and Time* presents itself solely as "the business of philosophers" (p. 24), and this truncated self-understanding and delimited sense of intertextuality left it blind to the play of other ideological forces.

As I intimated earlier, however, there is the wherewithal in *Being and Time* to counteract a conservative-revolutionary reading as well as the more trenchantly pro-Nazi use Heidegger made of the text in 1933–34. The philosophy of *Being and Time* is one of process and possibility, but the reflective, openly questioning, and self-questioning tenor in which problems are discussed, as well as an occasionally explicit statement, does serve as a guardrail against certain blatantly abusive readings. One may well question the text's underspecified and rashly generalized or even essentialized arguments, especially with reference to social and political criticism. And one may suspect its unsituated and relatively unchecked insistence on certain problems, such as the uncanny and Being-toward-death. But the way in which inquiry proceeds is distant from dogmatism, authoritarian closure, and the scapegoating of the other. As Heidegger explicitly puts it, "Existential Interpretation will never seek to take over any authoritarian pronouncement as to those things which, from an existentiell point of view, are possible or binding" (p. 360). Yet this is precisely what Heidegger himself attempted to do in his use of *Being and Time* in 1933–34. Furthermore, certain tensions in *Being and Time* are themselves not simply debilitating but enabling in keeping the text open and inviting readers to argue with it and attempt to carry further the process of thought it initiates—perhaps in directions other than those Heidegger pursues. I want to discuss some of these tensions that place *Being and Time* in a discursive context that is significantly

---

[17]Included in *Basic Writings*, ed. David Farrell Krell (New York: Harper and Row, 1977), pp. 193–242. See especially p. 207.

different—at times worlds apart—from that of the ideologically saturated, stereotypical pro-Nazi texts of 1933–34.

The texts of 1933–34 effect a one-dimensional "ontic" reduction and dogmatic application of the ontology and existential analytic of *Being and Time*. Yet in *Being and Time* there is a tension, even an undecidability, in the relation between the ontological and the ontic. The text presents itself as fundamental ontology, which is more primordial (*ursprünglich*) than the ontical inquiry of the positive sciences. It elaborates "basic concepts" that "determine the way in which we get an understanding beforehand of the area of subject-matter underlying all the objects a science takes as its theme, and all positive investigation is guided by this understanding" (p. 30). In a sense, fundamental ontology and the existential analytic of *Dasein* that is its *via regia* provide "*a priori* conditions" for sciences and regional ontologies (p. 31). But does this mean that a binary opposition separates the ontological from the ontic and that fundamental ontology occupies a separate sphere of inquiry that excludes investigation of the ontic? At times one may be tempted to draw this conclusion. But the more general argument of *Being and Time* would instead lead to the notion that the relation between the ontological and the ontic is constitutive of a problematic distinction—not a pure binary opposition—and that the ontological involves a particular way of questioning the ontic in terms of the latter's unexamined assumptions and conditions of possibility. Indeed, the relation between the ontological and the ontic might well be seen in terms of a process of mutual questioning and interrogation, even involving a possibility that Heidegger's animus against the everyday prevents him from entertaining: the possibility that the common sense so active in the everydayness he criticizes may itself question ontological inquiry, for example, by bringing it down to earth and forcing it to make sustained contact with problems that are commonly perceived as significant.[18] In spite of his blindness to this possibility, Heidegger's argument would nonetheless imply that the ontological and the ontic should not be conflated but neither can they be

[18]Heidegger himself one-sidedly stresses the way existential analysis does violence to common sense or at least seems to do so from the viewpoint of common sense. "Existential analysis . . . constantly has the character of *doing violence* [*Gewaltsamkeit*], whether to the claims of the everyday interpretation or to its complacency and its tranquilized obviousness. . . . Common sense misunderstands understanding. And *therefore* common sense must necessarily pass off as 'violent' anything that lies beyond the reach of its understanding, or any attempt to go out so far" (pp. 359, 363). The very exaggeration in his emphases almost prompts their reversal.

purely dissociated from or opposed to each other. Here a footnote in *Being and Time* is pertinent, for it also bears on Heidegger's critique of radical constructivism and his insistence that all understanding depends on preunderstanding and implication in a context or life-world.

> But to disclose the *a priori* is not to make an '*a-prioristic*' construction. Edmund Husserl has not only enabled us to understand once more the meaning of any genuine philosophical empiricism; he has also given us the necessary tools. '*A-priorism*' is the method of every scientific philosophy which understands itself. There is nothing constructivistic about it. But for this very reason *a priori* research requires that the phenomenal basis be properly prepared. The horizon which is closest to us, and which must be made ready for the analytic of *Dasein*, lies in its average everydayness. (P. 490n)

In this sense one might argue that Heidegger did not properly prepare the phenomenal basis of his critique of average everydayness insofar as he did not thematize the relation of the critique to conservative-revolutionary and displaced Christian motifs. More generally, one might argue that ontological inquiry may not simply bracket the ontic or relegate the application of its own insights to the empty category of "philosophical anthropology." When it touches on social and political issues, such inquiry is under the obligation to probe the problematic distinction between the ontological and the ontic and to avoid portentous vagueness by being specific in its analyses and criticism. In addition, the problematic nature of the distinction between the ontological and the ontic seems to be implied by Heidegger's conception of the hermeneutic circle itself. In terms of this circle, any primordiality or primal leap would presuppose prior leaps in a situated, repetitive temporality that combined breaks (including traumatic breaks) with insertion in a forestructure or preexisting (but not simply determinative) context of meanings and possibilities. As Heidegger puts it: "Interpretation is grounded in something we have in advance" (p. 191). Moreover:

> When one talks of the 'circle' in understanding, one expresses a failure to recognize two things: (1) that understanding as such makes up a basic kind of Dasein's Being, and (2) that this Being is constituted as care. To deny the circle, to make a secret of it, or even to want to overcome it, means finally to reinforce this failure. We must rather endeavor to leap into the 'circle,' primordially and wholly, so that even at the start of the

analysis of Dasein we make sure that we have a full view of Dasein's circular Being. (P. 363)

The existential analytic of *Being and Time* seems in important ways to be centered on Dasein and even to approximate a certain kind of anthropocentric "humanism"—tendencies from which Heidegger would later take his distance. Indeed, his own triangulation of problems in terms of presence-at-hand, readiness-to-hand, and Dasein, as well as his tendency continually to criticize one tendency or another for treating Dasein as if it were mere presence-at-hand or readiness-to-hand, seems to assume what Heidegger later termed a technological frame as the text's own unthematized frame of reference, for the argument does not apparently leave room for other possibilities of Being or for other relations between Dasein and the environment. Still, what is significant with respect to the pro-Nazi texts of 1933–34 is that in *Being and Time* Dasein is repeatedly seen as a being in question in its very Being—a being "which each of us is himself and which includes inquiring as one of the possibilities of Being" (p. 27). We are Dasein that is conceived in an essentially nondogmatic manner; but it is noteworthy that Heidegger never argues that Dasein is simply us. His very use of "Dasein" instead of "human being" would seem to preclude this simple identification and thus any unqualified form of humanism. (Nor is Dasein initially "decided" between the individual and the collective, and the interaction between the two is complex and problematic. Dasein is most individuated with respect to death, which is one's "ownmost," "non-relational," "not to be outstripped [*unüberholbare*]," uncanny possibility [p. 294], but even here, concern and mutual involvement are not altogether eliminated.) Although Heidegger in this text has a very limited idea of the relations between humans and nature and although his view of the status of animals may never get beyond the limitations of *Being and Time*, his thought has possibilities for envisioning humans as noninvidiously situated participants in a broader network of relations. Indeed, his later thought would at times almost seem to call for such a vision.

Emmanuel Levinas has argued that Heidegger's insistence on ontology tends to obscure the problem of ethics, and this contention does seem borne out by *Being and Time*. In one sense Heidegger's critique of "values," in the specific, radically constructivist sense of subjective human creations projected onto analytically reduced objects, is cogent (see, for example, p. 132). But it is unclear where this critique leaves ethics in other respects. The interface of ontology and ethics in *Being and Time* seems to touch on the questions of authenticity and inauthenticity, involving the key concept of "Entschlossenheit." There is an important place for the agency of Dasein as pro-jecting Being-in-the-world, but the norms Dasein should follow as an agent are never specified in substantive terms. One might conclude from Heidegger's approach that the height of inauthenticity would be to stipulate dogmatically the substantive content of authenticity in terms of norms or policies, which would once again place in radical doubt the texts of 1933–34. But this conclusion need not be taken to obviate the desirability either of an insistence on the role of limiting norms interacting with more transgressive, indeed uncanny forces or of sustained reflection about the substantive nature of such norms, which need not be dogmatically decreed but explicitly proposed as contestable regulative guides. Heidegger does not take thought in this direction, which in its own way runs along the fault line between the ontological and the ontic. But he does say enough about the authentic and the inauthentic to cast doubt on certain interpretations of his thought.

Authenticity and inauthenticity designate possibilities of being of Dasein. These possibilities may be differently realized by different people, but they are not reified and projected onto separate and distinct groups (such as the elite and the masses or Aryans and Jews). Here there may be a possibility of slippage in reading Heidegger insofar as inauthenticity is bound up with everydayness and the "they," whereas authenticity involves resistance that is at times seen as exceptional. But Heidegger does not move explicitly toward an elitist and mandarin conception of discrete groups. "Inauthenticity characterizes a kind of Being into which Dasein can divert itself and has for the most part always diverted itself; but Dasein does not necessarily and constantly have to divert itself into this kind of Being" (p. 303). Everyone is "proximally and for the most part" inauthentic and "fallen" but the possibility of authenticity is available not as a permanent state but precisely as a possibility that is seemingly at times attained (notably in an *Augenblick*, or moment of vision) but never simply possessed in all security. Authenticity seems to involve autonomy or "something of its own" (p. 68)—indeed, to be implicated in the various connotations of the *eigen*-words evoked by *Eigentlichkeit*. But it also seems to be radically open to others and to alterity within the self. In a sense, it might be construed to deconstruct the opposition between autonomy and heteronomy and to raise the question of their relationship. Here one's translation and interpretation of *Entschlossenheit* as a feature of authenticity is crucial.

"Authentic existence . . . constitutes itself in anticipatory resoluteness [*vorlaufende Entschlossenheit*]" (p. 370). And *Entschlossenheit* involves a certain way of confronting anxiety. "Anxiety can mount authentically only in a Dasein which is resolute. He who is resolute knows no fear; but he understands the possibility of anxiety as the possibility of the very mood which neither inhibits nor bewilders him" (p. 395). *Entschlossenheit* is also close to *Erschlossenheit*, which is generally translated as "disclosure"—notably in the interplay between disclosure and concealment or revealing and hiding. Heidegger himself gives two somewhat different "definitions" of *Entschlossenheit*, only the first of which would justify a translation and interpretation of it as empty "decisiveness": (1) "the choosing to choose a kind of Being-one's-self which, in accordance with its existential structure, we call '*resoluteness*' " (p. 314); (2) "the distinctive and authentic disclosedness [*Erschlossenheit*], which is attested in Dasein itself by conscience—this reticent self-projection upon one's ownmost Being-guilty, in which one is ready for anxiety—we call '*resoluteness*' " (p. 343). The second "definition," while still procedural, would relate *Entschlossenheit* to the ethical, and it would also suggest a relation to Freud's notion of *Angstbereitschaft*—the readiness to feel anxiety, whose absence for Freud made one susceptible to trauma. The second "definition" might also lead one to stress the role of an etymological translation of *Entschlossenheit* as literally "unclosedness" or even "openness"; it would also suggest a translation of it as "readiness." The latter was in fact proposed by Sartre in his notion of *disponibilité*. I suggest that *Entschlossenheit* involves at least all these meanings and that only an excessively decisive gesture can render it as "decisiveness" and present it as univocally leading to decisionism. Indeed, the term also involves a relation to *Gelassenheit*, which makes an appearance in *Being and Time* to mitigate and moderate without simply denying the importance of agency in Dasein. "Letting things be involved is something which we understand existentially as a letting-them-be" (p. 405). In fact, another of the unresolved tensions in *Being and Time* is the relationship between Dasein as an agent with projects in the world and the notion that care involves letting the world be.

Entschlossenheit is also intimately related to being-in-a-situation and to the problems of temporality and historicity. Karl Löwith reports that in his last meeting with Heidegger he said that he "was of the opinion that [Heidegger's] partisanship for National Socialism lay in the essence of his philosophy. Heidegger agreed with me without reservation, and added that his concept of 'historicity' was the basis of his political 'engagement' " (W, p. 142). Yet is it difficult to see why the concept of historicity as Heidegger develops it in *Being and Time* would in and of itself favor a commitment to the Nazis, particularly when one takes into account its multiple connections with other concepts and lines of argument that would place that commitment in question.

"The Situation," Heidegger tells us, "is the 'there' which is disclosed in resoluteness" (p. 346), and "authentic resoluteness . . . keeps repeating itself" (p. 355). Repetition links the past and the future through the activity of Dasein in a "present" situation that cannot be fixated punctually. "The resoluteness which comes back to itself and hands itself down . . . becomes the *repetition* [*Wiederholung*] of a possibility of existence that has come down to us. *Repeating is handing down explicitly*" (p. 437). In this sense, the authentic present is a "moment of vision" (*Augenblick*) that recovers a future-oriented possibility of the past—a "resolute rapture [*Entrückung*] with which Dasein is carried away" toward possibilities encountered in a situation as objects of concern—"but a rapture which is held in resoluteness." This moment of vision that relates past and present through a disclosive repetition "can *not* be clarified in terms of the 'now' [*jetzt*]" (p. 387). One may perhaps relate this moment of vision that occurs as repetition to the process of working-through in psychoanalysis—a process Freud contrasts to acting-out and the repetition-compulsion in which the traumatic past captivates or possesses one and is relived as if it were literally present. The moment of vision in this sense would be a certain kind of repetition in the face of trauma and the uncanny anxiety it brings. It would involve an effect of belatedness as one came to terms with a past that harbored unrealized possibilities that one might attempt to hand down and realize in the future. Deciding which possibilities merited realization would again confront one with the critical question of ethical and ethicopolitcal judgment—an issue concerning which *Being and Time* is of limited assistance.

The type of questioning in *Being and Time* does place in jeopardy an extreme logic of pure identity and difference that is crucial for the operation of a scapegoat mechanism whereby what causes anxiety in the self is projected onto the discrete, despised other. The unsettling of a logic of pure identity and difference is one aspect of the insistence on the hermeneutic circle—an insistence that becomes even more pronounced in Heidegger's later thought where the type of questioning goes beyond hermeneutics and becomes increasingly probing or mystifying, depending on one's point of view. Without entering into the intricate issue of precise dating or the analysis of problems of transition, one may nonetheless raise in a general way the question of the relation between Heidegger's Nazi turn and the Kehre in his thought. I am inclined to see the Kehre not as a simple discontinuity but as a repetition in the problematic sense of an intertwined repetition compulsion and attempt at working through problems in the face of trauma and posttraumatic effects. This complex and overdetermined repetition did, moreover, come with some significant changes in emphasis and articulation.

In *Being and Time* the role of Dasein is crucial if not central, and Dasein is an agent in its projects, including the project of recovering possibilities from the past through repetition. The stress on an existential analytic of Dasein as the primary undertaking of fundamental ontology comes with the primacy of hermeneutics, interpretation, and the attempt to disclose or render perspicuous the meaning of Being. The emphasis on *Durchsichtigkeit*—clear-sightedness or perspicuity—is pronounced in *Being and Time*, and it constitutes an explicit theme in the text. Indeed, even when there is a disproportionate emphasis on the uncanny or Being-toward-death, the tone and rhetorical mode of the text are nonetheless more Apollonian than Dionysian. And although there is a concern for the interplay of disclosure and concealment, the project is clearly one of disclosure. There is little sign of the role poetry, in its obscure dialogue with philosophy, will play in Heidegger's later thought, and there is virtually no indication that philosophy itself should be seen as a "poetizing" use of language. The one reference to poetry itself underscores the discursive nature of poetry and relates it to disclosure and communication. "The communication of the existential possibilities of one's state-of-mind can become an aim in itself and this amounts to a disclosing of existence" (p. 205). The problem of language itself is not ignored, but it is subordinated to discourse, interpretation, and disclosure. Little sense exists that language speaks Dasein rather than vice versa. By contrast, with the Kehre the turn to Being comes with an emphasis on poetry, the prevalence of concealment and erring, and the status of language as the uncanny house of Being whose evanescent disclosures are often unintentional or even beyond our ken. What seems radically downplayed, if not lost, is a sense of agency for Dasein. And the problem of the ethical and the ethicopolitical seems to have even less room than in *Being and Time*. It is, of course, tempting to relate these tendencies to an unworked-through trauma regarding the Nazi commitment and lingering illusions that Heidegger never fully confronted, indeed, to a tendency to deny, repress, or suppress aspects of the past rather than to work them through in an explicit, critical manner.

Although perhaps not entirely beside the point, such an interpretation would be too simple, especially insofar as it overlooked the dialogue between Heidegger's later thought and *Being and Time*, the insistence in his later work on the interplay between concealment and disclosure, and the challenge posed both by his arguments and by his stylistic performances. What would nonetheless bear repeating is the assertion that there is a diminished sense of agency in the later Heidegger. Here one may point to an arresting statement in the *Spiegel* interview:

> Philosophy will not be able to effect an immediate transformation of the present condition of the world. This is not only true of philosophy, but of all merely human thought and endeavor. Only a god can save us. The sole possibility that is left for us is to prepare a sort of readiness, through thinking and poetizing, for the appearance of the god or for the absence of the god in the time of foundering [*Untergang*]; for in the face of the god who is absent, we founder. (W, p. 107)

What is shocking and objectionable in this comment is not its assertion that "philosophy will not be able to effect an immediate transformation of the present condition of the world" or even that "all merely human thought and endeavor" cannot achieve such a feat. These assertions may be taken as welcome signs of sobriety and prudence in the conception of the limits of both philosophy and sociopolitical action. What is shocking is that Heidegger adheres to an encompassing, indiscriminately negative apprehension of the present world, is willing to use a Spenglerian term in characterizing its condition, seems to find no significant role whatsoever for human agency other than a John-the-Baptist function, is still longing for salvation, and can find his redeemer only in an absent god. This constellation of traits is indeed objectionable.

I think that other possibilities exist in Heidegger's thought, especially if one does not leave *Being and Time* behind but tries to explore further its tensions and take them in directions that may contest certain of Heidegger's own emphases that at times become more forceful in his later thought. But just as it is deceptive to see his turn toward Nazism either as a result of an insufficient deconstruction of metaphysics and humanism or, on the contrary, as a result of an insufficient affirmation of a humanistic metaphysic of radical freedom, it is equally deceptive to see his later thought either as pointing an exemplary way beyond his early humanistic "lapses" or as a mere symptom of his unworked-through Nazi past.[19] Among the more valuable aspects of the later thought are an insistent critique of anthropocentrism and a more nuanced attentiveness to the multiple possibilities of language. What recurs from *Being and Time* is a restricted view of animals and nature. And what is excessive is a shift from a philosophy centered on Dasein to an extreme decentering of Dasein in an at times incantatory and mesmerizing mode of thought that leaves little room for critical agency. In my own discussion I have periodically indicated relationships between aspects of Heidegger's thought and psychoanalysis. This is certainly not the only fruitful direction one may take, but I think an elaboration of these relationships might provide a de-

---

[19]In *Heidegger and Modernity*, trans. Philip Franklin (1988; Chicago: University of Chicago Press, 1990), Luc Ferry and Alain Renaut oppose the former options, which they somewhat caricaturally attribute to Philippe Lacoue-Labarthe and Jacques Derrida, only to affirm the latter ones. Their critique of Heidegger combines a militantly anthropocentric humanism, an endorsement of existing liberal-democratic systems, a general defense of immanent critique, an unqualified dismissal of modern mass culture in the worst tradition of "culture critique," and a regurgitation of an early Sartrean philosophy of radically transcendental freedom (which is incompatible with immanent critique). Their affirmation of extreme human autonomy tends to make politics a simple derivative of philosophy and is able to defend humanism only through invidious oppositions between humans and the rest of nature. They in fact share some of the most dubious features of Heidegger's thought, including its indiscriminate mode of "culture critique" and its inadequate examination of the relation between humans and animals. Their own version of spiritualistic freedom even leads them to assert: "This area of freedom is thus confounded with the infinite distancing from nature typified by the processes of education and politics" (p. 100). There are indeed difficulties in the responses to Heidegger of Derrida and Lacoue-Labarthe (notably the latter's tendency in *Heidegger, Art and Politics*, trans. Chris Turner [London: Basil Blackwell, 1990], to treat Heidegger as a fetish in an argument that oscillates between castigating and "lovingly" identifying with him). But Ferry and Renaut hardly provide a viable alternative.

fensible way of rereading Heidegger and of forging stronger links among psychoanalysis, philosophy, and sociopolitical thought.

POSTSCRIPT. Since the completion of this chapter, several important discussions of Heidegger's politics have appeared that have a special bearing on the mooted question of Heidegger's anti-Semitism and its relation to his published work.[20] Regarding the question of anti-Semitism, a critical investigation of all the evidence concerning Heidegger's practice is clearly needed, one that attempts to establish the degree of credibility in hearsay and the extent and bearing of more solidly documented material, such as letters signed by Heidegger. What is also needed, as I have intimated, is an inquiry into the questions of whether and how anti-Semitism manifests itself in Heidegger's published work.

In *The Politics of Being*, Richard Wolin, relying primarily on the work of Ott and Farías, addressed "the vexing question of Heidegger's anti-Semitism" (p. 4) without thematizing the problem of distinguishing among and critically weighing various types of evidence. He referred to "Toni Cassirer's 1950 autobiography, *Mein Leben mit Ernst Cassirer*, where she speaks of having heard of Heidegger's 'inclination toward anti-Semitism' as early as 1929" and the "longstanding rumor that while Rector, Heidegger barred his former teacher, Edmund Husserl, from utilizing the university libraries on the grounds that Husserl was a Jew"—a rumor, as Wolin observed, that was denied by Heidegger in the *Spiegel* interview. He also referred to more recent evidence that "weighs heavily against the philosopher's self-exculpatory strivings." There was, for Wolin, an "exclusively pragmatic basis" on which Heidegger interceded in July 1933 on behalf of two Jewish professors" (Eduard Fraenkel and Georg von Hevesy) because Heidegger was concerned with the negative impact of dismissal on "Germany's foreign policy interest." In a letter of 12 July 1933, Heidegger "assured the Ministry of Education of his full support for the National Socialist ordinance barring Jews from civil service professions" (p. 4). Wolin also pointed to Ulrich Sieg's disclosure in *Die Zeit*, on 29 December 1989, of a letter of recommendation Heidegger wrote in 1929 on behalf of one of his students, Eduard Baumgarten. In it Heidegger promoted Baumgarten by arguing that "at stake is nothing less than the urgent

[20]See Tom Rockmore and Joseph Margolis, eds., *The Heidegger Case: On Philosophy and Politics* (Philadelphia: Temple University Press, 1992), and Tom Rockmore, *On Heidegger's Nazism and Philosophy* (Berkeley: University of California Press, 1992).

awareness that we stand before a choice: once again to provide our *German* spiritual life with genuine, indigenous [*bodenständige*] manpower and educators, or to deliver it over definitively . . . to increasing Judification [*Verjudung*]" (quoted on p. 5). Wolin also noted Heidegger's ironic reversal in his later attempt (December 1933) to block Baumgarten's appointment to Göttingen University on the grounds that Baumgarten "hailed from a 'liberal democratic' milieu in Heidelberg, had become excessively 'Americanized' during a sojourn in the United States, and, lastly, owing to his associations with 'the Jew [Eduard] Fraenkel.' " Finally, Wolin referred to Max Müller's statement (which may be found in an interview included in the collection by Neske and Kettering) that "from the moment Heidegger became rector, he allowed no Jewish students who had begun their dissertations with him to receive their degree" (quoted on p. 5). Wolin, however, argued that "it would be precipitate to conclude that 'racial thinking' occupied an essential niche in [Heidegger's] 'worldview' — let alone in his philosophy." He agreed with Jürgen Habermas that it is "more likely that Heidegger's anti-Semitism was of the 'customary, cultural variety.' " But he also asserted that it would be "misleading to deny that so-called 'cultural anti-Semitism' formed the necessary historical precondition for the racial-biological anti-Semitism that had been germinating in German society since the late nineteenth century." And he insisted on the contextualist view that informed his own interpretation of Heidegger's writings, to wit, that Heidegger's "intellectual world-view was much more profoundly conditioned than one might have initially believed by the vehement, latently fascistic 'critique of modernity' — of 'Western' values, the Enlightenment, 'cosmopolitanism,' and so forth — that was shared by both the German intellectual mandarinate and the provincial Volk alike" (pp. 5–6).

Relying on much of the same evidence as Wolin, Rockmore, in *Heidegger's Nazism*, goes further in linking anti-Semitism to Heidegger's thought by arguing that Heidegger indulged in "spiritual" in contrast with racial anti-Semitism. He also mentions in a note (p. 367) Edmund Husserl's reference (in a letter or 4 May 1933 to Dietrich Mahnke) to Heidegger's "in den letzen Jahren [. . .] immer stärker zum Ausdruck kommenden Antisemitismus" [ever more strongly expressed anti-Semitism in recent years — my translation]. And he points to Pierre Bourdieu's belief that "a close reading of Heidegger's work already [in the first edition of Bourdieu's book in

1975] revealed such themes as anti-Semitism" (p. 267). But Rockmore does not demonstrate how Heidegger's published texts might be read or interpreted as anti-Semitic.

In certain texts after 1933 (but not in *Being and Time*) Heidegger accords a dubious privilege to the German language as a medium of thought that has a special connection to Greek. But one cannot simply make a direct extrapolation from this view, which might plausibly be argued to underwrite a language-based, "ontological" ethnocentrism, to an "ethics of masters" or a "philosophical racism," as Victor Farías attempts to do.[21] I have remarked on Heidegger's unguarded criticism of tendencies that might have been culturally stereotyped as Jewish (such as idle chatter in *Being and Time* or the "noncommittal play of wit" in the Rectoral Address) as well as the more dubious aspects of his fascination for the abyss and the sublime. One may also note that he remained at least a nominal member of the Nazi party until the end of the war and continued to harbor illusions about the possibilities of a regime in which anti-Semitism and, after a certain point, the extermination of Jews were crucial features. And what may be most questionable about his postwar writing is the absence of a direct confrontation with the problem of the Shoah. But I reiterate that I think his philosophical thought in important ways places in doubt a logic of scapegoating that is essential for anti-Semitism.

John D. Caputo, however, argues that in Heidegger's later history of Being (in partial contrast to the analytic of Dasein in *Being and Time*) there is no room for the victim whose call is silenced. He also raises the question of whether the victim is a victim of Heidegger's quest for essence that precludes his or her appearance. For Caputo, the victim in Heidegger becomes a "differend" in Lyotard's sense in that he or she lacks a voice that may be heard.[22] I would suggest that Heidegger attempts to take a distance from, or even to undercut, the logic of scapegoating and victimization (which are from his perspective perhaps to be interpreted as effects of the oblivion of Being)—but to do so in so "essential" a manner that there may be no place from which to counter victimization as a historical phenomenon and to work through one's own implication in it. For someone who takes Heidegger's thought seriously, the difficulty is how to argue or intervene against

[21]See "Foreword to the Spanish Edition, *Heidegger and Nazism*," in Rockmore and Margolis, eds., *The Heidegger Case*, pp. 337, 341.

[22]"Heidegger's Scandal: Thinking and the Essence of the Victim," in Rockmore and Margolis, eds., *The Heidegger Case*, especially pp. 276–79.

anti-Semitism and comparable phenomena without simply becoming arrested in a binary logic of opposition and reversal. To the extent that this line of interpretation is convincing, it would indeed be necessary to take Heidegger's thought (especially in *Being and Time*) in directions—notably ethical and political ones—different from those Heidegger takes.[23]

[23]See also the discussion of Heidegger in Richard J. Bernstein, *The New Constellation: The Ethical-Political Horizons of Modernity/Postmodernity* (Cambridge: MIT Press, 1992), especially pp. 118–36, where Bernstein argues that the later Heidegger concealed the possibilities of *phronesis* (practical wisdom) and political praxis and relied instead on the dichotomy between technological action, on the one hand, and poetical revealing in its relation to "thought," on the other. Note also that Jacques Taminiaux sees severe limitations in the role of phronesis even in *Being and Time*—a perspective that might be related to Levinas's view that the concern with ontology tends to marginalize the problem of ethics, "Heidegger and *Praxis*," in Rockmore and Margolis, eds., *The Heidegger Case*, pp. 188–207. Hans Sluga's important study, *Heidegger's Crisis: Philosophy and Politics in Nazi Germany* (Cambridge: Harvard University Press, 1993), appeared too late for me to be able to take it into account. Sluga not only provides a nonreductive contextual reading of Heidegger which delineates the latter's relations to figures such as Alfred Bauemler and Ernst Kriek. He also analyzes the manner in which Nazis appropriated the thought of earlier philosophers, notably Fichte and Nietzsche.

SIX

❧

The Return of the Historically Repressed

A mooted question is the applicability of psychoanalytic categories to social and cultural phenomena, in particular, the extent to which certain modern sociocultural phenomena can be seen as a return of what has been historically repressed. This question, which is often answered in reductive and oversimplified ways, confronts one with a number of problems. In addressing them, my own approach is only suggestive, and I at most indicate avenues of investigation that require further inquiry and research. In other words, I am not claiming to be—and I doubt if one can be—demonstrative in indicating (or negating) the role of the returning repressed in history. I am only contending that things sometimes seem to happen as if the repressed were returning in disguised and distorted form, and such a hypothetical construction of events can be correlated with a different understanding of temporality or the movement of history itself (one suggested in related ways by Freud, Heidegger, and Derrida).

My focus is secularization involving the relation between religious and secular phenomena, notably modes of secular explanation or ideology that seem to invoke displaced religious categories. Psychoanalysis itself has been construed (at times by Freud himself) as a full explanation of religion that reveals the nature of earlier religious practices or beliefs as "really" a matter of mystified psychology. This narcissistic self-conception may well be ideological in its own blind, uncritical reliance on categories such as full disclosure or revelation (in opposition to mere illusion), and it constitutes psychoanalysis as a totalizing discourse that appears (however deceptively) to fully englobe and master its objects as well as to provide an authoritative, godlike identity for the analyst.

Secularization involved conflict between emergent forces—such as science, anti-ritualistic forms of religion, and productively "rational" modes of economic or bureaucratic behavior—and earlier religious and social beliefs or practices. It also involved conflict between groups that were primary carriers or propagandists for these forces. Psychological conflict and repression were themselves mapped onto sociopolitical conflict and repression. And nascent psychology, psychiatry, and psychoanalysis struggled for turf earlier and, to some extent, still occupied by religion as they offered explanations and therapies for phenomena otherwise interpretable in religious or more broadly traditional terms. Psychoanalysis seemed to have an ambivalent, hybridized, and uneasy status between religion, which it warded off, and science, with which it flirted or even desired to lawfully wed.[1] In their important book, Peter Stallybrass and Allon White argue that "science only emerged as an autonomous set of discursive values after a prolonged struggle against ritual and it marked out its own identity by the distance which it established from 'mere superstition'— science's label for, among other things, a large body of social practices of a therapeutic kind."[2] They further note that Freud did not do full justice to "the whole range of festive material scattered through various studies on hysteria and which together create a subtext irreducible to nursery games" (p. 175). Freud's patients were not simply victims of the isolated, Oedipalized family romance but "again and again

[1]See Peter Homans, *The Ability to Mourn: Disillusionment and the Social Origins of Psychoanalysis* (Chicago: University of Chicago Press, 1989).

[2]*The Politics and Poetics of Transgression* (Ithaca: Cornell University Press, 1986), p. 174. Despite its many qualities, this thought-provoking book has several limitations that may be typical of recent work combining the perspectives of new historicism and cultural studies. It tends to conflate dominant and elite culture while drastically downplaying critical tendencies in the latter. It also tends to conflate popular and mass culture and even has a basically early modern conception of popular culture, the problematic effects of whose transformations in the last few centuries, notably with the rise of commodification and, more recently, the media, receive insufficient attention. It is, moreover, remarkable that in a book focusing on transgression, the Holocaust is ignored. The book is nonetheless a basic contribution to cultural history that helps one to reconceptualize the nature and effects of displacement over time.

. . . suffer[ed] acute attacks of disgust, literally vomiting out horrors and obsessions which look surprisingly like the rotted residue of traditional carnival practices" (p. 174). More generally, "the carnival material of the case studies witnesses an historical repression and return. The repression includes the gradual, relentless attack on the 'grotesque body' of carnival by the emergent middle and professional classes from the Renaissance onwards" (pp. 175–76). This attack led not to the simple disappearance of carnival in the modern period but to complex processes in which repression interacted with fragmentation, marginalization, and sublimation (p. 178). What Stallybrass and White argue with specific reference to carnival may in certain ways be applicable to ritual and related belief in general, notably including sacrifice and the immanent sacred which, already highly sublimated in Christianity, became even more sublimated with the attenuation of ritual mediation in the Reformation and Counter-Reformation. Moreover, to the extent that the breaking-away from earlier signifying practices was traumatic and intertwined with economic and social crisis, there would be a propensity for the repressed to return in distorted or disguised form, particularly in a movement such as Nazism, which, in its scapegoating and victimization, both actively proclaimed its neopagan impetus and drew on popular Christian anti-Semitism.[3]

Both ideology and the critique of ideology in any specifically modern sense arise simultaneously in a context of secularization wherein one confronts the problem of the displacement of religion, the repression of certain of its elements, and the seeming return of the repressed. And one prevalent kind of ideology in modernity is the redemptive narrative or theory wherein one's saving, identity-forming values are projectively figured as realized in empirical fact, whether diachronically through a process of development or synchronically through a totalizing conceptualization that reductively "explains" the other while fully validating the self. In a more particular sense (that should not become a pretext for facile generalization), Nazi ideology may with some justification be interpreted as secular religion with a redemptive message for the in-group of committed believers (or even

---

[3]For a recent, theoretically limited, but informative attempt to treat these problems, see Gavin I. Langmuir, *History, Religion, and Antisemitism* (Berkeley: University of California Press, 1990). Langmuir stresses the way the Nazi Aryan anti-Semitic myth displaced and incorporated prevalent traditional Christian anti-Jewish stereotypes and fantasies in the context of a new surrogate religion and biologist ideology.

would-be believers) and a deranged, drastically desublimated sacrificial component, involving scapegoating and victimization, in the treatment of certain oppressed others as impure elements or contaminants in the body politic.[4] This radical desublimation might, however, allow for a negative sublime in the form of unheard-of, traumatizing transgression that is presumed to be unrepresentable and to be met only with silence. One might also point to particularly perverse aspects of grotesque and "carnivalesque" behavior in the treatment of victims in the camps that would warrant close study (entry rituals of

[4] I think there is much to be learned from the work of René Girard, especially his *Violence and the Sacred*, trans. Patrick Gregory (Baltimore: Johns Hopkins University Press, 1979). The difficulty in this particular book is that Girard seems to be offering (and even to be repeating in a blind transferential manner) a general theory of culture and society in which ritual is the essence of culture, sacrifice is the essence of ritual, and scapegoating and victimization are the essence of sacrifice. Moreover, the book seems to leave one with only two options: generalized sacrificial crisis (and rampant violence) in secular society or controlled sacrifice (and explicitly sacralized violence) in religious society. (In later work Girard turns to a seeming third way in Christian love that presumably holds out the promise of transcending all implication in a sacrificial, scapegoating mechanism.) I am making none of these hyperbolic and reductive claims but instead am concerned with (and attempt to offer a critique of) victimization and scapegoating that may involve modern secularized sacrificialism.

Here I might also mention Mary Douglas's *Purity and Danger: An Analysis of the Concepts of Pollution and Taboo* (1966; London: Routledge, 1984). Douglas provides a wealth of material on ritual purity and "polluting" threats to it. Although at times sensitive to complexities, her own general interpretation relies overmuch on a binary opposition between "them" and "us"—"primitives" and "moderns"—that underplays differences within each category and posits questionable contrasts between the two. Especially dubious is Douglas's belief that "primitive cultures" have a "personal, anthropocentric, undifferentiated world-view" (p. 92), notably with respect to religion, whereas modern cultures separate religion from secular life and therefore attain greater objectivity and a nonanthropocentric understanding of the world. Thus, according to Douglas, "dirt avoidance for us is a matter of hygiene or aesthetics and is not related to our religion" (p. 35). Douglas also has a reductive understanding of psychoanalysis as universalizing, ahistorical, and socially unspecific (pp. 121–25). Moreover, she conjoins a not altogether consistent emphasis on cognitive factors (dirt as "matter out of place" that disrupts orderly patterns of meaning) with a social pragmatism that construes "the primitive world-view" as a practical, even unreflective, "appanage of other social institutions" (p. 91). What this combination of factors prevents Douglas from fully appreciating is the role of religion in modern cultures and the extent to which religious and ritual considerations are displaced in secular practices or ideologies in ways psychoanalysis might help to elucidate. It is perhaps no accident that she seems to write in oblivion of the Nazi period and has but one passing reference to anti-Semitism via Sartre's analysis, which she criticizes for not recognizing that the "yearning for rigidity" is "part of our human condition" (p. 162). Robert A. Pois's *National Socialism and the Religion of Nature* (New York: St. Martin's Press, 1986), which emphasizes the role of secularized religion in modernity, came to my attention too late for me to make use of it in this book.

degradation involving the extreme reversal of "ordinary" expectations—beating, stripping, shaving the entire body, outfitting in camp garb—prisoners forced to make music to accompany their victimization, guards making abusive jokes about naked bodies or about prisoners cleaning filthy latrines, and so forth).

Any use of psychoanalysis with reference to society and culture raises the preliminary problem of the applicability of certain concepts—for example, the return of the repressed—beyond the clinical context involving discrete individuals as subjects.[5] Freud tended to see this applicability as analogical, and the analogy between the individual and society may be enough to warrant the exploration of the interpretive value of certain concepts, especially if that applicability is explicitly presented as problematic and suggestive, not grounded in the idea that ontogeny recapitulates phylogeny, and related to the continual need for detailed research into specific processes of sociocultural and historical transmission. While insisting on the problematic status of sociocultural uses of psychoanalytic concepts and the need for research to substantiate, qualify, or even contest one's assertions, I would nonetheless point out that a purely analogical conception of the applicability of psychoanalysis may be based (at times in Freud himself) on unexamined individualistic ideological assumptions. Especially in this context, it may be worth contending that psychoanalysis is misconstrued as a psychology of the individual: its basic concepts should be understood as undercutting the binary opposition between the individual and society because these concepts apply to social individuals whose relative individuation or collective status is a problem for investigation and argument. Such a contention would, if anything, further reinforce the insistence on specific inquiry and research in elucidating the extent to which psychoanalytic concepts, such as the return of the repressed, are indeed applicable to various phenomena. Individuation is in certain respects pronounced in the modern West, but even here what happens to the individual may not be purely individual, for it may be bound up with larger social, political, and cultural processes that often go unperceived. And there obviously are events that have a differential impact on different groups,

[5]For an admirably researched, illuminating, but undertheorized attempt to apply concepts such as unfinished mourning, obsession, repression, and the return of the repressed to groups in postwar France, see Henry Rousso, *The Vichy Syndrome: History and Memory in France since 1944*, trans. Arthur Goldhammer (Cambridge: Harvard University Press, 1991).

as there are collective processes of interaction, mutual reinforcement, and censorship that further repression, denial, or avoidance in responding to such events.

Moreover, the question of the interpretation of sociocultural phenomena in terms of the return of the repressed is, arguably, related to the understanding of the variable workings of repetitive temporality in (or as) history. Here the notions of simple continuity or discontinuity are deceptive, for "continuity" involves not pure identity over time but some mode of repetition, and change is not a totally discrete process even in extreme forms of trauma. Indeed, trauma is effected belatedly through repetition, for the numbingly traumatic event does not register at the time of its occurrence but only after a temporal gap or period of latency, at which time it is immediately repressed, split off, or disavowed. Trauma then in some way may return compulsively as the repressed. Working through trauma brings the possibility of counteracting compulsive "acting-out" through a controlled, explicit, critically controlled process of repetition that significantly changes a life by making possible the selective retrieval and modified enactment of unactualized past possibilities.

The concept of displacement, including the displacement of the religious in the secular, raises the problem of repetitive temporality and directs inquiry toward the specific and variable articulations of repetition and change or "continuity" and "discontinuity" over time. Ascertaining the precise nature of the interaction between repetition and change also requires research into given cases and configurations. The problem should not be prematurely resolved by conflating displacement either with basic continuity (as in M. H. Abrams or Northrop Frye) or with pure discontinuity (as in certain of Michel Foucault's explicit theoretical statements). Furthermore, one should engage the complex interplay not only of past and present but of similarity and difference among approaches to understanding and reading in the contemporary context as well—an interplay that implicates the observer or analyst, poses the question of how to respond to such implication, and underscores the problem of the possibilities and limits of the recovery of meaning.

What I term "repetitive temporality" should not be essentialized or hypostatized as a purely abstract process happening "out there" and determining the behavior of historical agents. There may indeed be constraining processes that are all the more determining to the extent that they operate unconsciously, notably through the symptomatic acting out of repetition compulsions. But these processes (prominently including the return of the repressed) raise the question of the interaction between compulsion and responsible agency or choice, for example, in the retrieval of past possibilities and the attempt to begin again. They also raise the question of the relation between reconstruction of the past on the basis of a reading and interpretation of its artifacts and a dialogic exchange with it—an exchange that is more responsible and controlled to the extent that it is attuned to the problem of transferential displacements over time and the need to work through them critically rather than to remain fixated in at times necessary processes of acting-out. In this sense, historiography involves work on memory that inquires into its operations, attempts to retrieve what it has repressed or ignored, and supplements it in ways that may provide a measure of critical distance on experience and a basis of responsible action.

Freud himself was preoccupied or even obsessed with the problem of secularization and its relation to the return of the repressed. He even indicated that psychopathological symptoms might be displaced versions of earlier religious practices. Not only did he assert that a psychopathological symptom was a kind of intrapsychic institution that attempted to effect on a private and self-punitive level what had earlier been undertaken on a collective and perhaps ceremonial or celebratory one. In an even more circumstantial manner, he tried, at times in oversimplified or hyperbolic fashion, to relate specific symptoms to former religious practices or problems. For example, he wrote to Wilhelm Fliess: "By the way, what have you to say to the suggestion that the whole of my brand-new theory of the primary origins of hysteria is already familiar and has been published a hundred times over, though several centuries ago? Do you remember my always saying that the medieval theory of possession, that held by ecclesiastical courts, was identical with our theory of a foreign body and the splitting of consciousness?"[6]

[6]*The Origins of Psychoanalysis: Letters, Drafts, and Notes to Wilhelm Fliess, 1887–1902* (Garden City, N.Y.: Doubleday, 1957), p. 90. One particularly interesting treatment of secularization that includes discussions of Freud and Nazism is Jean-Joseph Goux, *Les iconoclastes* (Paris: Editions du Seuil, 1978). Goux insists that the very structure of Nazism was religious and that its relation to Judaism was that of an enemy-brother contending for the position of the "chosen people." He does not, however, analyze the role of scapegoating in Nazi ideology and practice, although such an analysis would accord with certain aspects of his argument. Moreover, with reference to iconoclasm, the taboo on images, and the radical transcendence of divinity, he draws a stark con-

Although it has the virtue of pointing to possible relations between psychopathological symptoms and religious belief or practice in general—as well as between psychoanalysis and earlier theories, Freud's formulation is misleading. Indeed, he apparently falls prey to Hans Blumenberg's critique of an "identitarian" concept of secularization, for the medieval theory of possession is not identical to Freud's theory of the splitting of the ego, nor is possession identical with hysteria.[7] In this passage, Freud leads one to believe that there is some essence of the phenomenon that endures in an identical or basically invariant state over time, and this essence simply receives different names over time—possession in the one case and hysteria in the other. The typical inference from this view is that psychoanalysis has identified and explained the true essence or meaning of the phenomenon that was earlier perceived in deluded, mystified, or (what we

---

trast between Judaism and Christianity and does not differentiate among tendencies within these religions that would mitigate the binary opposition between them. Similarly, in his often brilliant discussion of Freud and Marx, he does not address the issue of currents in their thought that do not conform to his thesis on the role of displaced Judaism with its animus against the image.

[7]See Hans Blumenberg, *The Legitimacy of the Modern Age*, trans. Robert M. Wallace (1966; Cambridge: MIT Press, 1983). Blumenberg himself elaborates a grand narrative of legitimation around the epochal significance of the "modern age," and he at times takes his critique of the "secularization thesis" to hyperbolic extremes complementary to those of the defenders of essential identity between religious and secular phenomena whom he attacks. Blumenberg makes only a few rather general if not vague allusions to the Nazis (see, for example, p. 117). He does not use the Holocaust as one acid test of this thesis about the "legitimacy" of the modern age. Nor does he treat the bearing of secularization on Nazi ideology. His only reference to Hitler is circuitous and comes in a footnote on Campanella that concludes a long discussion of Carl Schmitt. The relevant portion of the note reads: "In the *Dubitationes* iv . . . an opinion is cited according to which animals too would have to have religion: 'Necque enim posset politica absque religione existere.' Hitler, according to Speer's recollection, observed that ' . . . it has been our misfortune to have the wrong religion' " (p. 604n14). It might not be too much of an exaggeration to suggest that the Nazi phenomenon is the ghost in the closet of Blumenberg's immensely learned book. In addition, while it is useful as a corrective to the thesis he challenges, Blumenberg's own attempt to argue that in the relation between religious and secular phenomena over time, one at most has essentially different answers to comparable questions tends, in my view, to decide the issue of the relation between repetition and change in an overly neat and analytically reductive manner. More interesting is an argument he makes that is not entirely accommodated by this analytic reduction—an argument in which he does not so much accept a "weak" version of the secularization thesis as provide a way of interpreting the process of secularization itself. This is his reoccupation thesis, according to which secular phenomena may be seen as reoccupying, reinvesting, or recathecting ground formerly occupied by religion. This formulation has the merit of raising rather than prematurely resolving the problem of the variable articulations of repetition and change over time.

belatedly see as) "ideological" terms.[8] The equally typical reaction to this inference is that it involves a simple projection of contemporary categories onto the past and conflates this projection with explanation. The further move—the standard historicist move, which is also dubious—is to argue that one has two essentially different phenomena and that the earlier one can only be understood in its own terms and for its own sake. I suggest that these seeming alternatives are not really alternatives but rather complementary aspects of a larger framework based on an essentialist logic of identity and difference. They share a disavowal of the process of displacement as a complex interaction of repetition with change; they also disavow the complex nature

[8]The understanding of a phenomenon as ideological may itself have traumatic effects, and the temptation is to repress or deny them by turning to a new ideology to fill in for the loss. For example, a believer who comes to see religion as ideological faces the possibility of collapse of the symbolic world, and the temptation is to turn immediately to a surrogate ideology in order to rebuild a life. In this way, the possible implications of critique may be foreclosed or drastically curtailed. In addition, the recognition that aspects of science may at any given time be ideological and shaped by sociocultural and political considerations places in question the idea that science is an inviolate sphere of activity that is invariably pure, value-neutral, or aligned with desirable values in some global concept of "modernity." The designation of race as a pseudoscientific concept should not obscure the fact that it was until recently widely taken as legitimately scientific. Nazi scientists were not anomalous in their understanding of it, and racially or otherwise biased experiments on humans have taken place outside Nazi Germany. Mario Baggioli even argues that "the processes (though not the results) of Nazi science were not exceptional": "Science, Modernity, and the 'Final Solution,' " in Saul Friedlander, ed., *Probing the Limits of Representation: Nazism and the "Final Solution"* (Cambridge: Harvard University Press, 1992), p. 205. Baggioli also criticizes the tendency to scapegoat Nazi scientists or doctors as individuals but to exculpate science and medicine themselves in one's analysis of unacceptable practices involving racial selection, hygiene, and eugenics. He observes that "when the Nazis took over, the preexisting scientific discourse allowed the doctors to become the priests of the cult of the German blood as well as its medical keepers and the exterminators of its potential polluters" (p. 193). He further notes that "Mengele was using Auschwitz as a scientific institution which offered exceptional possibilities to study usually rare individuals," and he suggests that "the symbiosis between the discourse of racial hygiene, the medicalization of the Final Solution, the institution of the concentration camps, and the development of experimentation on humans was too tight and effective to be considered accidental" (p. 202). Despite certain overstated aspects of his analysis, Baggioli is rightfully concerned that "the dangerous naiveté of the historiography that tries to prevent science from being implicated in the Final Solution" may lessen one's ability to "understand how science became (and could again become) implicated in a tragedy such as the Final Solution" (pp. 204–5). Indeed, the study of Nazi science may reopen the basic questions of the actual and desirable articulations of science as a historically variable activity, their relation to ethicopolitical norms, and the legitimate limits of experimentation (including, in my judgment, experimentation or biotechnological manipulation that freely "sacrifices" animals in view of self-centered human needs or even curiosity).

of one's implication in and tendency to repeat aspects of the processes one studies—a transferential relation to the past that should ideally be worked through in a critical manner. Especially valuable in coming to terms with transference is Blumenberg's psychoanalytically informed understanding of displacement through a notion of reoccupation whereby older religious or theological ground is repossessed or "recathected"—reoccupied—by a secular practice or ideology.

Here it is useful to look briefly at two recent books, Rudolph M. Bell's *Holy Anorexia*[9] and Caroline Walker Bynum's *Holy Feast and Holy Fast: The Religious Significance of Food to Medieval Women*.[10] Bell argues a rather straightforward identity thesis. For him, the extreme ascetic form of fasting that was seen as a mark of exemplary holiness in women of the Middle Ages was essentially the same as what was termed anorexia in the nineteenth century. The same phenomenon was simply reclassified as a medical condition, and it was converted in the popular imagination from an object of wonder and awe to a pitiful, psychopathological condition. Catherine of Siena, Clare of Assisi, Margaret of Cortona, Angela of Foligno, and other saintly women were simply "holy anorexics." Catherine of Siena, for example, ate only bread, uncooked vegetables, and water as a teenager, and as an adult she reportedly subsisted on the eucharist, water, and bitter herbs. She spit out the herbs, and when she was ordered to consume food by her spiritual directors, she became very ill and vomited it. Catherine of Siena and women displaying comparable behavior were for Bell afflicted with a personality dysfunction. They benefited from the mystifications of their time and were granted a holy status. But their behavior is exactly the same as that defined as anorectic in modern medicine. Bell seems anachronistically to present past religion as pure ideology and to see modern science as the totally successful critique and transcendence of ideology that reveals the truth through full secular enlightenment.

In her widely acclaimed book, Caroline Walker Bynum takes a significantly different tack. She focuses on cultural symbols and offers a striking case of anthropological "thick description" in conjunction with massively documented historical research. Her broader concerns are the special role of food as a symbol for women and the specific qualities of spirituality—particularly asceticism—in women's "experi-

[9]Chicago: University of Chicago Press, 1987.
[10]Berkeley: University of California Press, 1987.

ence" in the later Middle Ages. Anorexia is addressed in the later portion of the book as one part of this larger network of issues. One may, however, ask whether the ideological role of redemptive narrative in her account helps to induce certain questionable tendencies.

Bynum painstakingly attempts to describe, evoke, and at least implicitly validate the nature of the "experience" of women in the Middle Ages. For example, she states: "It is not particularly helpful to know that Catherine of Siena can be said to be, in the modern sense, anorectic or even bulemic (although the statement is clearly true). The question is: why is food so central to women? Modern definitions of anorexia, while helpful in pointing out that 'control' is a key issue in anorectic behavior, obscure our perception of such behavior by glossing over the fact that *food* and *corporeality* are at stake" (p. 207). At least within the context of the Middle Ages, there is for Bynum something essential and essentially different about women's experience, and in her attempt to determine what it is, she even asserts that "what [she] suggest[s] about the continuity of woman's sense of self into her symbolic language in medieval texts could be explained very much as Luce Irigaray has explained present feminist discourse in 'The Sex Which Is Not One' " (p. 416n). What one threatens to have here is an unmediated, unworked-through combination of historicist contextualism (attempting to understand the past in its own terms and for its own sake) with presentist projection onto the past of contemporary meaning, desires, and values.

I suggest that certain dimensions of Bynum's account lend themselves to nonessentializing theoretical reformulation as involving an intricate process of repetition and change that cannot be decided in terms of either a simple divide between past and present or some identical core (or essential experiential phenomenon), on the one hand, and certain delimited, chronologically datable changes, on the other. For example, Bynum makes the following astute observations:

> It is not quite true (although there are elements of truth in it) to say that fasting was theologized in the Middle Ages and is secularized today. As the cases I discuss above make clear, medieval people did not see all refusal to eat as "fasting" (i.e., asceticism) or all extended abstinence as miraculous. And the case of the modern mystic Simone Weil and her many admirers, like the case of the German stigmatic Theresa of Konnersreuth, makes it clear that not all female abstinence in the twentieth century is medically or psychologically interpreted. (P. 195)

Bynum further notes that medieval writers had a number of paradigms for explaining extended periods of not eating, including miraculous or demonic causation, natural causation, and deliberate fraud or self-delusion. Her observations have the general value of pointing out that there are significant differences as well as similarities both at the same time and over time and that any valid comparison of "experiences" must take them into account. The notion of historical displacement or repetition with (perhaps drastic or traumatic) change would help to account for the "elements of truth" to which Bynum alludes by elucidating significant similarities with differences over time; it might also qualify our understanding of seemingly direct continuities (such as that between modern and earlier mystics) or seemingly total discontinuities (such as that between ascetics and those diagnosed as anorectic). Modern mystics such as Simone Weil go against the grain and have to contend with conditions and diagnoses that did not present themselves to earlier mystics, and they may attempt to imitate or emulate earlier mystics and retrieve earlier possibilities in a specific fashion that differs from behavior in the past. Moreover, as Bynum notes, the diagnosis of anorexia may induce a narrowly one-dimensional understanding of phenomena and the denial of symbolic dimensions of behavior that receive distinctive recognition in religious interpretation.

Here I would note that an indiscriminate critique or facile "undoing" of binarism may itself have various consequences: a denial or obscuring of its historically variable actual role, for example, in processes of exclusion, scapegoating, and victimization that may at times be quite pronounced and effective in both texts and social practice; a tendency to avoid the problem of the status and normative implications of one's critique; and an unguarded repetition of binarism and uncontrolled equivocation in one's own argument. The last-mentioned consequence is, I think, especially pronounced in Bynum's account. Thus, Bynum herself not only divides sharply between past and present in the interest of reconstructing empathetically yet objectively a past experience that nonetheless often seems to be construed in projective and presentist (more specifically, new historicist and contemporary feminist) terms. She also tends to conflate (rather than explore the problematic relations between) the masculine and the male as well as to draw a stark, binary opposition between male and female experiences, thereby occluding the role of other modes of gender and sexuality. Moreover, in her desire to accentuate the positive in women's experience, she insists somewhat gratuitously that elements of dualism and misogyny in medieval asceticism and in women's self-perceptions are not basic or dominant. Instead, what is presumably basic and dominant is the role of asceticism as "an effective way of manipulating the environment," "a rebellion against the moderation of the high medieval church," and a way of "fusing with a Christ whose suffering saves the world" (p. 218). Indeed, female asceticism, far from being substantially affected by hegemonic masculine views, is primarily an expression of women's experience; it is simultaneously an affirmation of the body. It should be seen as a matter of "changes rung on the *possibilities* provided by fleshliness than as flight from physicality" (p. 6). Or, as Bynum puts it in another formulation: "Late medieval asceticism was an effort to plumb and to realize all the possibilities of the flesh" (p. 294).

One might suggest that an either/or logic is out of place here and that the problem for interpretation is how both world-rejection and self-exploration or protest interacted and were at issue in asceticism. One might also suggest that Bynum's idea of the autonomy and affirmative nature—indeed the authenticity—of woman's experience seems remarkably unhistorical in its tendency to downplay the relation between oppressed or subordinated experience and hegemonic structures and in its elision of the problem of how precisely counter-hegemonic activity relates to dominant forms in ways that may variably combine symptomatic reinforcement of the dominant with more or less effective critiques and transformations of it.

The opposition Bynum draws between men's and women's experience relies on terms that are not elucidated. For Bynum, late medieval men thought and experienced in dichotomized or binary terms, relied on reversals of dominant oppositions, and saw life in the light of decisive crises, turning points, or conversion experiences. Women preferred continuity, synthesis, and paradox. In making this analysis, Bynum does not situate the status of her own binary tendencies. Nor does she indicate exactly how continuity, synthesis, and paradox went together in thought and experience, for they would hardly seem to be identical or even easily reconciled (or synthesized) terms. It should, however, be observed that this relationship may not pose a problem for Bynum insofar as she not only repeats a (presumably masculine) binarism but empathetically renders what she presents as a "logic" of total identity, including the total identity of seeming opposites such as humanity and divinity in Christ and in those who

identify with him through imitatio. In this sense, to imitate is to become and ultimately to be the other, and imitation may involve repeatedly and compulsively acting out Christ's persecution, torment,
and suffering (p. 256). (Here a logic of full identity—which of course
complements a binary logic of total difference between identities—
would seem bound up with the acting out of a repetition compulsion
wherein the past is not worked through but experienced as fully relived or present.) Indeed, in Bynum one has a series of metaphoric
identifications in which fasting, feeding, and feasting are synony-
mous (p. 250), and eating the eucharist which is Christ means eating
and so becoming Christ's crucified body (pp. 256–57). As Bynum observes in what she believes to be properly "nonjudgmental" terms,
such views accompanied "a Christian enthusiasm for bodies, especially mutilated dead bodies, as loci of divine power" (p. 255).

Bynum also tends to underemphasize the significance of the
thought of men who do not simply rely on binaries or conform to the
binary opposition on which she relies in contrasting medieval men
and women. As she puts it:

> All this is not to say that male mystics never use paradox (one thinks of
> Nicholas of Cusa) or that male theologians never push such paradoxical
> synthesis to the point of reconciling heaven and hell (one thinks of
> Origen) or that male penitents never substitute continuity of self in Jesus
> for passage up the hierarchy of the cosmos to God (one thinks of
> Francis). But the explosion of paradox in a Hadewijch, a Margaret
> Porete, or a Catherine of Genoa, the agonized rejection of the existence
> of hell in a Mechtild of Magdeburg or a Julian of Norwich, the delicious
> groveling in the humiliations of being human that characterizes virtually
> every religious woman of the later Middle Ages—these form a consistent
> pattern that is found only infrequently in religious men. And behind the
> pattern lies a confidence that all is one—all is, as Julian said, a hazelnut
> held in the palm of God's hand—because it is finally the humanity that
> we most despicably are that is redeemed. It is our "Me" that becomes
> God. (P. 290)

To use explosiveness or agonized rejection as differential criteria is
at best tenuous and requires extensive textual analysis of the type Bynum does not provide. And to refer, in an analysis stressing the affirmative nature of woman's experience, to "the delicious groveling in
the humiliations of being human that characterizes virtually every religious woman of the later Middle Ages" is itself somewhat paradox-

ical; at the very least, it requires some elucidation of the "affirmative" nature of abjection as well as of the working of a sacrificial logic even when the "victim" is a voluntary one. In addition, the charismatic or prophetic role of certain woman saints might indeed constitute a challenge to established religious authority (p. 233), but aspects of fasting, even when taken to disconcerting extremes in more or less admired and collectively supported individual practice, need not upset the social or religious order in any basic way and might, as Bynum notes, even be praised by male authorities and hagiographers themselves.

Bynum herself insistently engages in a redemptive reading of phenomena involving women and identifiably female experience—a type of reading that is perhaps epitomized in Tania Modleski's rehabilitation of soap operas as spaces in which women can think.[11] As soaps are to Modleski, saints are to Bynum, and the elements of truth and even the power of provocation in their accounts would, I think, be enhanced rather than denied by a more complex, qualified, and self-questioning analysis of the phenomena in question. Indeed, one may agree (as I do) with the ethical and political motivation of Bynum's (or Modleski's) account yet disagree with aspects of the approach to history and even contend that a different approach might better serve both feminism and the critique and rearticulation of sexual or gender relations.

I turn now to Charles Taylor's *Sources of the Self: The Making of the Modern Identity*[12]—a book in which a markedly redemptive reading is applied not to a particular group's "experience" but to the vast sweep of Western history itself. Taylor's is a breathtakingly ambitious and magisterial work that Jerome Bruner (on the dust jacket) praises as "surely one of the most important philosophical works of the last quarter of a century." Bruner adds: "Charles Taylor emerges as one of the truly great practitioners of philosophy in our century." In his review for the *Journal of Modern History*,[13] the noted historian Michael

---

[11]*Loving with a Vengeance: Mass-produced Fantasies for Women* (New York: Methuen, 1982).

[12]Cambridge: Harvard University Press, 1989. For a more sobering and self-critical view of some of the problems touched on by Taylor, see Jerome J. McGann, *The Romantic Ideology: A Critical Investigation* (Chicago: University of Chicago Press, 1983).

[13]64 (1992), 119–21. In addition to Ermarth's review, see the full and generous appreciation of Taylor's book in Craig Calhoun, "Morality, Identity, and Historical Explanation: Charles Taylor on the Sources of the Self," *Sociological Theory* 9 (1991), 232–63. Calhoun stresses the manner in which Taylor conjoins historical inquiry and social philosophy in the attempt to rehabilitate normative reasoning and practical judgment.

Return of the Repressed 183

Ermarth asserts: "Charles Taylor has outdone himself with a work of sustained brilliance. Even grateful readers of his previous studies on Hegel and social theory will be much impressed, for the present book is a landmark by any measure. It sets a new standard in intellectual history and will inspire future inquiry along the clear lines he lays down" (p. 119).

Taylor's book is distinctive in that it frames its wealth of material in a reaffirmed master narrative and even a qualified Eurocentric perspective after these initiatives have been subjected to seemingly devastating criticism. Taylor is also engaged in a hermeneutic voyage of recovery, and he convincingly makes the case that knowledge of the past is not irrelevant to philosophical understanding or argument in the present. More debatably, he tends to rehabilitate religion in general and Christianity in particular through the indirect route of hermeneutics, indicating that the privileged criterion of meaning tips the scales in favor of religion, which provides what secular displacements can never fully offer. Moreover, although he would like to unite philosophy and a certain use of history, he sharply opposes philosophy to literature. He does so with apparent self-effacement and humility, for he seems, in a neoromantic gesture, to elevate art to an epiphanic status and to confine philosophy to the clarifying work of the under-laborer or even the inept mechanic (p. 512). But such comparisons and rhetorical flights are never innocent, and this one serves implicitly to reinforce Taylor's predominantly negative treatment of certain figures, such as Nietzsche, or summary dismissal of others, such as Derrida, who have a different understanding—and practice—of the relation between philosophy and literature. For Taylor, deconstruction is a mere "vogue emanat[ing] from Paris" (p. 487), and he does not so much as grace it with a careful attempt at interpretation and criticism.

Taylor at times broaches an understanding of temporality as repetition with change or displacement, particularly with respect to secularization, whose role he recognizes and extensively discusses. But he tends to neatly separate continuity from discontinuity over time and

---

I think this is a crucial undertaking and agree with certain aspects of what Calhoun or Ermarth find valuable in Taylor's book. But given the marked praise the book has already received, I have chosen to focus on what I think are its limitations, especially with respect to issues that I raise in this study. There should be no doubt, however, that *Sources of the Self* is in many significant respects a very important and impressive work.

to present differences as quite distinct if not detached from similarities. Thus, rather than see a complex displacement of the religious in the secular, he envisions a process whereby what was once presumably a cosmic order or an unmediated and "objective" public world is radically ruptured, so that forms, meanings, and processes of identity formation are internalized. Taylor may be justified in stressing the importance of "inner" processes and even narcissism in the modern world, however difficult it may be to provide a cogent account of their quantitative or qualitative relations to earlier practices and modes of experience. But he tends to misconstrue the effects of trauma and to offer another rendition of the journey to the interior (or the internalization of what was once the outer world) that threatens to repeat uncritically the ideology it discusses. Taylor's entire narrative at times seems to be an overwhelmingly erudite genealogical reconstruction and valorization of now dominant self-images and clichés—a monumental refamiliarization of the all-too-familiar.

What Taylor in effect does is, first, to avoid the issue of how any reconstruction of the past is a problematic inference that at most delineates a variable configuration of more or less dominant and subdominant beliefs and practices and, second, to accept in his own voice the ideologically freighted or even mythical conception of the past-we-have-lost—a past presumed to be a more integrated, holistic, public world. Indeed, he offers a liberally upbeat, neo-Hegelian rendition of the history of ideas, culminating in the present Western, Eurocentric world. He explicitly envisions this world as enjoying a "moral exceptionalism" (p. 397) in that it insistently affirms and presumably has realized more than any other culture the ideals of benevolence, justice, equality, universality, and so forth, whose meaning Taylor has tried to recover. "We feel that our civilization has made a qualitative leap" with respect to such virtues as benevolence (p. 396), and for Taylor this feeling is apparently justified. If "we" might have some doubts about who exactly "we" are in this insistently culturalist and hermeneutic account in which class, race, gender, and species make only episodic appearances, "we" are not exactly reassured when Taylor circularly designates "us" as "those committed to goodness and benevolence" in "our" civilization (p. 448). Although Taylor does acknowledge some of the less edifying aspects of recent Western history and even refers a few times to the Nazis (pp. 415, 471, 484, and 575—but an entry does not appear in the index), he wants to affirm the moral superiority of the West (p. 397). His references to facts and factors that lessen the plausibility of his invidious valorization of the West as he understands it—what might perhaps be called his song of ourselves—tend to be made in passing and to function at most as relatively subdued qualifications of a largely celebratory argument. For example, one of his references to the Nazis situates them as an unsuccessful interruption of a victorious ethic of reducing suffering (p. 575). Taylor is apparently unaware of the manner in which this argument is close to a relativizing and dubiously "revisionist" interpretation of the Nazi period.

To make these points is not, however, to subscribe to the opposite view that presents Western history as one long, unmitigated story of destruction and decline. It is rather to argue for a more complex account of the various, at times conflicting, dimensions of that history, one in which the relation between empirical events or developments and one's values is explicitly problematized and made a matter of critical inquiry and argument. Instead of providing this kind of account, Taylor elaborates a massively redemptive master narrative in which empirical reality is portrayed as the progressive realization of values.

Taylor's undertaking is facilitated by at least four interlocking features of his approach, which are at least worth passing mention: (1) he remains on the level of generalized synoptic content (or, with respect to literature, character) analysis and rarely attempts a close, critical reading of texts or events; (2) he tends to dissociate and treat in relative isolation cultural meaning and humanitarian ideals rather than to explore systematically and critically the very tendency toward dissociation of spheres in modern life, including the dissociation and mutual corroboration of humanitarian ideals and practical inhumanity; (3) he does not thematize the problem of a split between internalization and objectification as complementary, mutually reinforcing processes whereby the modern period has witnessed not only internalization but also some of the most extreme forms of "externalistic," objectifying, and deterministic explanations of human action in currents such as positivism and behaviorism; (4) he notes the features of modern art and literature that depart from an epiphany of expressive being in the recovery of meaning but treats them in a dubious and domesticating fashion (for example, in terms of the concept of spatial form or framed epiphany). He also insists that modern artistic initiatives still involve variations on the inward turn even when they contest or displace it radically and—rather than resting content with what Taylor perceives and praises as a personally indexed vision of things—seem to seek a significantly different way of articulating relations or formulating problems. Indeed, even the insistently counterepiphanic literature of the Holocaust is for Taylor "just a step towards the new kind of epiphany" (p. 487). Perhaps the most dubious dimension of Taylor's account is epitomized in this unearned, benevolently bland, and judicious "just," for it is typical of the manner in which Taylor's own approach to problems and his very subject-position, notably including his use of language, tend to remain untroubled by the dislocations, challenges, and "inner" turmoil he notices in modern works. The serenely traditional if not conventional nature of Taylor's own discourse may make it impossible for him to engage and attempt to work through the problems he mentions, and it tends to disempower his admirable desire to affirm a needed existential shift in response to basic problems that would help to overcome cynicism.

In his *Holocaust Testimonies: The Ruins of Memory*,[14] Lawrence Langer concludes his account with a searing critique of Taylor's approach. He sees Taylor's book as a prolonged ideological nostrum that denies or represses the problems of deep, anguished, humiliated, tainted, and unheroic memory that Langer discusses with reference to video archives of survivor testimony in the Yale Fortunoff collection. More generally, Langer places in radical jeopardy any redemptive narrative that presents history as the realization or teleological unfolding of "positive" values. As he puts it:

> For Taylor, modern identity suggests "the ensemble of (largely unarticulated) understandings of what it is to be a human agent: the sense of inwardness, freedom, individuality, and being embedded in nature which are at home in the modern West." The videotaped oral testimonies we have studied develop an image of modern identity rooted not in theory but in experience, an image that articulates with more or less vividness what it meant (and means) in our time to exist *without* a sense of human agency. They reveal the consequences of a gradual attrition of the qualities of inwardness, freedom, and individuality, an estrangement from nature until one is alienated from the very self that Taylor equates with identity. (Pp. 198–99)

One may observe that the Shoah is an extreme instance of a traumatic series of events that pose the problem of denial or disavowal, acting-out, and working-through. In different ways this problem has

---

[14]New Haven: Yale University Press, 1991.

affected victims, perpetrators, bystanders, and those born later who have various subject-positions with respect to those more immediately involved in the events of the Holocaust. In this context, I suggest that the Shoah has often been in the position of the repressed in the post–World War II West and that those trying to lift this repression have faced incredible difficulties and temptations both in terms of the resistance of others and in terms of their own problems in putting things into acceptable language.

Much recent debate in critical theory and historiography is recast if the Holocaust is perceived as at least one more or less repressed divider or traumatic point of rupture between modernism and postmodernism. In this light, the postmodern and the post-Holocaust become mutually intertwined issues that are best addressed in relation to each other. The question to be posed to the postmodern critique of certain presumed modern projects such as totalization and liberation then becomes whether or to what extent various postmodern initiatives constitute symptomatic intensifications of generalized disarray—at most the acting-out of posttraumatic stress—or, serving to some extent as an antidote, become ways and means of recognizing and reinscribing prevalent conditions so as to further the possibility of counteracting a fatalistic repetition compulsion and thus of responsibly working through problems. (Habermas is closer to the former construction of postmodernism and Lyotard at times to the latter.[15])

Both the Holocaust and the post-Holocaust raise the question of a return of the repressed. I have already maintained that one issue in the Holocaust itself is the role of scapegoating and victimization, perhaps related to a distorted sacrificialism in the Nazi treatment of Jews. There is also the problem of the manner in which scapegoating interacts with an extreme, secularized instrumental or bureaucratic rationality. (One obvious link between the two is the way in which the victim was seen as racially "alien" in both ritualistic terms and in those of pseudoscience or "bureaucratese." The concept of race operated in at least two registers—pseudoscientific and ritualistic. As a result, the victim was never treated in the same terms as oneself,

---

[15]See especially Jürgen Habermas, *The Philosophical Discourse of Modernity*, trans. Frederick Lawrence (Cambridge: MIT Press, 1987), and Jean-François Lyotard, *The Postmodern Condition: A Report on Knowledge*, trans. Geoff Bennington and Brian Massumi (1979; Minneapolis: University of Minnesota Press, 1984) and *The Differend: Phrases in Dispute*, trans. George Van Den Abbeele (1983; Minneapolis: University of Minnesota Press, 1988).

thereby either neutralized as an object or made into a repository for the projection of one's repressed anxieties and self-doubts.) The scapegoating component has often tended to be denied for a variety of reasons, for example, a restricted idea of the banality of evil, a reliance on a conception of modernity in terms of bureaucratic rationality or a technological frame of reference, and a general desire to avoid any view that might seem, however remotely or unintentionally, to legitimate events or jeopardize secular rationality. But certain features of the Nazi treatment of Jews, such as the projective desire to remove a putative source of pollution from the community, make the role of scapegoating difficult to deny.

In the recent past, the repressed has seemed to return in a complex fashion that has induced renewed disavowal in certain quarters (for example, among revisionist historians) and commodified, commercialized, politically tendentious, and self-interested (if not pornographic) representation in other quarters. Beyond the question of representation, events in central and eastern Europe have had extremely equivocal consequences. The apparent desire in these areas for democracy, liberalism, pluralism, a market economy, consumer goods, and other features of "our way of life" has at times led to the one-sided construction of extreme crisis as a sign that the West has won, that Marxism in any and every form has been vanquished, and that history has ended. Yet the collapse of existing forms of socialism has enabled the resurfacing of everything that authoritarianism kept down, and the less promising revenants include anti-Semitism, rabid nationalism, ethnocentrism, and intolerance for others—revenants that may allow for the regrouping and reassertion of older communist forces. These developments might induce the sober conclusion that existing communist regimes may have lost, but nobody has won. As Dan Diner has put it, "From the depths of Europe, voices many thought had long since been forgotten can be heard once again: *Volk, Nation, Minorität.*"[16] In the light of occurrences in the former state of Yugoslavia, one may now add "ethnic cleansing" to Diner's list of returning voices.

Diner also notes that the traditional tendency to assimilate Jews and communists has made the anticommunist reaction aggravate resurgent racism and anti-Semitism. And the stress on traditional structures,

[16]"Problems of Periodization and Historical Memory," in *New German Critique* 53 (1991), 167.

national rivalries, and anti-Bolshevism in the interpretation of the past has itself furthered tendencies to forget and deny other features that disrupt reassuring visions of continuity and ideological identity. "An easily repressed abstract event such as the mass extermination, which in any case is difficult to retain in memory, will, along with an identification of communist antifascism and the Soviet victory over Hitler's Germany, be submerged in an ever-deepening amnesia" (p. 174). Curiously both those (like Arno Mayer) who would center the explanation of the Holocaust on anti-Bolshevism as well as criticize the communist scare that was so important in the Cold War and those (like Ernst Nolte) who would emphasize anti-Bolshevism in order to underscore continuous Western solidarity and keep the communist scare alive—at least by finding some surrogate for the lost or drastically diminished world-communist enemy—have an interest in downplaying or repressing certain features of the Holocaust (such as the distinctive nature of Nazi racism and anti-Semitism in a policy of mass extermination); both may thereby succumb to a view that does little to focus critical attention on and counteract the displaced return of elements that had disastrous effects.

One may relate the foregoing considerations to the question of the nature of theory and its critical potential. There are at least three intricately interacting—perhaps inseparable but nonetheless distinguishable—ways to construe theory. The first is theory as a totalizing discourse that makes sense of everything. Theory in this sense has itself been the object of stringent criticism in the recent past, notably in various poststructuralisms and postmodernisms. But its allure—or even its ineluctable if hidden return—has also been a preoccupation. Theodicy in religious interpretation and speculative dialectics as well as redemptive narrative in secular thought are some of its foremost avatars. Here irrationality and paradox may be acknowledged but only to be transcended or sublated, hence both comprehended and legitimated.

A scapegoat mechanism may be active in all totalizing practices. Through the process of scapegoating, identities are purified into binary opposites (notably between self and other or victimizer and victim) on the way to a higher identity or totality. And any irrationality redounds to the benefit of the community and ultimately of the sovereign, although such benefit may require the sacralization of violence and the role of an abject victim. From this perspective, the sovereign—including the secular sovereign or leader in a typically decisionist political theology—cannot make a mistake, and there is no such thing as a miscarriage of justice on the part of a sovereign agency. The sovereign is and must always be in the right.

Ideologically, the achievement of full identity or closure is the telos of totalization, and the full redemption of meaning and value is the very essence of discourse. Mourning in this sense is a process that succeeds to such an extent that it negates or overcomes itself, and (to paraphrase Hegel) the wounds of the past are healed without leaving any scars. The result may be the imaginary attainment of a "beautiful" whole. From this perspective, the critical distinction between fact and value easily becomes superficial, and the process of analysis or of theoretical inquiry cannot be distinguished from the issue of redemption or perdition, transfiguration or disfiguration.

This extreme version of totalization may of course take more modulated and attenuated forms, but even in them there may be a pronounced effort to accentuate the positive, notably through what I have termed redemptive readings or narratives. The extreme version of totalization may also be elaborated in order to serve as a foil to its radical undoing. An extreme and compulsively repeated undoing may nonetheless bear witness to the attraction of totalization and remain within an "all-or-nothing" frame of reference. For the extreme reaction to the assumption that everything ultimately makes sense may be the assumption that ultimately nothing makes sense. Or, through an overly generalized theory of romantic irony, one may believe that one always remains suspended between sense and nonsense in a manner that stymies all possible judgment and action.[17]

---

[17]For example, Andrzej Warminski writes the following with particular reference to Paul de Man's Word War II journalism: "Of course, everything changes as soon as we begin reading the texts—that is, begin reading *as* text—even the newspapers. For as soon as we begin to do so, we lose the possibility of using the referential moment inscribed in the newspapers as a reliable model for a cognition on the basis of which we could take action—for instance, like the action of judging de Man as either guilty or innocent. Reading suspends: it suspends knowledge and it suspends judgment, and it suspends, above all, the possibility of ever knowing whether we are doing one or the other. Reading suspends the decisions between the thematic, referential meaning and the rhetorical, allegorical function that turns upon it. This is why reading is truly threatening and truly terrible—not because it suspends you between two meanings, but because it suspends you between meaning and the material, linguistic conditions of meaning that always dis-articulate it radically as they make it possible"; "Terrible Reading (preceded by 'Epigraphs')," in *Responses: On Paul de Man's Wartime Journalism*, ed. Werner Hamacher, Neil Hertz, and Thomas Keenan (Lincoln: University of Nebraska Press, 1989), p. 392. Warminski seems insensitive to the apologetic implications of his

Here deceptive transfiguration is necessarily supplemented if not displaced by what may be an equally deceptive disfiguration or disarticulation. This reaction becomes particularly compelling in a posttraumatic context, particularly when the object of mourning is concealed or foreclosed and the process of mourning is arrested by (or even identified with) continual melancholy and the acting out of a repetition compulsion. Theory itself in this context may take necessary critical and self-critical inquiry—including inquiry into one's own assumptions—and autonomize or fetishize it until it becomes an externally predictable but internally compelling process of disarticulation, disorientation, destabilization, dismemberment, and so forth. The discursive symptom of this understanding of theory is the repeated, moth-to-flame movement toward the paradox, aporia, or impasse that "sublimely" brings language to a halt and renders impossible (or situates as hopelessly naive) any form of recovery or viable agency.

At times theory is restricted to these two options, which may be correlated with two complementary ways of responding to trauma that may mistakenly be seen as alternatives. One response involves denial or repression, for example, in a redemptive, fetishistic narrative that excludes or marginalizes trauma through a teleological story that projectively presents values and wishes as viably realized in the facts, typically through a progressive, developmental process. As Charles Taylor's *Sources of the Self* shows, this tendency (pace Lyotard) is hardly a thing of the past, and there is an avid audience for it. Indeed, even historians who shy away from the type of master narrative that Taylor relies on may nonetheless offer redemptive accounts and

---

own excessively generalized reading of reading, and what "meaning" is made possible on his analysis itself remains radically unclear. He forcefully brings out a possibility in all texts but one that is actualized in different ways and to different degrees in different texts and in different conditions. The danger in his approach is that deconstruction may become a homogenizing reading technology with sectarian overtones—a technology that reprocesses all texts in its own disarticulating terms, thereby breaking down all distinctions between texts. Reading something as text becomes tantamount to putting on a certain set of blinkers, so that reading a propagandistic newspaper article is essentially the same as reading the most intricate, self-questioning poem, novel, or philosophical text. Moreover, one may agree that one may not be in a position to make a definitive judgment about de Man as an individual, but such agreement does not imply that reading is totally unrelated to problems of deliberative and forensic—in contrast with narrowly judicial—judgment that may have certain mediated relations to ethical and political action. The attendant issue is the relation between decidability and undecidability with reference to different texts and situations.

implicitly code their stories through an often blind projection onto events of their wishes and values—a process that may convert past figures into one's own unmediated spokespersons. This process is facilitated by the tendency to avoid an explicit encounter with normative problems and to restrict historical discourse to seemingly empirical and analytic uses of language.

The second and complementary response tends intentionally or unintentionally to aggravate trauma in a largely symptomatic fashion. This may be done through a construction of all history (or at least all modern history) as trauma and an insistence that there is no alternative to symptomatic acting-out and the repetition compulsion other than an imaginary, illusory hope for totalization, full closure, and redemptive meaning. Acting-out and the repetition compulsion are frequently related to an affirmation or acknowledgment of posttraumatic fragmentation, disjunction, and instability wherein the impossibility of any final unity or "suture" may become tantamount to the unavailability or elusiveness of any durable bonds or "suturing" at all. Indeed, our straining for a politically and socially relevant mode of thought, which is not relegated to an inferior position or even experienced as mere divertissement with respect to an impossible redemption, may face strong internal inhibitions and blockages insofar as we are very much attached to our symptoms.

One may nonetheless insist on a third sense of theory related to Freud's notion of working-through.[18] Theory in this sense would prompt an attempt to combine criticism and self-criticism with a practice of articulation that would resist redemptive totalization. It would not deny the irreducibility of loss or the role of paradox and aporia. But instead of becoming compulsively fixated on or symptomatically reinforcing impasses, it would engage a process of mourning that would attempt, however self-questioningly and haltingly, to specify its haunting objects and (even if only symbolically) to give them a "proper" burial. It would also involve a tense interaction between

[18]This third sense of theory may also be related to what Jacques Derrida terms "generalized displacement," which must accompany the reversal of hierarchically arranged binary opposites if one is not to remain entirely within their frame of reference. In the wake of trauma, the problem is how to effect a "double inscription" of acting-out and working-through, melancholy and mourning in the attempt to come to terms with problems. One may also see this problem in terms of an attempt to relate performativity to double inscription and to a notion of the normative that should not be conflated with normalization—a notion requiring that the question be posed of the actual and desirable interaction between limits and transgression.

seeming opposites such as stability and the risk of trauma—an interaction that would raise the question of desirable alternatives to one's
object of criticism, notably in terms of the relationship between normative limits and transgression.

Working-through was obviously crucial for Freud, although he provided relatively little sustained investigation of its nature and at times
was even inclined to conflate it with totalizing remembrance.[19] Moreover, in post-Freudian critical theory, the process of working-through
has received relatively little explicit attention. This state of affairs is
undoubtedly related to the difficulty of even envisioning an effective
process of working-through in a posttraumatic context in which
agency cannot simply be assumed but must be reconstituted. But it
may also be related to symptomatic acting-out (often reinforced by too
restricted a theory of performativity) and to the widespread assumption that one is caught between the illusory attempt at theoretical or
narrative totalization and a compulsive repetition of trauma, double
binds, or utter fragmentation. At the very least, one should try to
question these fixations, however tentative and provisional one's formulations must be.

Langer avoids theory—notably psychoanalytic and deconstructive
theory—and relies on a sensitive ordinary-language approach to
problems. Especially in light of his topic, this approach is quite defensible. But he focuses on Holocaust testimonies with such an intensity
and sense of their inherent truth that he tends to bracket or avoid the
problem of the relation between testimony and historical understanding and self-understanding. He also has a rather unmediated view of
"experience" (in contrast to "theory") and its authentic rendering in
oral testimony (in contrast to "literary" writing with its conventions).[20] In addition to its idealization of "experience," Langer's view
obscures the role of rhetorical conventions in oral discourse and the
interaction between "literary" writing and speech. And it carries
over into what may be an uncritical relation to his own position as
secondary witness who is presumed to transparently render the experience of the original witness as victim—a position that is particularly

[19]See especially "Remembering, Repeating and Working Through," in *The Standard
Edition of the Complete Psychological Works of Sigmund Freud* 12, trans. James Strachey
(London: Hogarth, 1958), pp. 145–56.

[20]For example: "Oral testimony is distinguished by the absence of literary mediation"
(p. 57). "Beyond dispute in oral testimony is that every word spoken falls directly from
the lips of the witness" (p. 210n).

untenable given the riven experience and the belatedness of witnessing for victims of trauma themselves. Moreover, Langer's account seems to share with certain sophisticated theoretical endeavors the extreme, all-or-nothing assumption that there are essentially only two (impossible) options: totalizing, redemptive meaning (now seen as illusory if still alluring) and symptomatically staying within trauma by acting out a repetition compulsion with its fragmentation or fracturing of all possibilities of bonding and renewal. At points he even gives way to rare hyperbole and generalizes what he sees as a survivor "ethic," whereby one has no alternative but to identify in a *sauve-qui-peut* fashion with a situationist, impromptu self for which "ordinary" morality involving obligations to others is simply irrelevant. Thus, for example, he writes:

> Self-esteem is crucial to the evolution of heroic memory; the narratives in these testimonies reflect a partially traumatized or maimed self-esteem, lingering like a non-fatal disease without any cure. Heroic memory is virtually unavailable to such witnesses, because for them remembering is invariably associated with a jumbled terminology and morality that confuse staying alive with the intrepid will to survival. Such remembering replaces the Sisyphean gesture of defiance against a hostile universe with particular circumstances that chip away at inappropriate images of a heroic self. Those circumstances in turn give birth to a diminished self that demands a whole cluster of redefinitions and fresh perceptions, a modernized or modernist view of verbal and moral possibilities and limitations that need not be restricted to Holocaust reality alone. (Pp. 176–77)

Here one gets at least a hint of the rather leveling if not ahistorical idea of all modern history as holocaust or trauma. As Langer puts it in his conclusion:

> A kind of unshielded truth emerges from the[se narratives], through which we salvage an anatomy of melancholy for the modern spirit—part of our anguish and our fate. For the former victims, the Holocaust is a communal wound that cannot heal. This is the ailing subtext of their testimonies, wailing beneath the convalescent murmur of their surface lives. We have little trouble listening to that surface murmur. When the subtext of their story echoes for us too as a communal wound, then we will have begun to hear their legacy of unheroic memory and grasp the meaning for our time of a diminished self. (Pp. 204–5)

One may agree with the view that the Holocaust is, in a manner that would have to be further differentiated, "a communal wound that cannot heal." But does this view entail that countervailing tendencies in the lives of victims—and by seeming implication in modernity in general—are merely constitutive of a surface life or murmur that is somehow less authentic than what is argued to lie beneath? In line with his emphases in interpretation, Langer is even led to infringe his hermeneutic principle of attentive, respectful listening. For he tends to downplay, see as flatly contradictory, or even discount as illusory, testimony that either insists on acts of defiance and resistance during the Shoah or perhaps tensely combines the reliving of a traumatic past with a counterideological attempt to recount a history, reconstruct a sense of agency, and rebuild a life. Langer's view is compelling insofar as the unexpected shock of trauma—what surges up in the absence of what Freud termed *Angstbereitschaft* (the readiness to feel anxiety)—typically paralyzes or numbs the victim and makes immediate resistance impossible. But when there are signs of resistance, particularly in a posttraumatic situation, one might expect the analyst to be attentive to them and to inquire into their genesis, for they may be indicative of an effort to work through problems. Indeed, like quite a few others, the final testimony (of Philip K.) that concludes Langer's book and follows immediately on the passage I have just quoted does not unequivocally support Langer's very active interpretation:

> I often say to people who pretend or seem to be marveling at the fact
> that I seem to be so normal, so unperturbed and so capable of
> functioning—they seem to think the Holocaust passed over and it's done
> with: It's my skin. This is not a coat. You can't take it off. And it's there,
> and it will be there until I die. . . .
> If we were not an eternal people before, we are an eternal people after
> the Holocaust, in both its very positive and very negative sense. We
> have not only survived, but we have revived ourselves. In a very real
> way, we have won. We were victorious. But in a very real way, we have
> lost. We'll never recover what was lost. We can't even assess what was
> lost. Who knows what beauty and grandeur six million could have
> contributed to the world? Who can measure it up? What standard do
> you use? How do you count it? How do you estimate it . . . ?[21]

[21]Compare the words of Nietzsche's madman concerning the death of God: "How could we drink up the sea? Who gave us the sponge to wipe away the entire horizon? What were we doing when we unchained this earth from its sun? Whither is it moving

We lost. The world lost, whether they know it or admit it. It doesn't make any difference. And yet we won, we're going on. . . .

I think there are as many ways of surviving survival as there have been to survive. (Quoted on p. 205)

Without even attempting to do justice to this statement, I want simply to observe that in it one has the strongest conceivable formulation of an essential tension or undecidability between conclusions to be drawn as well as between parts of the self. There is no simple opposition between depth and surface, and the assertion that the Holocaust is not a coat does not imply that the reconstructed self is. The comment about the many ways of surviving survival points to the danger of homogenizing or overgeneralizing about the experience of victims and survivors. I think one may also argue that it indicates the danger of massive generalizations about modernity and points instead to the importance of careful comparative history.

There may be a sense in which Langer himself remains too much within a displaced and secularized religious framework—a framework he shares with Taylor whose emphases he reverses. Langer is justifiably concerned with righting an imbalance created by salvationist attempts to make us feel good by portraying the experience of Holocaust victims as an uplifting testimony to the heroic strength of the spirit and the indomitable human will, but at times he may go too far in the opposite yet complementary direction. He at least implies that if values do not redeem the past, purify memory, and validate a conception of full heroic identity, autonomy, and agency, then values are

now? Whither are we moving? Away from all suns? Are we not plunging continually? Backward, sideward, forward, in all directions? Is there still any up or down? Are we not straying as through an infinite nothing?" *The Gay Science*, trans. Walter Kaufmann (New York: Vintage, 1974), p. 181. On the question of resistance, the testimony of Helen K., which Langer does not discuss, is of special interest. As all members of her family are killed or die, she forms the resolve to resist and survive if only to show Hitler that he cannot succeed in destroying her. She participates in the Warsaw ghetto uprising and recalls with pride the explosion of one of the Auschwitz crematoria (see Fortunoff Video Archive Tape A-35). Nor should one simply take at face value Primo Levi's hauntingly self-effacing assertion that the true witnesses died. This is the kind of assertion a Primo Levi may make but that people without comparable experience may not take up in their own voices. Indeed, those who survived extreme conditions might in a legitimate sense be said to have resisted a state of affairs designed to destroy them even if they did not take part in uprising or sabotage. See, for example, the excruciating testimony of Leon S., who underwent trying situations, including torture, but for moral and religious reasons does not regret having never raised a hand against his tormenters (Fortunoff Video Archive Tape A-25).

themselves altogether unredeemed and irrelevant not only to the past but also in some way in the present. He explicitly states that historical investigation of the Holocaust "cannot promote life" and that "the 'knowledge' [humiliated memory] imparts crushes the spirit and frustrates the incentive to renewal" (p. 79). Langer here indicates possibilities—forceful possibilities—but possibilities that should in certain significant ways be resisted, not furthered or enshrined. One may, moreover, contend that if experience or facts depart drastically from values—as they may in certain circumstances—this departure does not invalidate the values but indicates the extremity (which does not mean the dismissable anomaly) of the circumstances and the repeated need to do everything possible to prevent the recurrence of similar circumstances. One may also suggest that the study of the Holocaust may serve life not by reinforcing a misplaced, self-congratulatory sense of one's unearned worth but in the limited and mediated sense of helping to engender a nonfanatical determination to prevent anything comparable from occurring again.

Langer's conclusions may seem uncompromisingly radical or even rigorous, but their generalization is questionable. They remain purely interpretive, and it is difficult to see how they can be associated with social action or even a qualified and variable sense of agency (as limited liability) other than through a blind decision or act of faith. While in no sense denying the role of trauma in history or the significance of losses that cannot be made good, one may ask whether one may counter ideologically saturated, redemptive narratives by attempting to pose problems in a manner that does not tend to remain within a strategy of reversal.

Acting-out may well be necessary and unavoidable in the wake of extreme trauma, especially for victims. With all due respect to those for whom this risk may be too frequent and too great, I suggest that perhaps the interviewer and the analyst (without pretending to the possibility of purely transparent rendering of the "unshielded truth" of survivor testimony) should try—or allow themselves—to become what Langer aptly terms secondary witnesses in a specific sense, that is, in and through a labor of listening and attending that exposes the self to empathetic understanding and hence to at least muted trauma. In other words, one would attempt to put oneself in the other's position without taking the other's place. (It does no one any good simply to become a surrogate victim, however compelling the inclination may at times be.) This possibility of self-exposure is one crucial reason why inquiry is often avoided or has such extremely depressing effects. (One must admire Langer for his exceptional undertaking and appreciate the possible reasons for certain of his conclusions—conclusions one may at times be inclined to share.) Insofar as it is traumatic, repetition involves an uncanny, radically destabilizing excess that threatens the breakdown not only of "literary" conventions but of all conventions of language use, indeed the possibility of breakdown in every sense. Yet the radical ambivalence of repetition—its "undecidability" if you prefer—implies the possible role of countervailing forces that may not entirely heal wounds but that allow mediated ways of surviving survival—forces such as mourning itself, where grief is repeated in reduced, normatively controlled, and socially supported form. In the latter sense, the victim and, in a more distanced manner, the analyst or historian may also address explicitly and attempt to bring about the working through of problems. Here one has a significantly different work of memory and of mourning that can never fully overcome the extremely destabilizing or radically fragmenting effects of trauma and the need to act them out. But this work may nonetheless more or less effectively engage them and enable, however haltingly and incompletely, a limited renewal of life.

It would be jejune either to offer recipes for working-through or to present the process as reaching closure with the attainment of a fully integrated self or personhood. I do, however, suggest that one component of the process is the attempt to elaborate a hybridized narrative that does not avoid analysis or ideologically deny trauma by projectively representing empirical reality as the simple realization or teleological unfolding of wishes and values. This narrative would not deliver an untroubled "pleasure in narration" in the form of either essential continuity in exposition (paralleling identity-forming continuity with the past) or aestheticized montages of precious moments (sugar-coating nonidentity in the present). Rather, the nonfetishistic narrative that resists ideology would involve an active acknowledgment and to some extent an acting out of trauma with the irredeemable losses it brings, and it would indicate its own implication in repetitive processes it cannot entirely transcend. But it would also attempt to conjoin trauma with the possibility of retrieval of desirable aspects of the past that might be of some use in counteracting trauma's extreme effects and in rebuilding individual and social life. This effort would be deeply problematic and, particularly for nonvictims, easily subject to ideological abuse. But it should not simply be foreclosed through an overly restricted conception of possibilities. Here one should note a major inhibition to this effort that Langer may not sufficiently elaborate. Victims of trauma may experience not only "guilt" about surviving but intense anxiety about rebuilding a life and beginning again. One basis of anxiety is the feeling that building a new life is a betrayal of loved ones who died or were overwhelmed in a past that will not pass away. This feeling of betrayal must, I think, itself be explicitly recognized in the attempt to work through it, notably in processes of mourning.[22]

Working-through also requires a sustained, problematic relation between witnessing in Langer's sense and a critical comparative history that marks differences, including those between the present and the past; it also involves the attempt to acquire some perspective on experience without denying its claims or indeed its compulsive force. But experience should not be hypostatized as the source of authenticity and authority. It certainly has a crucial role in defining a subject-position that is distinctive and in some cases (notably that of victims) worthy of the utmost respect and sustained attentiveness. Yet working-through, as it relates both to the rebuilding of lives and to the elaboration of a critical historiography, requires the effort to achieve critical distance on experience through a comparison of experiences and through a reconstruction of larger contexts that help to inform and perhaps to transform experience. One's sense of one's own problems may change to the extent one comes to see their relations both to the experience of others and to a larger set of problems, some components of which may escape one's purview. (Two limiting features of Langer's phenomenological approach—perhaps of the interviewing procedure in general—are that he by and large isolated survivor experience from other dimensions of the Shoah—for example, the role of perpetration, collaboration, bystanding, and resistance—and he interviewed witnesses themselves primarily in isolation. He apparently did not ask whether support groups among survivors, functioning to some extent as empathic communities for mourning, made any difference in one's relation to the past and in one's present life. A broader problem is of course posed by what confronted survivors in postwar society, for example, in the United States, where avoidance or denial was prevalent in the dominant society and there were few if any social "rites of passage" from former existence to the current way

[22]The feeling of betrayal arises in a few testimonies, notably that of Leo G. on p. 146.

of life. In Germany, the "economic miracle" and, in France, the myth of the Resistance—that is, the idea, furthered by both de Gaulle and Communists, that all of France with only marginal exceptions was essentially involved in resistance—functioned at the very least as mechanisms of denial with respect to Nazism, the Shoah, and collaboration.)

In addition, working-through requires acknowledging the problem of values and norms and recognizing their distinction from empirical reality, which they do not redeem or transfigure but which they enable one to evaluate and possibly to transform. Here one has a work on memory that is crucial for the constitution of agency and addressed to the specific nature of the weak messianic power of secular values—a power that can readily assume an ideological role. One should, I think, resist the temptation to project values onto empirical reality through ideological narratives as well as to deny the pertinence of values when circumstances suspend their applicability or make their viable realization impossible. (One might tentatively suggest that the distressingly paradoxical situation of many victims was that values were for them relevant but often not applicable or realizable.) One should also resist the inclination (present in one dimension of Heidegger's thought) to radically undercut values or see them as merely superficial symptoms of modernity, for example, through a fundamental ontology that misleadingly excludes or brackets the "ontic" (or empirical) and repeats blindly both unacknowledged Christian motifs (such as fallenness or worldly activity as divertissement) and the antimodernist slogans of conservative-revolutionaries. Rather, the critical distinction between values and empirical realities is required both for nonfetishistic narrative and for any responsible attempt to pose the problem of reconstruction or beginning again in terms of desirable modes of life that viably live up to values they can never totally embody. Indeed, older forms of immanent critique may themselves have to be retrieved and transformed precisely because one can no longer simply assume values as givens and criticize existing practices in their light. Although one should not exaggerate the extent of the process to apocalyptic proportions, values have to a significant extent been jeopardized by trauma and evacuated by banalization, and they may be invoked as mere clichés or rhetorical topoi by those who do not believe in them and may not be shocked when they are radically distorted or transgressed. In this respect, there is a need for a discourse on values that is not purely transcendental or detached from social and historical inquiry but critically related to problems of empirical research as well as to the rebuilding of agency, which is required for the situational transcendence of existing relations toward more desirable possibilities. With reference to historical discourse addressing extremely traumatic events, such as those of the Shoah, there may also be a valid need for ritual uses of language that engage the process of mourning—a need that does not simply eliminate but should be tensely conjoined with the critical and self-critical nature of historical understanding. It should also be admitted, however, that such a need places a demand on the use of language that many historians (including myself) may be unable to answer.

My remarks may, for those who are discussed in Langer's book, seem to be little more than what Freud termed a menu offered to people in a time of famine. And my discussion of *Holocaust Testimonies* has perhaps concentrated too much on what I find to be the dominant—or at least the most pronounced—tenor of Langer's argument, particularly when he seems intent on reversing Charles Taylor's redemptive narrative. But there are nuances in his argument that indicate that the alternative to redemptive narrative is not an unqualified, melancholic writing of disaster or at best the belief in a total disjunction between values as an "irrelevant luxury" for victims in the camps and a valid luxury for us except when we listen to Holocaust testimonies (p. 121). (Indeed, if such a total disjunction were possible, certain problems would not exist either for victims or for attentive listeners and interpreters.) The nuances in Langer's argument may suggest something different, notably the sense that we are still in search of a language with which to render, however inadequately, both what happened to people in the camps and what implications we may draw from these events. (In this suggestion, with which I very much agree, Langer may be seen as converging with Lyotard.) I want to end by quoting two passages in which Langer is himself more qualified in drawing conclusions from the material he has so closely studied:

Implicit in this groping but thoughtful appraisal of a defamiliarized reality is the dismissal of a whole lexicon of safeguards for the security of the integrated self: choice, will, power of deliberation, confidence in predictive certainty. This is not to say that these faculties could not be or never were asserted. They were, as Chaim E. admits; but unheroic memory exposes as an illusion the avowal that they retained their absolute value and meaning even in a deathcamp like Sobibor. (P. 177)

Rejecting nihilism *and* heroism, the diminished self lapses into a bifocal vision, as its past invades its present and casts a long, pervasive shadow over its future, obscuring traditional vocabulary and summoning us to invent a still more complex version of memory and self. (P. 172)

Conclusion: Acting-Out and Working-Through

In ending this book, I return to certain issues that play an important part in the argument of earlier chapters but call for further thought. Perhaps the most obvious bear on acting-out and working-through. I have insisted on the importance of working-through because of my belief that it has been underemphasized and relatively undeveloped in post-Freudian psychoanalysis. Even in Freud it did not receive much theoretical elaboration.[1] I cannot claim to have made up for these deficiencies, but I nonetheless think it is important to point them out and to pose problems in a fashion that may stimulate the thought of others.

I would emphasize that the relation between acting-out and working-through should not be seen in terms of a from/to relationship in which the latter is presented as the dialectical transcendence of the former. I have noted that, particularly in cases of trauma, acting-out may be necessary and perhaps never fully overcome. Indeed, it may be intimately bound up with working through problems. But it should not be isolated, theoretically fixated on, or one-sidedly valorized as the horizon of thought or life.

In the texts of Jacques Lacan the problem of working-through is not placed in the foreground, nor does it tend to be in the work of those

---

[1] Two of Freud's most important studies here are "Remembering, Repeating and Working-Through" of 1914 (*The Standard Edition of the Complete Psychological Works of Sigmund Freud* 12, trans. James Strachey [London: Hogarth, 1958], pp. 145–56) and "Mourning and Melancholia" of 1917 (*Standard Edition* 14 [1957], pp. 237–60).

looking to him. Lacan's own prose style seems to serve as a vehicle to act out problems by "performing" the unconscious or emulating the movements of dream-work itself. A similar point might be made about the most prominent contemporary Lacanian who addresses problems of ideology and the sublime: Slavoj Žižek. Whereas Lacan takes Mallarmée's poetic prose as a lodestar, Žižek employs a discursive analogue of cinematic jump-cuts in associately bringing together often brilliant yet disjunctive insights into contemporary popular culture. Neither Lacan nor Žižek confronts the problem of the Holocaust in a sustained manner, and in the case of Lacan (1901–81) this omission is particularly noteworthy because he was an adult during World War II. In reading Žižek, one is hard-pressed to detect constructive ethicopolitcal possibilities that might complement often searing critiques of existing phenomena, and the Lacanian and Marxist senses of alienation are conflated to become a seemingly unsurpassable horizon of thought and practice. The "sublime object of ideology" itself emerges as the Lacanian Real—an unsymbolizable limit or unrepresentable kernel of experience.[2] Indeed, in Žižek the sublime seems to involve fixation on a radically ambivalent transvaluation of trauma as the universal hole in Being or the abstractly negative marker of castration.

One might argue that Žižek brings Lacan to the breaking point by eliciting his dominant tendencies and phantasmatically identifying him with Hegel as the negative dialectician who subverts speculative synthesis or wholeness (*Aufhebung*) and validates alienation and infinite desire as the horizon of thought and action. For what seems dominant in Lacan is the insistence on the misrecognition (*méconnaissance*) of truth—truth that is elusive yet allied with fragmentation, helplessness, and lack, which inform human (non)identity as the narcissistic,

[2]See *The Sublime Object of Ideology* (London: Verso, 1989). Žižek underscores the danger of reductive contextualization, but he runs the risk of an equally reductive hypostatization and leveling of problems: "All the different attempts to attach this phenomenon [concentration camps] to a concrete image ('Holocaust', 'Gulag' . . .), to reduce it to a product of a concrete social order (Fascism, Stalinism . . .)—what are they if not so many attempts to elude the fact that we are dealing here with the 'real' of our civilization which returns as the same traumatic kernel in all social systems? (We should not forget that concentration camps were an invention of 'liberal' England, dating from the Boer War, that they were also used in the USA to isolate the Japanese population, and so on" (p. 50). One should also not forget that these various historical cases have different valences and pose specific problems that cannot be covered through the locution "and so on." Žižek's stance often seems to be that of the high-altitude theorist obsessed with the Real and its putative effects.

nihilitating instance of self-punitive desire. The ego is not, as in Freud, a mediating agency that both tests reality and is subject to the pull of the id, the demands of the superego, and the illusions of phantasmatic projection. It is the construct of the Imaginary, totally consumed by illusion and compulsion—particularly the compulsive illusion of its own wholeness or identity that masks and exacerbates its inner divisions, self-rivalry, and mimetic deceptions. The only escape from entrapment in the sadomasochistic, aggressive rivalry of the Imaginary presumably comes with Oedipal sublimation through the intervention of the problematically gendered, culture-bearing, paternal superego (or "name/no [*nom*] of the father") as the vehicle of the Symbolic, whereas the Real is a continually inaccessible asymptote that refigures the id or, more basically, names the unnameable, impossible Other that is "liberated" in psychosis. Indeed, the focus of psychoanalysis shifts to a delusional, rigid, paranoid, self-immolating ego threatened by fantasies of dismemberment, and the Symbolic itself often seems to be sucked into the vortex of the Imaginary and the Real insofar as agency is evacuated and misrecognition or self-deluded speech becomes the uncontrollable force radically destabilizing, if not obliterating, the distinctions among the three "orders." In any case, it is difficult to find in this patriarchically biased, linguistically oriented, often bewildering theoretical formation a place for critical, responsible agency within a noninvidious normative framework, even if one carefully distinguishes the desirability of such agency from its self-serving, indiscriminate use that is justifiably criticized by Lacan: the nonexplanatory, moralizing tendency to blame the victim by seeing ethical failure as the "cause" of "pathology."

It is tempting to conclude that Lacan's "return to Freud" involved a reformulation of psychoanalysis wherein certain possibilities were more subtly and deceptively obscured or precluded than in Freud himself. But Lacan's thought is complex enough to raise doubts about any brief summary attempting to capture its basic direction, although his tendency to undo performatively his seeming assertions often increases the force of misrecognition in reading him. One may nonetheless suggest that certain discursive movements—if only when read against the grain and oriented through a selective reworking of Lacan's self-contestations—indicate how one might approach the issue of working-through in its relation to acting-out. A principal conceptual means would be the relation of the Imaginary to the Symbolic (with the notion of the Real defetishized to allow for other possibilities in the response to trauma). To act out is to remain within the self-punitive Lacanian Imaginary, although acting-out—if it is not made into an object of fixation or rashly generalized and validated as an all-consuming "fate"—may be required for processes of working-through. Actively disengaged from patriarchal assumptions and related instead to a transformed notion of normatively regulated interaction, the Symbolic would mark the entry into language in the specific sense of usage that would not definitively transcend all blind spots, bring total integration, or even serve as a "cure" for "psychosis" but would at least enable (while never ensuring) a viable role for critical judgment and responsible action. Decisive here would be the problematic interaction between obsessive compulsion and a re-petitioning that constitutes or reconstitutes agency and raises the question of desirable social and political institutions.[3]

In their useful codification of psychoanalytic terminology which combines Freud and Lacan, J. Laplanche and J.-B. Pontalis address directly the problems of acting-out and working-through.[4] They discuss problems largely from a clinical perspective that may not be directly applicable to the more generally theoretical issues that have been my concern. But their analyses are of interest to the extent that they address psychoanalytic processes that may not be confined to clinical contexts or to the individual alone. They define acting-out "according to Freud" as "action in which the subject, in the grip of his unconscious wishes and phantasies, relives these in the present with a sensation of immediacy which is heightened by his refusal to recognize their source and their repetitive character" (p. 4). They also observe that Freud most often referred to repetition in the transference as acting-out and that acting-out betokened the return of the repressed (pp. 4–5). Of working-through, they write:

---

[3]See the discussion of repetition in Žižek, *Enjoy Your Symptom!* (New York: Routledge, 1992), especially pp. 78–105. Žižek's forte nonetheless remains the analysis of alienation from within, and his stress even in his discussion of working-through tends to remain on acting-out. Thus he writes: "Transferential repetition cannot be reduced to remembrance, transference is not a kind of 'theater of shadows' where we settle with past traumas *in effigia*, it is repetition in the full meaning of the term, i.e., in it the past trauma is literally repeated, 'actualized.' The analyst is not father's 'shadow,' he is a presence in front of which the past battle has to be fought out 'for real' " (p. 102). Žižek often assumes there are but two options: remembrance as an impossible, imaginary attempt to totalize experience through dialectical transcendence and the repetition compulsion that repeats or relives the trauma in at best a lucidly theorized fashion.

[4]See *The Language of Psycho-Analysis* (1967; New York: Norton, 1973).

Process by means of which analysis implants an interpretation and overcomes the resistances to which it has given rise. Working-through is taken to be a sort of psychical work which allows the subject to accept certain repressed elements and to free himself from the grip of mechanisms of repetition. It is a constant factor in treatment, but it operates more especially during certain phases where progress seems to have come to a halt and where a resistance persists despite its having been interpreted.

From the technical point of view, by the same token, working-through is expedited by interpretations from the analyst which consist chiefly in showing how the meanings in question may be recognised in different contexts. (P. 488)

Although they present working-through as countering compulsive acting-out, Laplanche and Pontalis do not give way to a simple ideology of liberation from the constraints of the past. They mitigate the opposition between acting-out and working-through by noting that "working-through is undoubtedly a repetition, albeit one modified by interpretation and—for this reason—liable to facilitate the subject's freeing himself from repetition mechanisms" (pp. 488–89). Working-through would thus seem to involve a mode of repetition offering a measure of critical purchase on problems and responsible control in action which would permit desirable change. Laplanche and Pontalis also indicate how working-through is not a purely intellectual process but requires a form of work involving not only affect but the entire personality. Indeed, for them "working-through might be defined as that process which is liable to halt the repetitive insistence characteristic of unconscious formations by bringing these into relation with the subject's personality as a whole." (p. 489). They also quote Melanie Klein as observing that "patients, who at some time have gained insight, repudiate this very insight in the following sessions and sometimes even seem to have forgotten that they had ever accepted it. It is only by drawing our conclusions from the material as it reappears in different contexts, and is interpreted accordingly, that we gradually help the patient to acquire insight in a more lasting way" (p. 489).

In my own discussion, I have suggested a linkage in recent theory of acting-out not only with possession by the repressed past, repetition compulsions, and unworked-through transference but also with certain modes of performativity, inconsolable melancholy, and the sublime. The Holocaust itself has often tended to be repressed or encrypted as a specific series of events and to be displaced onto such general questions as language, nomadism, unrepresentability, silence, and so forth. Such a process obviates the investigation of the relation between the particular and the general. It also generates a quasi-theological situation in which problems lose all specificity by being everywhere and nowhere—a situation that easily lends itself to apologetic uses. The discovery of Paul de Man's World War II journalism or the revival of the question of Heidegger and the Nazis functioned in certain quarters as a kind of return of the repressed. But at times reactions have involved the reiteration of modes of reading and interpretation that abet the tendency to trope away from specificity and to reprocess problems in terms of reading technologies that function as discursive "cuisinarts." Such reactions inhibit processes of working-through and learning from the past.

I have also tried to take the concept of working-through away from a narrowly therapeutic framework and to relate it to ethical and political considerations. Working-through implies the possibility of judgment that is not apodictic or ad hominem but argumentative, self-questioning, and related in mediated ways to action. In this sense, it is bound up with the role of distinctions that are not pure binary oppositions but marked by varying and contestable degrees of strength or weakness. In Freud, working-through was normative and related to the problem of the interaction between limits and transgression, but its normative status was often occluded by seemingly neutral, medicalized notions of normality and pathology. The problem posed by working-through is to render explicit the question of normativity and to avoid the pathologization of certain phenomena (such as homosexuality and femininity) on grounds that often replicate current stereotypes and prejudices. This process would require one to pose the problem of normativity in noninvidious ways and to assist in elaborating a network of norms or values that cannot be conflated with normalization (in the sense of the dubious postulation of the statistical average as normative).

The foregoing analysis indicates that the undoing or undercutting of binary oppositions is insufficient insofar as it is not consistently related to an analysis of their actual empirical role, the effort to counteract their functioning in its historical specificity, and the articulation of distinctions that are necessary for such efforts as well as for any reconfiguration of thought and practice. Thus, deconstructing the opposition between the beautiful and the sublime or, in another register, between perpetrator and victim should not remain within a strategy of reversal, which leads to the automatic valorization of the supposedly suppressed member of the pair or even to a disorienting displacement and generalization of the latter that may induce an obliteration of distinctions. Aside from an investigation of the actual role of oppositions in thought and practice, one would need distinctions to differentiate between types of thought or activity; one would also need a strategy of intervention both to resist illegitimate relations and to work out alternatives. Hence, for example, there is a significant difference between the self-sacrificing asceticism of a saint who willingly emulates Christ as victim and the victimization of Jews during the Shoah, however much the latter was in certain cases related to a deranged sacrificialism or the former to institutionalized oppression. There are also crucial differences between modalities of the sublime as well as disparate relations between them and ethical limits. One cannot simply amalgamate Wordsworth before Mount Snowdon and Himmler before the spectacle of exterminated Jews. Nor can one move without careful and contestable mediation from the most daring experimentation in art to ethical and political assertion or action that directly affects the lives of people. Yet any generalized aesthetic of the sublime threatens to eventuate in such conflations.

One of the foremost historians of the Shoah, Saul Friedlander, has addressed the problem of working-through in terms that are instructive.[5] He observes:

> The major difficulty of historians of the Shoah, when confronted with echoes of the traumatic past, is to keep some measure of balance between the emotion recurrently breaking through the "protective shield" and numbness that protects this very shield. In fact, the numbing or distancing effect of intellectual work on the Shoah is unavoidable and necessary; the recurrence of strong emotional impact is also often unforeseeable and necessary.
>
> "Working through" means, first, being aware of both tendencies, allowing for a measure of balance between the two whenever possible. But neither the protective numbing nor the disruptive emotion is entirely accessible to consciousness. (P. 51)

Friedlander's remarks are especially valuable because he makes

[5]"Trauma, Transference and 'Working Through,' " in *History and Memory* 4 (1992), 39–55.

them from the position of a theoretically sophisticated historian who has actually tried to write accounts of the Shoah. He also notes the proximity of certain of his concerns—such as "the avoidance of closure, the ever-questioning commentary and the 'excess' carried by the *Shoah*" —to deconstruction. While being sensitive to the rhetorical dimensions of texts and even to "the impossibility of establishing any direct reference to some aspects at least of the concrete *reality* that we call the *Shoah*," Friedlander nonetheless puts forth a noteworthy qualification: "Coming closer to a *significant historical linkage* seems to me to be necessary; it is the corollary of my previous remarks about the growing fragmentation of the history of the Nazi period as a defensive mechanism or as the result of some paralysis on the side of the victims. In a sense, what is suggested here is the simultaneous acceptance of two contradictory moves: the search for ever-closer historical linkages and the avoidance of a naive historical positivism leading to simplistic and self-assured historical narrations and closures" (pp. 52–53).

Friedlander thus sees an essential tension between the valid resistance to closure and the need for articulation among accounts in the attempt to counteract dubious modes of fragmentation. He also calls for a combination of narrative and commentary in self-aware historiography of the Nazi period, and he even sees a possibility of linking critical (but not narrowly positivistic) historiography with certain dimensions of memory. Here it is worth quoting him at some length, for his views provide a somewhat different perspective on arguments I made earlier:

> Whether . . . commentary is built into the narrative structure of a history or developed as a separate, superimposed text is a matter of choice, but the voice of the commentator must be clearly heard. The commentary should disrupt the facile linear progression of the narration, introduce alternative interpretations, question any partial conclusion, withstand the need for closure. Because of the necessity of some form of narrative sequence in the writing of history, such commentary may introduce splintered or constantly recurring refractions of a traumatic past by using any number of different vantage points.

Friedlander continues:

> The dimension added by the commentary may allow for an integration of the so-called "mythic memory" of the victims within the overall

representation of this past without its becoming an "obstacle" to "rational historiography." For instance, whereas the historical narrative may have to stress the ordinary aspects of everyday life during most of the twelve years of the Nazi epoch, the "voice-over" of the victims' memories may puncture such normality, at least at the level of commentary. (P. 53)

Indeed, Friedlander insists not only that memory and critical historiography be combined but that *"working through means confronting the individual voice* in a field dominated by political decisions and administrative decrees which neutralize the concreteness of despair and death. The *Alltagsgeschichte* of German society has its necessary shadow: the *Alltagsgeschichte* of the victims" (p. 53). Testimonies are one way of confronting individual voices, but any archival traces of such voices would of course be valuable. Friedlander observes that "at the individual level, a redemptive closure (comforting and healing in effect), desirable as it would be, seems largely impossible," and at the collective level he fears a public erasing of the "excess" of unbearable events—an erasing that creates "a tendency towards closure without resolution, but closure nonetheless" (p. 54). While in many basic ways agreeing with Friedlander, I have tried to argue that a broader theoretical awareness of possibilities, although in no sense assured of public resonance or even of limited effectiveness in the life of the individual, may nonetheless enable a more modulated response to problems of analysis and judgment.

A crucial problem in relating acting-out to working-through is the connection between melancholy (or melancholia) and mourning. In Freud's "Mourning and Melancholia" it seems that melancholia is ambivalently both a precondition to (or even necessary aspect of) mourning and that which can block processes of mourning insofar as it becomes excessive or functions as an object of fixation.[6] Here at least two preliminary questions can be raised. First, does modern society have suitable public rituals that would help one to come to terms with melancholia and engage in possibly regenerative processes of mourning, even if in extremely traumatic cases an idealized notion of

[6]In addition to Freud's essay, see Eric L. Santner, *Stranded Objects: Mourning, Memory, and Film in Postwar Germany* (Ithaca: Cornell University Press, 1990); Alexander Mitscherlich and Margarete Mitscherlich, *The Inability to Mourn: Principles of Collective Behavior,* trans. Beverley R. Placzek (New York: Grove Press, 1975); and Peter Homans, *The Ability to Mourn: Disillusionment and the Social Origins of Psychoanalysis* (Chicago: University of Chicago Press, 1989).

full recovery may be misleading? Second, who is it that one mourns and how can one specify the object of mourning in ways that are both ethicopolitically desirable and effective in reducing anxiety to tolerable limits? Regarding the second question, it is important that the need to specify the object of mourning be recognized as a crucial problem. In the case of postwar Germans, it was often unclear to what extent Hitler was the lost loved object. The occlusion of this object facilitated avoidance or denial, and it was accompanied by a tendency to obscure the problem of Jewish victims who were not valued recipients of emotion. It seems necessary here not only to recognize the lost object in order to allow for processes of mourning to be engaged, as Alexander Mitscherlich and Margarete Mitscherlich argued, but perhaps to criticize the inclination to remain invested in—as well as the very need to mourn—unworthy objects. By contrast, the difficult problem for public education and practice would be to reorient both emotion and value in the direction of victims who are indeed deserving objects of mourning. In this sense, any attempt to facilitate processes of mourning and to further the emergence of viable public rituals would require an effective critique of anti-Semitism and related forms of scapegoating and victimization. It would be a mistake to concentrate all attention on postwar Germany, for anti-Semitism and scapegoating as well as the more particular problem of working through denial and repression with regard to the Holocaust arise in other countries, including the United States.

Melancholia is an isolating experience allowing for specular intersubjectivity that validates the self in its desperate isolation. In the best of cases it may allow for insights that bear witness to questionable conditions and have broader critical potential. To be effective, mourning apparently requires a supportive or even solidaristic social context. In this respect Eric Santner has observed in *Stranded Objects*:

> Both the child trying to master separateness from the mother and the
> trauma victim returning, in dream, to the site of a shock, are locked in a
> repetition compulsion: an effort to recuperate, in the controlled context
> of symbolic behavior, the *Angstbereitschaft* or readiness to feel anxiety,
> absent during the initial shock or loss. It was Freud's thought that the
> absence of appropriate affect—anxiety—is what leads to traumatization
> rather than loss per se. This affect can, however, be recuperated only in
> the presence of an empathic witness. In the case of the child playing
> *fort/da* [the famous game of the child throwing away and fetching a
> bobbin on a string that is a mother-surrogate—a game Santner

suggestively analyzes in terms of mourning] it is the parent/observer, and in that of the trauma victim the empathic analyst, who co-constitute the space in which loss may come to be symbolically and affectively mastered. Homeopathy without appropriate affect becomes a purely mechanical procedure that can never lead to empowerment; without a social space in which this affect can be recuperated, the homeopathic operation becomes a sort of elegiac loop that must repeat itself endlessly. (P. 25)

In the spirit of Santner's own self-questioning analysis, one may ask whether the social space of the empathic witness is sufficiently occupied by a one-to-one relationship or whether it requires—for any publicly effective (and perhaps for any individually durable) process of mourning—the role of more widely instituted practices. One may also note the difficulty of applying the homeopathic logic of the antidote to anxiety insofar as the latter is totally unspecified in its object and amounts to a disoriented if "sublime" response to radical nothingness. Any process of mourning, it seems, would require some degree of specification of the object, which anxiety would always exceed and in relation to which Angstbereitschaft itself would run the recurrent risk of getting out of control. But one might still contend that a readiness—or a recovered readiness—could counteract trauma and function as an antidote to the extent that anxiety did not remain altogether diffuse but was related to objects that could be illuminated by historical understanding and subject to informed judgment, even if never susceptible to total mastery or fully adequate representation. Some combination of critical historical investigation, ethicopolitical judgment, and social ritual would increase this possibility, although the secular site of such a combination would at present seem limited to the only partially effective psychoanalytic (or more generally psychotherapeutic) relationship and the activity of various support groups. Insofar as historiographic discourse could itself validly have a ritual dimension without sacrificing its critical nature, it too might assist in some small way in facilitating warranted public processes of mourning. At the very least, one might point out that the idea of an appropriate language—indeed, an acceptable rhythm between language and silence—in attempting to render certain phenomena depends on ritual as well as aesthetic criteria.

In *The Ability to Mourn* Peter Homans treats the genealogy of psychoanalysis itself in terms of its implication in mourning the loss of traditional symbols and shared ideals. This process gave rise to a specific space for thought and practice between religion and science. Summarizing his argument, Homans writes:

> Psychoanalysis and the "understanding" forms of social science not only owe their origins to science and religion, but they are always also breaking away from both. For this reason their structures and processes have had to be forged anew, eschewing both simple imitation of science and simple repetition of religion. Freud and Weber both imitated science, and this style has failed. Transposing their work back into philosophy and religion will also fail. Learning about the origins of psychoanalysis has taught us something important about its structure: the way it individuated out of both science and religion. Of the two fixed spaces or spheres the religious one seems the more important, at least for the present moment, but only because it is far less recognized by those who study psychoanalysis and psychology. The best guarantee of the uniqueness, irreducibility, and autonomy of psychoanalysis, both as a form of investigation and as a profession, and the best assurance that it will not continue in its now-customary splendid isolation from the communities of knowledge which surround it, lie, paradoxically, in recognizing its complex, double relation to its religious and social context—how it began as "a part of" these and how it came to "part from" them. (P. 343)

Homans provides valuable historical and contextual insight into Freud's own preoccupation with the problem of secularization which affected the nature and status of psychoanalysis itself. And one can agree with his insistence on the fruitlessness of attempts at simple imitation of science or simple repetition of religion as well as his caveat about the transposition of psychoanalysis or other social sciences into philosophy and religion. But he is perhaps too lapidary in his characterization of science and religion as "fixed spaces" and in his assertion of the "uniqueness, irreducibility, and autonomy" of psychoanalysis, "both as a form of investigation and as a profession." There may well be significant tensions in psychoanalysis itself as a form of investigation and as a profession—tensions that make it intersect with other modes of inquiry and interrogation. Homans's own argument would lead instead in the direction of a notion of psychoanalysis and neighboring social sciences as hybridized activities that continually rethink their procedures, boundaries vis-à-vis other disciplines, and very understanding of religion and science. Furthermore, Homas explicates and defends the role of the participant-observer, and this dual role itself seems to call for inquiry into such problems as transference and the need to work through it.[7] Indeed, such inquiry would be necessary to resist scientistic self-understanding without sacrificing critical reason as a mode of deliberation and judgment that cannot be reduced to mere calculative or instrumental rationality.

For Heidegger, a key problem was thinking through the relation between the same (which was not the identical) and the different. His own understanding of this relationship became most dubious when he relied on a notion of essence that threatened to subordinate differences to similarities and, at the limit, to obliterate the voices of specific victims. Heidegger addressed problems without an explicit theory of repression and in a manner that construed ethics and politics as superficial and threatened to foreclose serious consideration of them. Freud, of course, did provide a critical and self-critical theory of repression, and although the notion of displacement also harbored the danger of conflation, the role of trauma indicated that repetition itself might come with radical change or difference. The challenge was to specify the nature of desirable change in given circumstances, and this challenge was if anything insufficiently met by a generalized therapeutic ethos even when the modest goal of this ethos was to return people from hysterical misery to everyday unhappiness.

This goal was of course Freud's as a professional clinician who encountered people seeking help on a one-to-one basis and in a setting where his authority was generally unquestioned. But there was in Freud a valuable role-tension between the clinician and the critical social theorist who addressed broader and more contested problems in collective life. We are, to be sure, still confronted with the need to address the relations between the same and the different both synchronically (for example, with reference to relations among the disciplines) and diachronically (notably in terms of the return of the repressed). And although we may recognize the limitations of Freud as a critical social theorist, the role-tension he embodied still has something to say to us. Indeed, a comparable tension exists between the roles (or subject-positions) of historian and critical theorist or, more generally, between those of scholar and intellectual—roles that may (and in my judgment should) be played by the same social individuals.[8]

[7]See the interesting discussion in Homans, *The Ability to Mourn*, pp. 253–56.
[8]I am of course not disqualifying other sites for the emergence of intellectuals but

The scholar is able to rely on expertise and established criteria of research in the production and evaluation of knowledge. The intellectual goes beyond an area of professional expertise to address problems that are of broader social and cultural interest, and in that sense he or she does not simply mind his or her own business. The activity of the intellectual is more tentative and controversial than that of the scholar. It is especially open to contestation when it includes not only critique but the suggestion or recommendation of alternatives to existing practices and frames of reference. Still, it may both indicate problems for further scholarly inquiry and touch on concerns of more general public interest. Conversely, research is most acute and stimulating when it poses, or at least helps to generate, questions for critical reflection. I have intimated that the relation between history and theory is itself most valuable when the two enter into a sustained and mutually challenging exchange—in fact, when their relation is seen as a variation of that between scholarship and critical intellectual activity. The point is not to resolve the role-tension between the intellectual and the scholar—or between the theorist and the historian—but to make it as thought-provoking as possible.

With respect to the history of the Holocaust, this study raises at least two sets of issues with which I want to conclude. First, I have indicated that the history of the Holocaust requires a sustained attention to the interaction of groups and tendencies during the Nazi period as well as to the relationship of historians or other contemporary

---

stressing the need for professional scholars to combine expertise with critical intellectual activity. In addition, I would note that my emphasis on problems such as acting-out and working-through or on the need for a historically informed, ethicopolitical discourse is in no sense intended as a substitute for concern with social and economic issues. On the contrary, the development of an acceptable ethicopolitical approach requires judgment bearing on socioeconomic practice. It should be obvious that working through the past in any viable, durable, and politically relevant manner would itself demand a careful critical analysis of social and economic institutions both over time and in contemporary life. A view of psychoanalysis that took it from a purely individual or clinical perspective only to keep it within restricted psychological or theoreticist categories would be of little value for critical theory. It is in this sense that the older attempt by the Frankfurt School to join Freud and Marx, although open to criticism in the precise form it took, is still a challenge to intellectuals who do not simply substitute Freud (or Lacan) for Marx or affirm uncritically the practices of existing liberal-democratic regimes. To make this point is not to endorse totalizing attacks on these regimes or to believe that they form "carceral archipelagos" worse than Old Regime France or even modern dictatorships. But it is to insist both on the importance of immanent critique with respect to them and on the tendentious complacency of approaches that take them as an unquestioned locus of moral superiority.

analysts to the past. The latter consideration requires a sensitivity to the implications of certain emphases in a present context of inquiry and debate as they bear on possible and desirable futures. In this sense, the Historikerstreit, which professional historians often see as of minimal interest because it generated "more heat than light" and did not reveal new evidence or methodological perspectives concerning the Shoah, is of crucial historical and critical concern in its bearing on how individuals and groups at present come to terms with the past. Moreover, in inquiring into that past—a past that cannot be dissociated from present problems and choices—we need sensitive studies of life in the camps and ghettos as well as a renewed investigation of perpetrators such as Hitler, Himmler, and the SS. Holocaust testimonies may prompt new questions for the former inquiry because they raise in a pointed manner the problem of the intricate relation between memory and the reconstruction of events. Regarding the history of perpetrators, the early concern with ideology, anti-Semitism, and racism was compromised when it was associated with the approach of prosecutors during the Nuremberg trials in which the narrow incentive to demonstrate the monstrously criminal nature of perpetrators was combined with a self-serving inclination to exonerate or even celebrate "our side." There was an understandable reaction to the deficiencies of the "Nuremberg view" that led initially to the emphasis on the "machinery of destruction" or the "banality of evil." More recently, positions have been codified into "intentionalist" interpretations, which stress the explicit intentions of figures such as Hitler and often conflate ideology with intention, and "functionalist" interpretations, which stress (in general accord with the "machinery-of-destruction" approach) the transindividual role of impersonal institutions, "polycratic" bureaucratic power, and social structures. Recognition of the obvious limitations of either approach in isolation from the other has at times (for example, in the work of Christopher Browning) led to a synthetic perspective that focuses on the experience and activities of "little people" at the bottom of the hierarchy of the "machinery of destruction" who carried out the execution of millions of victims. While I recognize the value of this research, I also suggest that there is a renewed need for a study of the prime movers among perpetrators (perhaps also of those "little people" who were able to overcome inhibitions about mass execution)—a study guided by some questions I have tried to raise, such as the role of ideology as secular religion and the relation of scapegoating and victimization to displaced, distorted sacrificialism.[9] Ideology here cannot simply be conflated with intention or with explicit plans laid by Hitler in the 1920s, but there is the question of how ideology operated (for example, in relating exclusion, ghettoization, and extermination within a scapegoat mechanism) and when a practice could be argued to become an explicit, intentional policy. The crucial issue, however, may well be the ideological and political legitimation of the desire to "get rid of" the Jews and other outsiders within the Volksgemeinschaft, for scapegoating facilitates the step from exclusion or ghettoization to extermination.

The second set of issues are comparably difficult. The Shoah was a reality that went beyond powers of both imagination and conceptualization, and victims themselves could at times not believe what they went through or beheld. It posed problems of "representation" at the time of its occurrence, and it continues to pose problems today. It is in this sense a paradigmatically traumatic series of events related in complex fashion to the question of silence that is not mere mutism but intricately related to representation. In different ways in various disciplines or areas of discourse and representation, the Shoah calls for a response that does not deny its traumatic nature or cover it over through a "fetishistic" or redemptive narrative that makes believe it did not occur or compensates too readily for it.[10] In one sense, what is

---

[9]For a relatively early study of the SS that is to some extent sensitive to these issues and that introduces certain complications into the account of SS policy toward the Jews, see Heinz Höhne, *The Order of the Death's Head* (1966; New York: Ballantine, 1989). Höhne argues that Himmler and other important elements in the SS who became the key executors of extermination were not the originators of the idea. Indeed, they first supported the expulsion of the Jews and even opposed Goebbels when he triggered *Kristallnacht* on 9 November 1938. Yet Himmler was dedicated to the Führer and to the cult of self-sacrifice in the SS as a quasi-religious military order, and he came to see genocide as a component of a world-historical mission. He nonetheless was "so shocked by the disgusting scene" when he witnessed the Einsatzgruppe's execution of two hundred Jews in Minsk that he almost collapsed (p. 414). Out of a concern for the morale and psychological state of his men, Himmler advocated finding a less direct method of killing that eventuated in the use of gas vans. Höhne also refers to the case of Erich von dem Bach-Zelewski, "Himmler's most aggressive Eastern minion," who suffered a nervous breakdown and "haunted by his guilt . . . would pass his nights screaming, a prey to hallucinations" connected with the shooting of Jews and other experiences in the East (p. 411). In these respects, what I have referred to as a Nazi negative sublime was not a solitary force but an equivocal part of an overdetermined complex in which there might be a failure in transvaluing trauma, reinforcing "hardness," and averting the breakdown of the perpetrator.

[10]The notion of narrative fetishism is developed with great insight by Eric Santner in "History beyond the Pleasure Principle: Some Thoughts on the Representation of Trauma," in Saul Friedlander, ed., *Probing the Limits of Representation: Nazism and the*

necessary is a discourse of trauma that itself undergoes—and indicates that one undergoes—a process of at least muted trauma insofar as one has tried to understand events and empathize with victims. This process may, in the best of cases, serve as an antidote insofar as it is related to a broader attempt to work through problems and develop a perspective that addresses certain issues (including normative issues) in social and political life. But this process may also get out of control and not only reinscribe but even intensify fragmentation and disorientation. Such a possibility threatens to occur when one identifies trauma with history or modernity and elaborates an approach that insistently remains within trauma by endlessly enacting a repetition compulsion or generating aporias. The attraction as well as the limitation of such an approach is that it continually sacrifices the self, which may even be constituted as a surrogate victim.[11]

The concepts of modernism and postmodernism often seem to divert attention from significant problems rather than to illuminate them, particularly when they are confined to "aesthetic" concerns or become the pretext for an indiscriminate generalization of the notion of "aestheticization" in a manner that occludes the role of other forces, such as religion and its displacements. (There is an obvious sense in which we secular intellectuals are more comfortable with the notion of the aesthetic, even when we criticize its putative role, than we are with the idea of the continued importance of religion and its relation to secularization.) But if one is to critically reinscribe modernism and postmodernism, one may begin by pointing to the role of the

---

"*Final Solution*" (Cambridge: Harvard University Press, 1992), pp. 143–54. Santner writes: "By narrative fetishism I mean the construction and deployment of a narrative consciously or unconsciously designed to expunge the traces of the trauma or loss that called that narrative into being in the first place. [. . .] [It] is the way an inability or refusal to mourn employs traumatic events; it is a strategy of undoing, in fantasy, the need for mourning by simulating a condition of intactness, typically by situating the site and origin of loss elsewhere" (p. 144). Fetishistic narrative thus attempts to reinstate the pleasure principle prematurely, without inscribing trauma and the work of mourning.

[11]Here one may note the importance of the work of Georges Bataille, who theorized the role of sacrifice and transgression, foregrounded the problem of displaced ritual and religion in modernity, had a problematic relation to fascism, and became a crucial reference point for "poststructural" thinkers in France such as Foucault and Derrida (who themselves did not pay adequate attention to the political dimensions or contexts of his thought). One may also wonder whether the essays of Derrida and Felman on de Man (discussed in Chapter 4), which include atypically weak argumentation, involve a sacrificial constitution of the self as surrogate victim that deflects "blame" from de Man as idealized figure.

Holocaust as one problematic, often repressed (which may also mean canonized) point of rupture between the two. Postmodernism has developed in the wake of the Shoah, which it has often explicitly avoided, typically encrypted, and variably echoed in traumatized, melancholic, manically ludic, opaque, and at time mournfully elegiac discourses.

Recent attempts to address more directly problems related to the Shoah, which I discussed in earlier chapters, have been fraught with problems. I would not defend an impatient dismissal of interest in the aporia construed as a marker of impossible desire or a point where paradox is most intense. Nor do I mean to imply that one should simply reverse perspectives by reducing postmodern or, more generally, poststructural approaches to symptoms of their often obscured genealogical contexts. But the disclosure of an aporia (or a strong internal self-contestation in a text or argument) is not the ultimate goal of analysis or the invitation to endless repetition. The aporia may indicate a problem that still needs to be worked through in the attempt to generate both better readings and more desirable tensions or modes of interaction in social life.

More desirable modes of interaction include the role of the carnivalesque, whereby impasses are somehow played out and existing norms or structures are periodically transgressed—ideally validated insofar as they are legitimate and prepared for change insofar as they are not. Indeed, the carnivalesque itself would have a crucial part to play in a viable process of working through problems, and it is one aspect of Jewish culture that warrants recovery and reaffirmation. During the Shoah, Nazis made sadistic use of carnivalesque processes stripped of their fruitful ambivalence and serving only to degrade victims, and gallows humor was one way in which the oppressed in ghettos and camps were able to confront an impossible situation and not be totally crushed by it. Even when the invocation of carnivalesque humor in one's own voice might pose difficulties for the historian of the Shoah, he or she could provide a critical analysis of Nazi uses and a sensitive rendering of victims' uses while exploring the larger problem of recapturing and making available broader, richly ambivalent, and potentially healing dimensions of the carnivalesque in history.[12]

[12]Some of these problems are broached by Terrence Des Pres, "Holocaust Laughter?" in Berel Lang, ed., *Writing and the Holocaust* (New York: Holmes and Meier, 1988), pp. 216–33. For a more extensive discussion of camp conditions, see Terrence Des Pres, *The Survivor: An Anatomy of Life in the Death Camps* (1976; Oxford: Oxford University Press, 1980). Des Pres notes the Nazi tendency to literalize or "act out" metaphors in their

Moreover, genealogical reconstruction might help to raise otherwise unapparent questions about recent approaches that should perhaps be rethought in terms of the relation between the events of the Shoah and more general issues on which these approaches tend to focus, such as the "traumatic" nature of the entry into language, the "trace" structure of inscription in relation to an inaccessible, continually deferred presence, and the ludic or even carnivalesque possibilities of undecidability. This relational question is often obscured in its own specificity when the particular is subsumed in the general, and history or modernity is construed as holocaust or trauma. When such a subsumption occurs, theory becomes theoreticism, and the danger is that problems will be blindly acted out without sufficient critical attention being paid to the way they are framed. I have indicated that this danger is perhaps most blatant with respect to an (an)aesthetics of the sublime that indiscriminately valorizes the un(re)presentable or the experimentally transgressive without posing the problem of the actual and desirable relations between normative limits and transgression. When acting-out is taken from a larger frame of reference, in which it may to some extent function as an antidote, and the unavoidable, disorienting possibility of the radically different or "other" is fixated on, one may unintentionally repeat the traumatizing, dispossessing, nonnegotiable strategy of victimizers who postulate an unsurpassable "differend" in their relations with unassimilable others—a "differend" that is now unhitched from any goals or "solutions" to be absolutized and valorized as a general condition of which everyone is, in some sense, a victim. One crucial undertaking for postmodern and poststructural approaches may thus be to be wary of certain posttraumatic inclinations and to explore more clearly their own relation to the Shoah in all its intricate dimensions while explicitly addressing the issue of specificity as a complex mediation between the particular and the general. Such an undertaking may further an understanding of how to attempt to work through problems without either bypassing their traumatizing potential or endlessly and compulsively repeating it.

"excremental assault" on victims, for example, by making victims eat excrement (p. 70). The literature on Bakhtin and the carnivalesque is of course immense. For my own view, see especially "Bakhtin, Marxism, and the Carnivalesque," in *Rethinking Intellectual History: Texts, Contexts, Language* (Ithaca: Cornell University Press, 1983), pp. 291–324.

INDEX

Wippermann, Wolfgang: *The Racial State: Germany 1933–1945*, 152–53

Wolf, Christa, 66n

Wolin, Richard, 38n, 151
  The Heidegger Controversy: A Critical Reader, 140
  The Politics of Being: The Political Thought of Martin Heidegger, 139–41, 165, 166

Wordsworth, William, 108, 211

Yerushalmi, Yosef Hayim, 11n–12n

Zagorin, Perez, 30n

Žižek, Slavoj, 206, 208n
  The Sublime Object of Ideology, 206–7